The Skillful Leader III

Strengthening Teacher Evaluation

Taking Action to Improve Ineffective Instruction

ALEXANDER D. PLATT ED.D.

CAROLINE E. TRIPP ED.D.

Ready About Press

Distributed by Research for Better Teaching, Inc.

Acton, Massachusetts

Dedicated with love and gratitude to our incomparable life partners Carolyn and Ray
for their collective 85 years of sustaining, nourishing, and inspiring us.

Distributed exclusively by Research for Better Teaching, Inc.
One Acton Place
Acton, Massachusetts 01720
978-263-9449 Voice
978-263-9959 Fax
www.rbteach.com

To order copies of this book or to request permission to reprint for any purpose, please contact Research for Better Teaching, Inc. See RBT publications listing at the back of this volume.

ISBN 978-1-886822-57-3

Cover and text design: Dean Bornstein
Composition: Dean Bornstein
Production management: Post Publishing Service
Development, copy editing, and indexing: Merry B. Post

CONTENTS

LIST OF FIGURES

in the text margin indicates a cross-reference.

LIST OF EXAMPLES

ACKNOWLEDGMENTS

We salute and send heartfelt thanks to two Frasers: our long-time writing partner, friend and sailing captain, Bob, whose research and patient instruction made the wealth of legal notes possible and Patty, the first mate and chief nurturer, the spiritual center of the six-pack.

This volume would not be possible without the collaboration and commitment of visionary school leaders. In Fresno Unified, special tributes go to Michael Hanson, Superintendent, and Julie Severns, Assistant Superintendent of Professional Learning, and to a group of admirable district leaders: Kim Mecum, Associate Superintendent for Human Resources; Cindy Tucker, former Associate Superintendent for School Support Services; Teresa Morales-Young, Director of Teacher Development; Rosario Sanchez, Assistant Superintendent; and Maria Mazzoni, Human Relations Administrator. We also thank the hundreds of dedicated Fresno administrators and the Turnaround School leaders—Ed Gomes, Kelly Wilkins, and Monica Alvarez—who invited us into their classrooms. In Everett, Washington, we thank Superintendent Gary Cohn and Executive Director for Human Resources Lyn Evans who, along with a wonderfully challenging group of school and central office leaders, pushed us to help them take teacher evaluation to a new level. Michelle Reid of the Port Angeles School District (Washington) and the entire Port Angeles administrative team did a terrific job of experimenting with and giving feedback on early concepts.

Jon Saphier, founder and President of Research for Better Teaching, has been our mentor, collaborator, teacher, and a role model of continuous learning for more than 30 years. Sandra Spooner's vibrant and consistent advocacy for children and belief in our efforts echoes in these pages. Nancy Love contributed invaluable advice and rescue work to help us think through the challenges of responsible data use. Ken Chapman lent us his ideas for the Progressive Discipline chapter. Jim Warnock, Deb Reed, and Mary Ann Haley-Speca helped us consider the evaluation challenges being faced by their client districts across the country. Our outstanding RBT colleagues (Marcia Booth, Jan Burres, Judy Duffield, Sue McGregor, Laura Porter, Fran Prolman-Zimmerman, Harriet Scarborough, Ruth Sernak, Ann Stern, Aminata Umoja, and Tracy Wright) have shown us what teachers and schools with high expectations can achieve in partnership with skilled consultants. Thanks also go to the RBT home team of Ivy Schutt, Carole Fiorentino, Joanne Krepelka, Kathi Knox, Cyndi Pennoyer, Gail Vettrus, and Marion Dancy, who keep the systems humming.

For applying their rich experience, high standards, and passion for equity to the task of critiquing early chapter drafts, we thank: Laura Cooper, former Assistant Superintendent of the Evanston Township High School District and now a colleague at Research for Better Teaching; Pia Durkin, Superintendent of the New Bedford, Massachusetts, Public Schools; and Kathy Spencer, former Principal of Carver High School and now head of Supervision and Evaluation programs at Research for Better Teaching.

ABOUT THE AUTHORS

Alexander D. Platt, Ed.D.

Alexander (Andy) Platt is a founding and senior consultant with Boston-based consulting firm Research for Better Teaching (RBT). In 2000, while he continued to be affiliated with RBT, he founded Ready About Consulting, dedicated to working with leaders of underperforming schools. He is the lead author of the first two books in the best-selling Skillful Leader series: *Confronting Mediocre Teaching* and *Confronting Conditions That Undermine Learning*. He specializes in coaching urban leaders on raising the quality of instruction through supervision and evaluation. Over his 35-year career, he has developed numerous long-term relationships with client districts and has taught courses to over 2,000 administrators in the United States, Europe, and Japan.

Caroline E. Tripp, Ed.D.

Caroline Tripp is also a senior consultant with Research for Better Teaching (RBT). A co-author of the first two books in the Skillful Leader series, she has spent more than 20 years training and supporting district and school-site leaders across the country. She specializes in long-term district development work that includes the design and implementation of supervision and evaluation systems for teachers and administrators, building effective leadership teams at all levels, training evaluators, and supporting the development of new administrators. She has presented nationally on a wide range of topics related to teacher quality and leadership development. Dr. Tripp served as the Director of Curriculum and Training for RBT's 10-year joint project on workplace excellence with the Montgomery County (MD) Public Schools. She was formerly a faculty member of the Boston Principal Fellows Program and Assistant Superintendent of the Shrewsbury, MA, Public Schools.

CHAPTER 1

INTRODUCTION

OUR WORK over the last decade and a half has been driven by a perpetual rallying cry: What you get to learn in America's public schools should not depend on who you are lucky enough to get as a teacher or a principal. It should not depend on what your family earns or whether you draw a good number in a lottery. It should not depend on whether you have mastered the business of "doing school" before you enter kindergarten or are encountering a book for the very first time as a five year old. Finally, it should not depend on what your teachers believe about the color of your skin or the capacities predicted by the neighborhood in which you live. But, of course, in many American schools, what you get to learn does depend on those things.

American policy makers and reformers have sought to close the gap in student learning and the quality of schooling for years. Each new wave of studies and legislation seems to fix its hopes on one or two new right answers—keys that will break the code and reveal what all of us in the field should do. When we first wrote about the challenges of confronting mediocre teaching, the answers of the moment involved testing-testing-testing (teachers and students), ensuring that teachers were appropriately credentialed or "highly qualified," and labeling failing schools so parents could flee them. Stimulating competition to improve schools through vouchers and charters was another favored solution to ineffective instruction and poor results. Putting teachers in "professional learning communities" or teams that could collaboratively analyze data and design new approaches to help students also seemed to hold great promise. So did RTI and Differentiated Instruction, Project-Based Learning, and Direct Instruction. Combinations of these reforms and programs carried out with skill and conviction have produced islands of excellence amidst a vast churn of initiatives, compliance, and confusion. By themselves, however, they have not resulted in widespread and sustained improvements in achievement.

Now we have entered the decade of much-heralded reforms to teacher evaluation. Like others before them, they are driven by the worthy vision of an expert instructor in every classroom. Years of research documenting the impact of good teaching back that vision. Federal funding and its accompanying mandates have provided fuel and a sense of urgency. Across the country Race to the Top states and coalitions of districts have been revamping their teacher performance standards and their evaluation procedures. They have debated or adopted complicated evaluation tools for assessing and rating teaching—all with the goal of "weeding out" the poor performers. They have embraced a new set of technical answers and "right ways" of doing business: performance rubrics, scoring sheets, 10-minute walks and sampling, tablet-based programs for data entry and sending quick feedback, portfolios, and SMART goals.

These "new" teacher evaluation systems also contain variations on what some educators consider a radical prospect and others consider a long overdue need. Student results or the outcomes of teaching must be used in some fashion when evaluators determine a teacher's rating and future employment. Countless hours have been spent arguing about the portion of a rating that will be determined by student performance: Should it be 50 percent or more? Should it count for only 30 percent of the final grade? Many more hours will be spent in trying to determine exactly how to measure impact. What is fair? What adjusts for differences in groups and resources? What takes into account all the variables teachers cannot control? The debate about *how* to link outcomes to teacher decisions and actions essentially obscures *why* we care about them. A good teacher can make an extraordinary impact on a child's life. That impact matters. Effective teaching is teaching that helps learners make substantive progress toward meeting curriculum standards. No child deserves to spend a year with someone who willfully or accidentally specializes in ineffective teaching.

First reports on how well new evaluation systems have done in identifying and "weeding out" teachers who do not perform at the highest levels have been discouraging. In states ranging from Florida to Michigan, 97 percent of teachers were rated as effective or better (Anderson 2013). We suspect that data from subsequent years will show little change in that pattern in most of the states surveyed but hope we are wrong.

The disproportionate attention to the technical aspects of teacher evaluation creates considerable noise and confusion. It may satisfy funders' and politicians' hunger for action, but it diverts attention away from some fundamental issues that educators and outsiders alike need to confront:

1. Do evaluators really believe that every adult and child in their schools is capable of changing and growing? If they don't yet believe that, can they act as if they do until the hope becomes a reality?
2. Are evaluators really convinced that the extraordinarily hard work required to name and take action against ineffective teaching will yield benefits for students? Do they believe that outcome is worth the cost in time and emotional energy?
3. Do the people who are supposed to making substantive judgments about teaching have rich and deep enough knowledge about pedagogy and data analysis to enable them to do so fairly and credibly? If not, are they willing to put in the time and effort to improve their own understanding and skills?
4. Have the institutions that should be preparing leaders to improve instruction provided the practical strategies, on-the-job experiences, and feedback that would enable evaluators to become skilled diagnosticians and problem-solvers?
5. Do district leaders provide the guidance, standards for leadership performance, support, and feedback to enable evaluators to stay the course in the face of political pressure? Are they willing to focus their own efforts and minimize the disruptions they can create?
6. Are politicians, school boards, and "helpful partners" willing to put aside a raft of competing (and often unimportant) urgencies to find and stick with a limited number of worthwhile priorities? Can they resist new fads that split district attention and pull instructional leaders away from their schools?

If the answers to any of these questions are "no," then we all need to examine our own roles in sustaining mediocrity.

Throughout our years of work with school districts, charter schools, and private schools across the country, we have repeatedly seen that the problem of inadequate learning cannot and should not be blamed on teachers alone. When children in one classroom do not have the same high-quality opportunities to learn as their peers, then all the adults responsible for their learning share the blame—and the obligation to change:

- The administrators, department heads, lead teachers, specialists, coaches, and consultants whose job is to help classroom teachers maximize the impact of their instructional decisions
- The grade-level or content-alike teams that tolerate broken promises and cover for or ignore low expectations and ineffective practice from some members
- The evaluators who do not have the competence or conviction to name problems and help teachers make the choice to fix those problems or to change careers—and therefore rate everyone as proficient
- The district-level leaders who do not support evaluators by holding high expectations, providing training and support, and backing them up when the going gets tough
- The central office behaviors that lead to Organizational ADD, fragmenting school leaders' focus and draining their time and energy
- The boards (and communities that elect them) that generate fear-based, politicized cultures that favor the narrow self-interests of adults bent on protecting their turf over the interests of children.

The problem of mediocre learning is an intricate and complicated one, a nested one with many layers suggested by the background rings in Figure 1.1. Strengthening teacher evaluation is one of the ways we can tackle this problem and take responsibility for improving our own profession, though certainly not the only one. Many variables, not the purview of this handbook, also affect students' opportunities to learn at high levels: rich and challenging curriculum such as that proposed by the Common Core Standards, access to technology, safe neighborhoods, freedom from hunger and fear, family and community engagement, to name just a few. But if we are going to invest considerable effort in teacher evaluation, what must happen?

Taking skillful action against ineffective teaching requires three key capacities, the "3 C's" illustrated in Figure 1.1:

Conviction:
Holding and consistently acting on a set of positive beliefs and stances about adults' and children's ability to learn and about one's own responsibility for acting when performance is not good enough

Competence:
Knowing and using research about teaching and schools and a repertoire of evaluation skills and strategies to help all adults perform at high levels

Control:
Providing and using adequate processes, standards, structures, and resources to make teacher evaluation substantive, meaningful, and effective

Figure 1.1 Confronting the Sources of Mediocrity

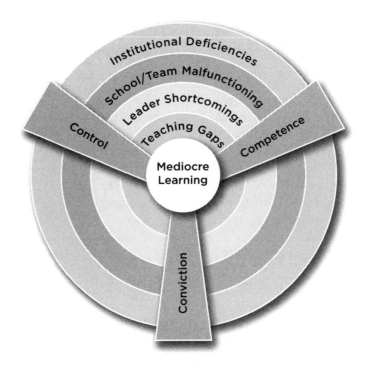

All three capacities must be present and working together for performance evaluation to be successful.

Thus far policy makers have been focused on improving what we call control: the systems, structures, and resources that guide or limit what you can do as an evaluator. They have encouraged new regulations that then necessitate new contracts, new standards, new procedures, and new rubrics and formulas for rating. Whatever their promise, all these changes will only be as effective as the people who implement them.

In earlier Skillful Leader volumes, *Confronting Mediocre Teaching* and *Confronting the Conditions that Undermine Learning,* we have written extensively about the role of conviction: holding beliefs and having the courage to act on them. In this handbook we focus the majority of our attention on competence. We have tried to compile what we have learned from studying skillful leaders at work, the practical strategies and habits of mind that help you do this part of your leadership job well. Evaluation is hard. Finding the time is enormously challenging. Staying the course can be daunting. The more skilled you are at data collection and analysis, problem diagnosis, communication, and the design of interventions, the more your conviction will grow about its potential to discriminate between levels of performance and improve opportunities for children.

Chapter 2 outlines the shifts in mindset and standard operating practices that need to be in place before you can effectively evaluate for impact on student learning. Chapter 3 introduces the action cycle for taking on ineffective teaching. These two chapters can form the foundation of your supervision and evaluation work no matter where you are on the continuum of evaluation reform.

Chapters 4 through 7 are all about how to carry out the key actions in the cycle. In Chapter 4A to C, you'll find strategies for using multiple sources of data to examine how well teaching is working to help students learn. There are suggestions for looking at teaching-focused data sources such as lesson plans, assessments, assignments, and tasks, as well as technology use and learning-focused data sources such as grading, achievement data, and progress reports. Acknowledging growing attention to professionalism and professional responsibilities, 4C suggests data sources and questions to help you examine and document those non-classroom responsibilities.

Chapter 5's sections A to G delve into the challenges of diagnosing problems in instruction and non-classroom responsibilities. Each section from B to F examines a specific teaching function such as managing the classroom, planning, and assessing, or setting and communicating high expectations that is found in almost all major evaluation systems currently being used across the country. Section G looks at diagnosing problems of professionalism.

Chapter 6 introduces a continuum for thinking about how you define and communicate problems to teachers. Each section of this chapter contains samples of what a skillful leader might say or write when communicating early worries (6B) or concerns (6C) or presenting a formal problem statement either in an evaluation document, a letter or memo, or an email (6D). In these sections you will recognize some familiar prototypes and cases from volume one, *Confronting Mediocre Teaching*. Sally Friendly, Frank Steel, Donna DeLimits, and others come back to serve again as useful examples of situations we all encounter.

Chapters 7 and 8 are all about selecting and designing interventions to break the cycle of ineffective practice and help teachers change. Chapter 7 presents a continuum of ways to intervene well before you get to the stage of needing to write a formal improvement plan for a teacher. We look at understanding how to match the intervention to the situation, the problem, and the individual and consider when and how to use oral or written suggestions, written recommendations, goal setting and Mini-Plans^{sm} to provide timely and targeted feedback and direction. Chapter 8 lays out when, why, and how to design improvement plans and includes a considerably modernized sample plan for Sally Friendly, who now faces the challenges of implementing Common Core curricula.

This is a handbook focused on producing growth—not on firing people. However, sometimes efforts are unsuccessful or an offense is too serious. The final two chapters deal with tracks to dismissal, resources that you may need if you find yourself dealing with issues of insubordination, contract violations, and the like that require progressive discipline rather than evaluation (Chapter 9) or if all other efforts to change the ineffective practice have failed (Chapter 10).

At the end of our courses on supervision and evaluation over the years, we've often asked new administrators to answer this question: "What do you want the people you supervise and evaluate to say about you after you're gone?" Their initial answers are usually consistent. They want to be seen as fair. They want to be seen as knowledgeable and competent. Then the groups divide. Some want to be remembered as supportive, accessible, or as good resources for helping teachers do their work well. Others want high expectations for students and adults and the ability to inspire others to rise to new levels to be their legacy. The debate crystallizes the challenges of teacher evaluation. Are they mutually exclusive? We think not. The commitment to name what is not working and offer help is a tribute to all the phenomenal teachers who show us what is possible in America. In the fundamental act of standing up and taking skilled action against ineffective practice, you offer the ultimate statements of conviction and focus. You assert that:

- Every child deserves an expert instructor
- Good instructors are made, not born
- Adults can grow, but . . .
- Time is short and children come first

EVALUATING FOR IMPACT

THE DRIVE to use student results in teacher evaluation has been grabbing headlines and gaining momentum for some time now. Its champions are ardent; its detractors are dismayed. If you work in a state whose first efforts have been clumsy, poorly conceived, or perhaps even irresponsible, you may already be weary of the turmoil and hope the whole movement will fizzle. Trying to solve the problem of ineffective practice with the heavy club of test scores, growth ratios, formulas, and newspaper lists is the latest effort to get our profession to take charge of its own performance. Like it or not, the shift to defining expertise through measuring impact is not going away.

CHANGES IN TEACHER EVALUATION

Forget the logistical wrangling, fear, and confusion produced from bumbling implementation and all the distracting charges and counter charges for a moment and concentrate on the parts of this reform that hold promise. We are in the midst of a significant evolution in the ways we think about and carry out teacher evaluation. These changes include:

1. Blurring or eliminating earlier distinctions drawn between acts of supervision and those of evaluation
2. Shifting from teaching-focused to learning-focused interactions in all phases of the process
3. Redefining and expanding what we mean by the terms *observation* and *data from an observation*
4. Increasing teachers' opportunities for regular, brief bursts of feedback and face-to-face conferencing—and correspondingly decreasing the heavy reliance on one-time encounters as the basis for evaluation
5. Expecting teachers to be skilled and engaged partners in the process of assessing effectiveness and modifying their own practices

All these changes have implications for your work. This chapter is a good place to begin if you want to

- Check your own operating assumptions about what high-quality teacher evaluation should be
- Identify topics for discussion and for calibrating your evaluations during your professional development for administrators
- Consider what might be included as part of the negotiation of a new contract or a revision of an existing evaluation system
- Think about the essential habits of mind and practice that should be in place to create a school culture focused on maximizing adult and student learning

The fundamental practices in the following pages can be used to implement a wide range of frameworks and approaches currently being adopted in states across the country. They lay the foundation for your credibility and competence as an evaluator. Watching skillful leaders, we have also learned that several key commitments provide the mortar for this foundation and are essential to your success:

- Talk early; talk often; listen more.
- Seek first to understand before you judge.
- Get and give the appropriate data to prove your point.
- Keep no secrets.
- Put students first.

As you consider both the new demands of evaluation and its traditional challenges, note how these commitments need to be alive and well kept.

1. Eliminating the Distinctions between Supervision and Evaluation

These first two changes in how we evaluate teachers are inextricably linked. To understand why, think about the assumptions that governed our work just over a decade ago. We found it helpful to distinguish between the two roles that leaders had to carry out under the heading of teacher evaluation: supervision versus evaluation. The former involved spreading a vision of high-quality teaching and learning through formative feedback, cheerleading, and suggestions for improvement. The latter involved making a judgment and giving a rating that theoretically assured the school board and community of a teacher's competence. Administrators who were skilled communicators and believers in transparency would make a point of telling teachers which hat they were currently wearing.

A decade ago only the rare supervisor—the individual charged with spreading a vision of high-quality learning—made explicit connections either in conferences or in writing between a teacher's actions and the outcomes of those actions. That enlightened supervisor might examine and raise questions about the work students produced or their performance on quizzes, unit tests, and standardized measures. Because that discussion was intended to stimulate the teacher's thinking, the results the supervisor and teacher talked about rarely appeared in the evidence for a final "evaluation": the judgment made about the caliber of the teacher's work. Certainly, most evaluation systems paid no *official* attention to whether or not teaching worked well for children: the impact of a teacher's decisions.

2. Shifting from a Teaching Focus to a Learning Focus

Both assumptions—about divisions between supervisory and evaluative roles and the use of results—no longer apply. Reforms to evaluation systems being proposed or just now being implemented are intended to make those systems learning-focused rather than teaching-focused. In a learning-focused system, the results produced by teachers' choices of action—not simply the fact that they took those actions— must be considered in feedback and in ratings. Therefore, teachers and evaluators should be engaged in a continuous, day-to-day appraisal of student performance in relation to agreed-upon, worthwhile targets. They should be talking about how effective the teachers' decisions are in helping them reach their self-identified goals for students. They should be discussing what adjustments the teacher might make and what data each might collect in order to assess students' progress. In other words, both parties should be making the kinds of judgments once considered to be the responsibility of the designated evaluator alone.

Figure 2.1 captures critical differences in emphasis and activities between teaching-focused evaluation and learning-focused evaluation. Throughout this handbook, when we use the word *evaluation* we mean it to represent the actions traditionally listed under supervision as well. We mean the actions detailed in the right-hand column of Figure 2.1, not simply the act of rating and ranking performance.

Figure 2.1 Making the Shift to Learning-Focused Evaluation

	TEACHING-FOCUSED EVALUATION	LEARNING-FOCUSED EVALUATION
Emphasis within analysis, conversation, and documentation	• What the teacher has done • How the teacher's performance relates to a set of standards • How the teacher "felt" the lesson went (i.e., liked/disliked) • How/what the teacher might change and why	• How teaching has affected what students know and are able to do • How the teacher's performance relates to a set of standards; how the students' performance relates to curricular goals and standards • What formative assessment showed about the instruction • Which instructional choices are helping or hindering student learning; what next steps need to be taken
Characteristic activities	• Classroom observation 1-3 times a year depending on years of experience • Requests that teachers submit "participation" info for non-classroom standards • Conference(s) to review supervisor's findings and "sign-off" on reports • Suggestions/recommendations focused on activities to do	• Frequent classroom visits of 5-20 minutes plus 1 or more formally scheduled full-length observations • Evidence gathering from job-alike or PLC meetings, LASW sessions, data analysis, artifacts showing student learning • Conferences to review student learning and reflect on teacher and school goals for students • Suggestions/recommendations specify desired outcomes as well as steps to take
Role of the evaluator	• Check the teaching against a set of "best practices," program requirements, or standards of performance • Fulfill minimum requirements for documentation in order to demonstrate compliance with contract	• Collaborate with the teacher to assess the impact of programs and practices on learners and identify what to change, how to make the changes, what data to collect, and how to monitor progress • Interact often to stimulate teacher thinking and problem-solving and to give feedback about performance in relation to a standard
Role of the teacher	• Provide a display of teaching prowess during required observations • Provide documentation of participation or compliance	• Analyze data, adjust instruction, collaborate with evaluator to identify next steps • Provide evidence of analysis, reflection, and improvement in outcomes

Ultimately learning-focused evaluation is based on a key assumption: teachers with a *longitudinal record* of helping students make progress meet performance standards. Correspondingly, teachers with a multiyear pattern of poor student performance that can be tied to deficiencies in instructional repertoire do not meet standards. Your responsibility as an evaluator is to make evidence about student growth in relation to agreed-upon benchmarks *one of the key variables but not the only variable* determining a teacher's official rating. The evidence you use must be drawn from multiple, credible data sources, *not single tests or achievement measures*. Taken together, these multiple data sources should reveal a pattern of decisions (or lack thereof), a picture of the impact of practice over time.

3. Expanding the Definitions of "Observation" and "Data from Observations"

Despite its imperfect history and limitations, direct observation remains the most common and immediately diagnostic source of information about the quality of a teacher's work. Given its inevitable influence, we propose expanding our shared vision of what effective, learning-focused observation is in two ways: including and using a wider range of events under the heading of *observation* and refining the traditional 30- to 45-minute classroom observation still required in so many contracts.

First, consider the following different types of activities that involve watching a teacher at work:

- **Announced or unannounced extended observations of 30 minutes or more in classrooms,** usually part of the process requirements or state regulations governing evaluation systems. Announced events are often preceded by a planning conference (sometimes called a pre-conference); both announced and unannounced observations are often followed by a reflecting (post) conference. Hereafter we refer to this type of event as a "formal observation" and consider it something like an annual physical.

- **Announced or unannounced observations of meetings** such as team or grade-level meetings, department meetings, special education team meetings, parent meetings, or professional development sessions where the purpose is to collect data about teachers' performance in meeting standards for professionalism and collaboration or community and family engagement. See Sections 4D and 5G.

- **Brief visits of 10 to 20 minutes to a classroom, meeting, or professional presentation.** These visits can be focused or targeted for specific purposes such as:
  — Following up on recommendations
  — Monitoring the components of a MiniPlan^sm or full-blown improvement plan
  — Collecting data about an individual or team's progress in meeting goals
  — Collecting data about a particular standard to flesh out the picture of a teacher's practice
  They can also be for purposes of discovery and diagnosis such as:

- — Determining the level of intellectual challenge provided by the everyday tasks students are doing
- — Assessing how well students are displaying target competencies critical to meeting Common Core Standards
- — Determining where further professional development may be necessary in order to ensure consistent high-quality practice across all classrooms

- **Mini-observations**, or short, unannounced classroom visits lasting 5 to 10 minutes whose purpose may be either for diagnosis or monitoring and range from "being visible" to sampling students' cognitive engagement or assessing the implementation of a single target practice or strategy (Marshall 2009).

- **Process and climate sampling**, watching and analyzing interactions between teachers and students in the common areas of the school such as the auditorium, cafeteria or hallways and during regularly recurring situations such as morning bus duty, dismissal, passing between periods, or walking to specials, lunch, and recess.

Each of these activities gives you different information and insights into how a teacher thinks, plans, interacts with students, and colleagues, and approaches everyday challenges and responsibilities. To create a fully rounded picture of what a teacher knows and is able to do and to make observation as useful as possible for both teacher and evaluator, you need a judicious mix of approaches from this repertoire. In some cases you may take detailed literal notes and analyze them for evidence of performance in relation to standards. In other cases, you may simply jot down a useful piece of evidence to support a rating on a standard, a question to ask, student responses that would interest the teacher, or an idea to discuss.

Leader Alert
Clearing Up Misconceptions About Data Use

You may already be collecting and discussing data from many different types of observations with teachers. We hope so. However, many school systems are still bogged down with old assumptions and strictures about what evaluators can and cannot do and what can be included in an assessment of performance. Leaders therefore waste valuable opportunities to provide teachers with concrete information and thoughtful feedback. Any activity conducted on school grounds during school time potentially provides data for documenting performance on a standard if you (1) inform teachers of your intent to expand data sources (2) keep responsible notes when you notice and want to follow up on a problem with a teacher, and (3) discuss those notes with the teacher. (See Legal Notes 9.1, 9.3.) ◆

We propose a more comprehensive picture of what should be involved in a so-called *formal* observation, the activity still listed in or required by most contracts and state regulations governing evaluation. Compare your district's current understanding of the term *classroom observation* to the multi-part event illustrated in Figure 2.2. Stages appear on the left of the diagram, and the data to be collected, discussed, and analyzed—in the spirit of seeking to understand and keeping no secrets—are on the right.

Figure 2.2 Data Collection in a Learning-Focused Observation

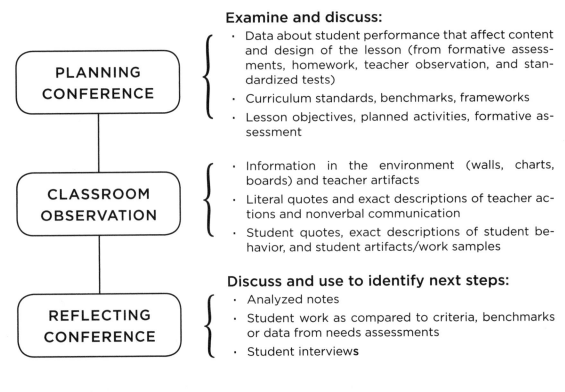

PLANNING CONFERENCE

Examine and discuss:
- Data about student performance that affect content and design of the lesson (from formative assessments, homework, teacher observation, and standardized tests)
- Curriculum standards, benchmarks, frameworks
- Lesson objectives, planned activities, formative assessment

CLASSROOM OBSERVATION

- Information in the environment (walls, charts, boards) and teacher artifacts
- Literal quotes and exact descriptions of teacher actions and nonverbal communication
- Student quotes, exact descriptions of student behavior, and student artifacts/work samples

REFLECTING CONFERENCE

Discuss and use to identify next steps:
- Analyzed notes
- Student work as compared to criteria, benchmarks or data from needs assessments
- Student interviews

As Figure 2.2 indicates, a formal, learning-focused observation involves:

- Substantive (not 5 minutes on the fly) discussion(s) of the data that have affected the teacher's plan, the important content and concepts students must master, techniques the teacher will use, and plans for assessment
- Collection of specific data during the lesson that show what students are doing and what students say in interviews. These data should document the caliber of student work and the level of academic language.
- Substantive analysis and planning of next steps in response to data about the impact of the lesson on students

Learning-focused observation requires teachers and evaluators to collect and consider mutiple sources of data. Anything that both parties examine together—from student portfolios to writing on exit tickets to the proposed contents and format of the upcoming unit test—is fodder for consideration in an evaluation. All of the relevant data sources discussed would show up in formal reports; they would be part of the assessment of the lesson's success in helping students reach worthwhile learning targets.

Leader Alert
Manage the Shift to Learning-Focused Observation Wisely

Whether announced or unannounced, formal observations must comply with collective bargaining agreements. Many contracts allow evaluators to consider other data sources. However, conflicts may arise if no one in the school district has done so before. Beyond the basics with which you must comply, keep several principles in mind. First, make your purpose clear: you are simply focusing on student learning as a way to make your assessments and feedback as useful as possible, not to punish teachers. Second, make the shift to a focus on learning the hallmark of all of your evaluations—not just those of one or two ineffective performers. Finally, be credible by committing to a goal of "no secrets and no surprises." Information that appears in formal documents should have been discussed and clarified with the teacher previously. ◆

Newcomers to the teaching profession usually have few preconceptions about what observation will entail. They can form the nexus of your reflective culture. The biggest challenge may be undoing old habits and stereotypes veteran teachers associate with traditional definitions of observation. Figure 2.3 suggest some strategies for changing tenured faculty's expectations.

Figure 2.3 Tips on Formal Observation for Tenured Faculty

- **Communicate early, often, and in multiple modes that you are widening the observation lens** from "Do you do all these teacher moves?" to "How are all these strategies and choices we make as teachers helping students?" Consider creating an activity (e.g., a brief, shared video or simulation) that allows the entire staff to experience what collecting and analyzing data about the students' responses will be like.

- **At the beginning of the year, carefully craft a memo outlining the purpose of observation and the ground rules and expectations for both participants.** End by explicitly inviting staff members to make suggestions and raise questions about anything that they find confusing. Before you send the memo, have a colleague or two read it critically to make certain you have been clear and perhaps to check that you are not violating any binding agreements. Send the memo to all staff and review it with each individual as you begin the process. Expect that in the early days of such a shift, there will be inevitable complaints about "not knowing" or "not being told" even when communication has been extensive. Veteran staff, assuming they "know how evaluation goes," may not look closely at the directions. By having expectations clearly laid out in writing, leaders can respond to the "you are picking on me" syndrome that sometimes develops if negative data surface as a result of the more stringent examination.

- **Start with an announced visit** despite the danger that low-performing teachers will resort to a "dog and pony" show that does not reflect a representative lesson plan. If we can communicate the expectations clearly enough (see Example 2.1), giving teachers a chance to do their best has some value. The announced visit may not reveal what the teacher does on a day-to-day basis; however, it does show what she or he can do. Whether instruction is good, bad, or mediocre, the announced observation gives you a benchmark performance. Comparing the data from an announced visit with that gathered from unannounced visits and other sources helps to validate judgments or highlight next steps.

- **Ask to see something from the heart of a unit (or a related series of lessons) that challenges students to apply or get better at a difficult skill or concept.** Emphasize that you prefer not to see either an introductory or "R and

R" (recall and review) lesson but rather something complex that will allow both of you to gain insight into the demands that current programs are placing on students and teachers. Or specify that you would like to see students practicing a key critical thinking skill necessary to meeting Common Core Standards.

- **Establish, communicate, and be consistent about upholding a policy that there are no penalties for a high-risk, rigorous lesson that doesn't succeed.** Save any response that carries pointed consequences for people who continue to produce low-level demonstrations. In the pre-conference, emphasize that you want to be able to provide valuable data about a part of the curriculum that repeatedly confuses students or slows them down or that you want to help a teacher think through other ways to handle a complex concept when you meet to debrief.

- **Collaborate with the teacher to identify what data on student understanding will be collected, by whom, and when before the observation begins.** You might collect a record of the kinds of questions students ask or answer incorrectly; the teacher might design and collect responses to a one-question quiz at midpoint in the lesson. You might interview students working in groups about their goal while the teacher would collect the problem set, essay, or lab report that results from several days of instruction.

- **Identify a clear mastery objective and some basic criteria for success before the lesson and have those statements ready to use when you begin to look at artifacts after the lesson.**

Example 2. 1 Sample Memo About Changes in the Focus for Observation

August 23, 20_

To: All Faculty

From: Frank Focused, Principal

Re: Formal Observations

Although I'll be in and out of your classrooms and getting to know your students in other ways this year, I will also be conducting two formal observations as part of the evaluation process. I want those events to be a productive learning experience for both of us and to make sure the time we spend results in students making progress toward the learning goals we have set for them. To that end, I want to be a useful "second pair of eyes" to help you with something that is hard for students to learn. Please invite me to a class where students will be challenged by having to work on a difficult concept or skill. Part of the class could certainly be direct instruction, but I would like to see students applying what you're teaching, either individually or in groups. That will give me a chance to ask them a few questions we will agree upon at the pre-observation meeting; it will get us additional data to think about as we debrief the lessons.

As a change from previous years when we would have met almost immediately, I would like to have the post-observation conference two to three days later to give you a chance to assess how students are performing in relation to your standards and objectives. You may or may not have final products, but I will be asking you to bring sample work related to this observation. We'll plan to look at the responses of one or two typically high-performing students, two or three students whose work represents average performance for the task, and a student who does not get it yet. We will make the progress of those students a topic of discussion as well.

Again, this shift is meant to have our discussions and the effort you put into these observations yield worthwhile insights about our learners and programs. We will talk in more detail as we set up appointments, but please don't hesitate to catch me with suggestions and questions about how this might work.

4. Increasing Feedback and Conferences

New approaches to evaluation place a premium on providing feedback. It is worth stopping to examine what that means. As an evaluator you can have many different responses to what you observe or learn about through your examination of artifacts, your conferences, or your interviews. These responses fall into rough categories:

- Judgments including praise
- Advice and guidance
- Feedback

The last term, *feedback,* is often used loosely to mean all three kinds of responses. However they are not equally effective and should not be conflated. In its purest sense, feedback is non-judgmental information about performance in relation to a standard, target, or goal the recipient is trying to reach. Feedback done properly enables teachers to make better decisions than they would have made without such information. Almost all the proficient and expert teachers we have ever met have professed themselves to be "starved" for genuine feedback, for the concrete information that a second set of eyes and careful data gathering can get for them. Although they may appreciate generic praise (*"That was great; I really enjoyed it!"*) for its momentary warmth, they note that it gives them nothing to build on, nowhere to go.

To be most useful, feedback needs to be specific (factual), timely, and targeted:

- The number of students who successfully used the past tense on the first try
- How much time the teacher talked versus the amount of student talk on a particular concept
- The exact question the teacher asked that illustrated her skill in implementing Common Core and provoked a spirited discussion

Feedback can be spoken or written, presented in an email, or dropped on a desk as a quick note. It can be provided during a scheduled conference. Or it can be discussed on-the-fly during a duty period or leaning on the wall together at the end of a long day. Feedback can be directed to an individual, a team, a department, or the school as a whole, as in what percentage of the faculty currently identifies and posts clear mastery objectives. It can be in response to a teacher's request or result from something you have seen that raises questions in your mind and merits follow-up. This kind of pure feedback does not have to be long and laboriously crafted. The point is that it arrives when it is most needed. It gives the data to illustrate where the teacher or team is in relation to their target. And, in the majority of instances, it leads to thoughtful examination of and worthwhile adjustments in practice.

As Kim Marshall has noted, providing useful feedback is a challenge when principals and other evaluators see such little teaching:

> The fact that administrators are in classrooms less than half a percent of their time should foster a little humility. Only principals with a very strong sense of their own power and persuasiveness would imagine changing a teacher's performance and students' achievement after peering through a narrow window. For evaluations to be credible with teachers, school leaders must first capture what is going on the other 99.9% of the time (2009 23).

In order to increase the number of classroom visits, Marshall suggests a strategy he calls Mini Observations (Marshall 2009). To take advantage of the Mini Observation strategy and to provide good quality feedback, you must be highly skilled at:

- Noticing what is important to student learning—not just what is easy to see
- Capturing data through notes and/or technology, not just using an iPad to check off behaviors
- Analyzing and categorizing that data using common frameworks that have meaning for teachers
- Selecting a worthwhile piece of what you have noted and communicating it quickly and respectfully

Think of the other implications for your work if you are to be able to increase teachers' opportunities to receive high-quality, growth-oriented feedback.

- Time has to be scheduled, made a priority, and protected.
- Office and support staff must be trained and expected to handle routine issues while you are in classrooms.
- You—and your team if you are in a school with multiple evaluators—will need systems for keeping track of where you have visited or observed, what you were looking for or discovered, and where to go next.
- You need a mechanism for getting the feedback to teachers that matches your work and learning style.
- You may also need a way to track which standards you have acquired adequate evidence for and which need more data.

If you have already made these changes, you are well ahead of the majority of American districts. If not, the need to do so will become an important focus for all the leaders in your district.

Time to talk and think together about teaching and its impact on students is a precious commodity. When you spend that kind of time with an individual or team, you signal your vision, values, and mission in the clearest possible way. And if you listen a great deal during a conference, you are likely to acquire all manner of new insights. We recognize that finding the time to listen and learn is truly difficult. The enormous caseloads most American evaluators carry coupled with the complicated demands on their time and attention make an extended "sit down" conference a luxury. If your district is like the majority we have encountered, conferences about teaching happen once or perhaps twice a year in tandem with the annual or biannual "formal observation." Most teachers and administrators we meet seem to agree that the feedback given and received during those encounters has limited utility.

Technology, with its lure of efficiency and its ability to override the constraints of the contractual work day, presents both a potential solution to finding "time to talk" and a danger. Without tone and body language to mediate a message or provide cues to the recipients' understanding, electronic communications fired off in haste can have unfortunate consequences. As we have all learned to our dismay, the time saved by not walking down the hall during the work day can be eaten up twice over by having to fix something that was misunderstood. Electronic checklists, copied to the teacher without further comment, may provide data but not necessarily meaning. The latter is made when people analyze the data together, raise questions, and ponder what to do next.

As you wrestle with the demands of evaluation systems that specify a minimum number of conferences or think about your personal goal of spending more time in learning-based exchanges with your teachers, focus on what is most important about events we call conferences. It isn't length. It isn't how smart you are or how much you know or how much you can talk—or even whether you are warm and friendly. What seems to be most important to helping teachers grow is first *what you focus on*: students, student learning, and important questions and insights that affect how well the teacher can work to advance that learning. And second, value is determined by *how you conference*: your respect, your intellectual curiosity about what they are doing and thinking, your ability to be an active listener, your ability to be fully present and focused for the time that you have. Under those conditions, many exchanges that you have could be called conferences if you gave yourself credit for them. Examples include

- The brief discussion about the caliber of students' latest writing samples you had with two teachers at the mailboxes
- The data analysis and problem-solving meeting you had with a subcommittee from your instructional leadership team
- The problem-solving around instructional modifications that you, the counselor, and a special education teacher did before a meeting with a distraught parent
- The excited back-and-forth discussion about studying a "flipped classroom" approach for potential use next year that happened spontaneously after a professional development session and kept you and six teachers standing in the hall for 20 minutes

At the moment, teachers may not think of these as conferences. However, if you label them as such, follow up, and refer to ideas you learned when you were talking to a teacher, you can begin to challenge old notions and shift the culture.

5. Making Teachers Partners in Evaluation

Teachers tell us that the evaluators they most respect know them and their work extremely well. Part of whether they feel known comes from whether the evaluator has spent sufficient time in their classrooms and in exchanges about teaching to be able to ask detailed questions and suggest pertinent additions—not boilerplate—to the teachers' repertoire. Part of feeling known also seems to come from whether they feel a sense of shared ownership and responsibility for assessing their own performance.

Increasing teachers' stake in and accountability for their own evaluation is also characteristic of some new systems. The rhetoric of partnership has often been present in discussions of traditional evaluation methods, but new processes and requirements now make shared responsibility essential. Teachers must set goals, in many instances with specific targets for student learning and specific data to be collected. They must make and carry out plans to meet those goals and figure out how to collect data to document progress at least. They must collect and provide the evaluator with relevant data to demonstrate their competence on particular standards that would not be readily apparent: on family and community engagement, participation in and application of professional development, or cultural proficiency, for example. In some instances they write midyear or end-of-year reflections and complete self-assessments.

Our very early sampling of the products of such partnerships suggests that we all have some distance to go in building both evaluators' and teachers' competence in using these new processes productively. Low-level compliance, a sort of survival strategy that is often a symbol of novice behavior, threatens their potential value. The tricky concept to define is "partnership." Like another famous "p" word, we know it when we see it. But we do not necessarily appreciate how difficult it is to create the real thing or how easy it is for good intentions to go awry. Partnership is not having teachers write their own evaluations or create and tote multiple binders full of evidence to an annual conference. It is not rubber stamping pointless goals so as not to offend the teachers' union or writing goals the principal wants and handing them to the teacher. Balance and persistence, time, and the ability to recognize failure and restart will all be needed. As good starting points in building partnership, we find the following tips in Figure 2.4 helpful:

Figure 2.4 Tips for Making Teachers Partners in Evaluation

- Memorize the broad terms of the teacher performance standards and use those terms to publicly label all kinds of positive examples you see around the school. Tell the teacher that a certain artifact will illustrate a particular standard or indicator, that you are taking note of it, and that she should too. Ask for other such examples.
- Build common language. Encourage teachers to learn and use the language of their new performance standards. Have fun with the task: make flashcards, have 2-minute quizzes in faculty meetings, create posters, invite teams to make up acronyms or mnemonics.
- Observe a video together and discuss with teams what might be important to raise in a follow-up discussion or what feedback would be most useful. Move from observing shared videos to peer observation, learning walks, rounds, or

other structures that allow teachers to watch one another at work and provide coverage.

- Hold a labeling party. You bring food. Have teachers bring all their collected artifacts for one week and label them with the standards they best match. Then facilitate a discussion on how to get or organize evidence on standards that were under-represented in people's collections.
- Give teacher groups the administrative standards and invite them to practice collecting notes, analyzing data, and figuring out feedback on a presentation you make or meeting you run.
- Use your phone or tablet to take pictures of all the examples of standards at work around the school and show them at a faculty meeting.
- Invite teachers to make presentations about their goals and goal plans or to serve as mentors for those who are struggling to figure out worthwhile targets.
- Operate under the principle of "no secrets." Communicate continuously about what you are doing in relation to new evaluation processes and why. If you make a mistake or need to change course, be open and honest about what it was, why it happened, and what you want to do next.
- Talk and question before you document. Use memos and forms to summarize agreements not to raise issues for the first time.

Good teachers, the ones that make a significant difference in the lives of students, the ones who never give up on looking for one more approach or one more refinement, evaluate themselves for impact every day. They know what their results are; they usually know how and why they got those results. They just need their leaders to join them in an intelligent consideration of what they have learned and what else might be brought to bear to help their students. Sometimes they just need us to get out of their way.

This handbook, however, is not about dealing with high performance but with taking action to get *in the way* of ineffective instruction. Shifting to learning-focused leadership in order to evaluate for impact requires a major change in your leadership priorities, not simply compliance with new evaluation procedures that include results. Reallocate how you spend your time and where you put your effort. Reframe your daily interactions to focus on student impact. Expand opportunities to seize feedback moments and conduct mini conferences. Practice collecting multiple sources of data. Build partnerships through relationships rather than mandates. If some of these practices seem awkward at first, enjoy the process and the learning. You'll know change is really happening!

Finally, if you are a principal supervisor, figure out how to align your supervision and coaching so that you conduct the same learning-focused conversations with your principals. If you are subjecting them to the old checklist activity–focused conversations and evaluations, how can you expect them to do otherwise?

CHAPTER 3

INTRODUCTION TO
THE ACTION CYCLE

The action cycle in Figure 3.1 represents what leaders do to identify and improve mediocre and unsatisfactory performance.

Figure 3.1 *The Action Cycle for Improving Ineffective Teaching*

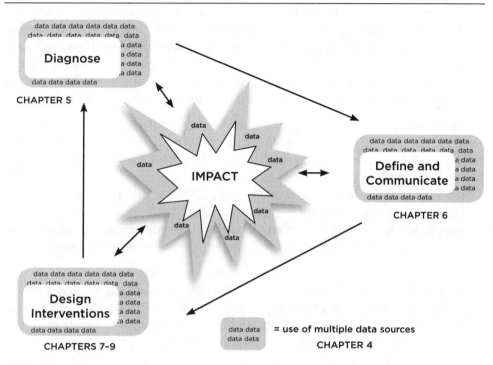

Each of the following chapters digs into one of the steps in this cycle. Seven key principles shape the model and are essential to its use:

1. **Assume that the work of improving ineffective teaching is not linear and that starting points will vary depending on the context.** As Figure 3.1 illustrates, steps interact with one another. You may begin with the most traditional of all entry points—a formal assessment of a teacher's performance dictated by your district's evaluation system. Or you may be compelled to action by data from external and school-based assessments that show students in some classes are being shortchanged. Those data would lead you to look more closely at the teaching that produced such an impact. A colleague from another school might, through a series of short, unannounced, diagnostic visits to classrooms, discover inequities in students' opportunities to learn. From there, she will cross-reference her findings with longer observations, artifact analysis, and student performance data.

2. **Gather and analyze data from multiple sources no matter where you enter the cycle and continue to do so throughout all the steps.** As you deepen your understanding of the nature of the problem and its causes, you will need to return to your pool of data sources to verify your hypotheses or to become more precise in your explanations of how teaching choices affect students' learning.

When you work with a teacher on goals, Mini-Plans^sm, or formal improvement plans, you will need to specify the data to be collected as evidence of success. Chapter 4 offers a menu of data sources that can be tapped for these purposes.

3. **Focus on the impact of teaching and school structures on students' current versus desired performance at all stages of the cycle.** Determining the impact requires a particular kind of analytical thinking: you start with the desired performance outcome for students and compare that to their present performance. That process is *establishing the gap*. Knowing the impact your school wants for its learners helps you tap into the sense of mission and moral purpose that brought many people to the work of teaching in the first place. If you and your leadership team are not clear about the performance outcomes and competencies—not test score gains—that you want for your students, you will be missing one of the most powerful tools that you have for confronting mediocrity.

4. **Think and behave like a diagnostician.** The critical diagnostic step, discussed in Chapter 5, helps you decide where and how to invest supervisory effort and the precious resource of time most effectively. Look for patterns of ineffective instruction across a school, department, or grade level: too much teacher talk, low expectations, lack of planning, or the failure to use assessment data. Or begin by asking why student performance in particular classrooms or teams is poor or inconsistent. In either case, you are trying to determine what factors are causing the poor student results and what interventions make the most sense.

5. **Find and use a common language and concept system to interpret your district evaluation standards or rubrics, describe the teaching needed, provide feedback, and shape interventions.** Otherwise, teachers feel pulled in all directions by competing voices, visions, and language. Administrative teams must work to make sure that they use the same framework to capture and communicate what they see happening in classrooms. Chapter 5 provides one such framework. It can be used in conjunction with district teacher performance standards, national standards or content guidelines, or program-specific pedagogy.

6. **Clearly define and communicate performance problems in terms of their impact on student learning before making detailed recommendations or specifying actions teachers must take.** Separating the problem definition step from the solution proposing step has several benefits. First, you increase the likelihood that teachers will understand the reasons for making changes, will be able to participate in identifying possible next steps, and will be able to "buy into" proposed solutions. Second, you reduce the emphasis on meaningless compliance as a way to satisfy an evaluator. As the examples in Chapter 6 illustrate, communicating a problem can fall on a continuum from the gentle expression of an early worry to a carefully worded paragraph following a negative rating on an evaluation. No matter what form the communication takes, defining the problem means precisely establishing two critical differences:
   - The gap between the kind of performance students ought to be demonstrating (the desired outcome) and the kind of performance students are currently displaying
   - The gap between the instruction students need in order to make progress in their learning and the instruction students are currently receiving

7. **Understand and strategically use a repertoire of approaches to intervention.**
Interventions to help a teacher improve can range from a set of precise recommendations that grow out of an observation or data conference to an elaborate, contractually dictated improvement plan that involves a team and one or more years of intensive work. In Chapter 7 you will see how being able to draw from a repertoire and match your response to the individual and context allows you to be more strategic and timely in your response to ineffective instruction.

The action cycle is our attempt to make public and concrete the kind of problem solving that skillful instructional leaders do and how they act on their convictions. Here we will confine ourselves to its usefulness in tackling the hardest parts of performance evaluations. However, we recognize that skillful teachers engage in the same process when they try to determine what they can do for their struggling students. This behavior shows up in teams that take charge of their own learning and in whole schools that have become learning organizations. Master the process, make it work for you in challenging situations, and watch it provide unanticipated benefits in other arenas of school life.

USING MULTIPLE

DATA SOURCES

4A
EXPANDING THE SOURCES OF DATA WE USE TO EVALUATE

Driven by "Race to the Top" requirements to include student results in teacher evaluation, virtually every state is moving to expand the sources of data used to assess teachers' performance. Using multiple sources of data enables you to develop a deeper and more precise profile of an individual's performance. It also increases the validity of your ratings by reducing the impact of bias and judgment errors. To assess the impact of teaching on learning, all tasks in the action cycle in Figure 4A.1 rely on having accurate and varied data:

- To diagnose need
- To define and communicate problems
- To design interventions

Each of these purposes will be described in detail in the chapters that follow.

Figure 4A.1 Using Data throughout the Action Cycle

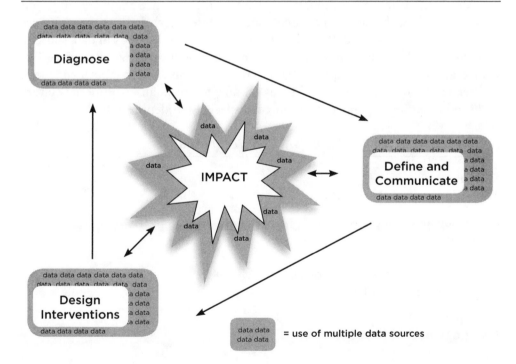

Chapters 4 and 5 provide two different but complementary resources to help you handle the evidence requirements for supervising and evaluating mediocre or unsatisfactory performers. Chapter 4 focuses on the data sources themselves: what they are, what they can tell you, and what questions you might want to ask about them. This chapter will help you navigate the data demands made by new evaluation standards, rubrics, and rating systems. Chapter 5 focuses on using a basic framework for teaching to diagnose the greatest area of need for a teacher with performance problems. Chapter 5 will help you select appropriate data sources matched to typical performance categories found in most evaluation instruments, such as management or planning. Begin with either chapter, based on your current needs and goals.

Chapter 4 is the best starting point when you want to expand your skill in using multiple data sources. Begin here when you want to do the following:

- Supplement observations and provide a fair rating of a teacher's performance
- Include student learning results in evaluations
- Provide evidence that an intervention is working or not working
- Make suggestions for data that teachers could collect to provide evidence of their performance or professionalism
- Specify evidence necessary to prove that a teacher has met the goals of an improvement plan
- Help content teams document the work they are doing to meet a team goal

For easy reference, the suggested data sources are organized by type: those that provide evidence about teaching, those that provide evidence about learning, and those that address the noninstructional aspects of a teacher's daily work (see Figure 4A.2). Sections 4B, 4C, and 4D will each deal with one of the types of data sources. You will find a brief description of the source, sample indicators for poor performance, and questions to help you dig into the source and the insights it can yield. The remainder of this section will focus on how to create an institutional culture that supports using expanded data sources, especially student results.

Figure 4A.2 Sources of Data

Section 4B
Teaching-Focused Data Sources

> Lesson and unit plans
> Homework and practice tasks
> Grading criteria
> Materials on walls, charts, or displays
> Technology and Internet use

Section 4C
Learning-Focused Data Sources
> Grading records
> Progress reporting
> Performance on formative assessments
> Feedback on student work
> Achievement data
> Student surveys
> Classroom interviews

Section 4D
Noninstructional Data Sources
    Professional growth plans and goal setting
    Meeting artifacts and observation notes
    Attendance records
    Arrival and departure records
    Communications to students, families, colleagues, or community
    Student placement data
    Discipline referral artifacts

BUILDING A MULTIPLE SOURCES CULTURE

The much-touted emphasis on using student results in teacher evaluation, though critical to making good decisions, has led to confusion, misconceptions, and fear in many districts across the country. In some cases hostile job actions and refusal to settle contracts have pointed out just how threatening some teachers perceive this type of evaluation to be.

As a skillful leader, you face a significant challenge. If you use multiple data sources and include student results only when you need to document mediocre performance, you will exacerbate the rumors and contribute to teachers' sense that they are under siege. Therefore, it is important to make consideration of multiple data sources, including student results, standard practice for all evaluations even if your state or school district has not yet adopted formal requirements to do so. So how do you build a culture in which supervisors and teachers expect to go well beyond one or two observations to determine the effectiveness of instruction and set individual goals for improvement? How do you shift from old assumptions and divisions of labor so that all teachers routinely take responsibility for collecting and analyzing data about the impact of their work? Figure 4.3 suggests some steps to change your school culture to one that uses data to improve instruction.

Figure 4A.3 How to Organize for a Multiple Data Source Environment

- **As you adopt performance standards, simultaneously identify data sources that could be used to collect data on each standard.** This is a critical activity to shift from a heavy reliance on observation and a teacher focus to evaluation that begins with the impact on learners. Whenever state regulations or local procedures permit, reserve complete management discretion in selecting and using data but make sure your suggested sources are carefully aligned to the standard.

- **Communicate clearly what sources of data can and might be used.** Whether the law in your state requires it or not, principles of fairness and equity dictate that supervisors inform supervisees about the data sources that could be considered in evaluating an individual's performance. (See Legal Note 4A.1.)

- **Embed any expectations regarding teacher collection of data in the contract.** If a district wants to require teachers to maintain a log or a portfolio for documentation, language to that effect should be clearly embedded in the contract. That step will help ensure that leaders are consistent when requesting that teachers produce certain high-priority data sources.

- **Conduct conferences that focus on data other than classroom observation.** For example, conferences could include data from the classroom walls, interviews with students, and formative assessment results. For a more detailed description of how to conduct these alternative conferences, see pages 188-201 in *The Skillful Leader II: Confronting Conditions That Undermine Learning* (2008).

- **Assess the degree to which use of data is embedded in your culture.** Provide feedback to the school to stimulate discussion about misconceptions and to identify professional development needs.

- **Design leadership training to focus on four interdependent skills:**
  1. Collecting data from a variety of sources
  2. Analyzing these data for meaning and impact on student learning
  3. Selecting areas for focus and action
  4. Communicating the gaps and areas for growth

Legal Note 4A.1 Data Gathering

When a district establishes its performance standards, appropriate data-gathering procedures must be identified. Ideally, as the evaluator or employer you want to preserve complete discretion in identifying and using data-gathering procedures. However, some states have adopted laws or regulations that prescribe what data gathering means and specify the percentage of a teacher's performance rating to be dictated by student results. Other states have left the determination of what data-gathering procedures can be used to local collective bargaining. Be certain to find out where your state and district fall on the continuum of either mandated methodology or open-ended discretion. For example, an appropriate statement might be something like the following language in a contract, policy manual, employee handbook, or other appropriately documented form: "In the Teacher Assessment Program, classroom observations are only one source of data. Additional sources of assessment data may include, but are not limited to, the following . . . " (Catalina Foothills School District Teacher Assessment Program [TAP] May 2012).

4B
TEACHING-FOCUSED DATA SOURCES

This category of data sources will help you move beyond relying on traditional observation as your sole source of data to diagnose, communicate, and document problems in teaching. It consists mainly of artifacts and includes

- Lesson and unit plans
- Homework and practice tasks
- Grading criteria
- Materials on walls, charts, or displays
- Technology and Internet uses

Artifacts are tangible representations of different aspects of teachers' complicated work. They vary in purpose and can provide valuable information about a teacher's depth of thinking and his or her decision-making process. Some artifacts, such as lesson plans or project guidelines, serve as indicators of planning. Others, such as a letter to a parent, a detailed syllabus, or a social contract hanging on the wall, reveal efforts to communicate and reinforce expectations. Still others, such as establishing grading criteria, relate to teachers' assessment of student learning.

LESSON AND UNIT PLANS

Lesson plans should be a high-priority data source. Examining written lesson plans (not just plan books) is essential:

- To explain why an observed lesson is fragmented and disjointed by identifying steps that were missed in planning
- To evaluate the alignment of intended instruction with state and district frameworks
- To analyze why students are consistently doing poorly on external accountability measures
- To document poor understanding of subject matter

Unit plans are essential sources if you are collecting data on whether the teacher or team produces competent lesson plans that include:

- Big ideas and essential understandings of the discipline that students should understand
- Prerequisite knowledge and skills students need in order to master the content of the new unit
- Activities that will get students actively involved in thinking about and applying the big ideas of a unit of study

- Pre- and post-assessments to determine what students are bringing to the unit of study and what they are taking away

Figure 4B.1 lists questions that are useful in analyzing the effectiveness of lesson and unit plans, discussing plans with teachers and teams, or coaching a struggling practitioner.

Figure 4B.1 Examining Lesson and Unit Plans

Lesson Plans
1. What **standard(s)** does this lesson address?
2. Does the plan include one or more clearly stated, worthwhile **student learning objectives** expressed in some variation of student-centered language such as "Students will be able to . . . as demonstrated by . . . .?
3. What **thinking skills**, tools, or processes will students learn or apply?
4. What will be the **grading criteria** (rubric) and exemplars that define student success?
5. What **prerequisite knowledge or skills** will students need to succeed in this lesson?
6. How will the teacher **frame the lesson** by making connections with previous learning and by giving the sequence and reason for the activities?
7. How will the teacher **assess prior knowledge** and identify student misconceptions and confusions? What strategies will the teacher use to reduce confusion?
8. What **formative assessment** is planned?
9. What **explanatory strategies** will be used to reach auditory, visual, and kinesthetic learners?
10. What structures are planned for the teacher to **check understanding** during the instruction in order provide data for possible re-teaching?
11. How will students have an opportunity to process or **summarize** their learning?

Unit Plans
1. What **central organizing ideas** does this unit address?
2. How is the unit **aligned** with state and district frameworks and with district benchmarks?
3. What **grading criteria**, including rubrics and exemplars, will define student success?
4. What **thinking skills**, tools, or processes will students learn or apply?
5. What **prerequisite knowledge or skills** will students need to succeed in this unit? How will these prerequisites be assessed?
6. What **pre and post assessments** and other formative assessments are planned?
7. What are the **opportunities for collaboration**, e.g., in developing common assessments, analyzing data, and conducting error analysis?
8. What will be the design for **summative assessment(s)**? What structures will be used beyond traditional tests?

> ### *Sample Indicators of Ineffective Practice*
>
> Lesson plans provided in writing or discussed during conferences
>
> - Contain no objectives or objectives expressed as lists of topics to be covered or activities to be done
> - Do not reference or make connections to standards
> - Equate objectives with doing activities rather than with mastering concepts and skills
> - Value covering content regardless of whether anyone learns
> - Do not show clear connections to organizing concepts and big ideas being studied
> - Often rely on activities that are not aligned to the goals of the curriculum or the intended daily objectives
> - Show no evidence of modifications as a result of data collected after or during previous instruction
> - Do not indicate that the teacher has thought about or intends to use formative assessment strategies to monitor student learning
> - Show little or no evidence of a planned sequence of questions that would help students develop higher order thinking and the ability to apply key concepts

HOMEWORK AND PRACTICE TASKS

"Tasks predict performance. What determines what students know and are able to do is not what the curriculum says that they are supposed to do or even what the teacher thinks she or he is asking them to do. What predicts performance is what students are actually doing" (City et al. 2009). This pithy statement highlights why you should examine the actual tasks that teachers select and design for their students. Take a quick walk around a classroom. Look at what is on the desks or tables and how students are interacting with the materials. Are students copying? Are they being asked to perform repetitive processes—the classic 100 long division problems—that test endurance rather than learning? Does the work challenge their thinking or merely keep them quiet? For example, notice the contrast between these two homework assignments:

1. Produce a creative illustration, chart, or model, or whatever that illustrates European exploration during the 15th through 17th centuries.

2. Create a visual representation that would help someone understand and remember one of the major themes identified during our study of European exploration. Consult your notes and text. Include in your visual at least five supporting events with a picture or diagram accompanied by short summary phrases.

Without even knowing the exact context for these assignments, you can see that the first one is likely to produce low-level thinking disconnected from a standard while the second one is at least tied to curricular concepts and requires some analytic work.

Figure 4B.2 illustrates the kinds of questions you could use to examine tasks.

Figure 4B.2 Examining Homework and Practice Tasks

Note that questions with an asterisk (*) might require a conversation with the teacher to supplement direct examination of the artifact.

1. What worthwhile learning target or objective does this task support?
2. Does the task clearly spell out what skills and knowledge are being practiced and the expectations for how students must complete the task?
3. *What prerequisite skills or knowledge are needed for this task, i.e., what would students need to have mastered previously?
4. *What are the criteria for success?
5. How would you characterize the level of rigor or intellectual demand required by each of these tasks? (Look for challenging "just right" work that demands effort but is not too difficult to render effort irrelevant.)
6. If you were the student who had to complete this task, what might be difficult for you?
7. What cognitive skills would students use to carry out the task? (Look for precise verbs such as "retell, listen, explain in your own words, copy, identify, or record" that will allow you to infer the cognitive demand.)
8. *What happens to the task after completion? Will students receive feedback? Will assignments be graded? Will there be a re-do opportunity? Will assignments be filed in notebooks or simply become fodder for paper airplanes and recycling bins?

Sample Indicators of Ineffective Practice

Homework and practice tasks

- Ask for rote recall, copying or simple paraphrasing, or repetitious practice of skills already mastered (a.k.a. "busywork")
- Are almost exclusively "canned" or purchased worksheets or study questions from the end of the chapter, often with little connection to major units, core skills, or the day's lesson
- Rarely include an objective or purpose for the work or criteria to help a student monitor his effort
- Show little or no evidence of modifications for students with limited English or Individual Educational Plans
- Show little or no evidence of adjustment or diversification to increase the level of challenge for students who are ready to stretch their skills

GRADING CRITERIA

What does it take to produce the highest quality ("A") work? Artifacts such as criteria for success checklists or scoring rubrics are helpful in answering this question. If you look at these artifacts in combination with grade books (described below), you get powerful data about expectations for learning. Keep in mind that merely having a rubric or criteria for success list is not enough. Most teachers are ill prepared to create such tools, and poor rubrics are easily downloaded from the Internet. These mediocre rubrics over-value low-level, "check-off" characteristics such as formatting and use vague distinctions between categories that cannot be readily measured, such as "enough details" versus "more than enough details." Many do not contain student-friendly language that would make them a useful tool for their intended audience. Figure 4B.3 suggests questions to help you evaluate grading criteria.

Figure 4B.3 Examining Grading Criteria

1. Do the criteria for success or rubrics align with key learning and high-priority standards?
2. Is the language clear and precise so that students could assess their own work or outsiders could easily make distinctions between levels of performance?
3. Is there a balance between compliance with technical demands (e.g., "must use three sources") and substantive learning (e.g., "must use evidence from the text to defend your argument")?
4. Is there any weighting assigned to criteria?
5. Is it clear how a final grade is calculated?

Sample Indicators of Ineffective Practice

Grading criteria

- Are based on poor-quality rubrics often downloaded from the Web or borrowed from a colleague
- Are disconnected from key targets and benchmarks
- Over emphasize easily measured procedures and formats (e.g., "Borders are lined up")
- Ignore state or district learning standards in determining final grades
- Contain vague language, e.g., "Grade on this project based on effort and accuracy"

CHARTS, DISPLAYS, AND MATERIALS ON WALLS

Artifacts on classroom walls provide a source of data for examining how teachers use visuals to support their instruction. This source can include expectation messages, models, exemplars, problem-solving protocols, grading criteria, and resources to consult during independent work. Figure 4B.4 suggests questions for examining how the wall data affect instruction.

Figure 4B.4 Examining Wall Data

Note that questions with an asterisk (*) might require a conversation with the teacher to supplement direct examination of the artifact.

1. What are the **criteria** for selecting student work to be posted? Is there a clear connection with standards, rubrics, or performance checklists?

2. Are **clear expectations** for classroom discourse in evidence, such as criteria for active listening or instructions on how to paraphrase?
3. Is there evidence of **thinking models or graphics**: charts such as "Steps for Problem Solving," "Writing Process Steps," or "Stems for Effective Leads"?
4. Are **standards posted** prominently in student-friendly language?
5. Is there any evidence of housekeeping routines and expectations for **student behavior**?
6. Is there evidence of **effort-based** "You can do it" messages?
7. Are there any indicators of **specific feedback** on student work (not simply smiley faces or "Awesome" stickers)?
8. Are there **curriculum-relevant content** artifacts such as word walls or individual charts showing progress on benchmarks (coded for confidentiality)?

Sample Indicators of Ineffective Practice

Charts, displays, and materials on walls

- Do not include models and resources to support instruction
- Are rarely refreshed and may have little or no connection to concepts being studied ("Getting to Know You" exercises from week 1 are still on the wall week 11)
- Are primarily commercial, chalk-filled, crinkled DC Heath charts and other ephemera from earlier eras
- Include student work not clearly aligned to criteria and standards, annotated with "Awesome" stickers and smiley faces
- Represent altars to the teacher and previous students such as pictures with every class s/he has taught or sports team s/he has coached

TECHNOLOGY, WEB PAGES, AND INTERNET SOURCES

Technology now provides classroom tools to support instruction that were not imagined in the 1990s: web-based demonstrations and instructional videos at teachers' fingertips, electronic response systems that allow instant access to how well students have mastered skills, interactive textbooks on tablet computers. Our purpose here is not to list all the possible classroom uses of technology but to emphasize that examining how teachers use technology provides a rich source of data about the quality of teaching. Clearly, this data source depends on the resources that the school provides. You cannot examine a teacher's use of student response systems (e.g., clickers) or SMART Boards^{tm}, for example, unless teachers have them available to use. This area includes how the teacher uses the Internet or develops classroom websites used to post assignments, conduct online discussions, or give individual feedback. Skillful teachers match the technology to their instruction and to the students before them. Mediocre performers waste technology potential and settle for low-level adoption.

Examining Website and Internet Sources

1. How do teachers integrate technology into their instruction?
2. In what ways do teachers use the Internet to support the objectives of their curriculum?
3. How do teachers use technology to communicate with parents?
4. How is users' confidentiality protected?
5. How do teachers use technology to support or enhance collaboration with colleagues and their own learning?

Sample Indicators of Ineffective Practice

Technology, web pages, and Internet sources

- Are not integrated into instruction or communication or not used at all
- Do not elevate the quality and rigor of instruction, e.g., using student response systems (SRS) to elicit answers for *recall* questions only
- Serve only the most elementary purposes such as using SMART Boards™ to list "Do Now" and homework)

Teacher-created data sources, usually in the form of physical artifacts that you can view or gather, provide invaluable insights into how an individual carries out daily work. They also become great starting points for conferences because the concrete items can help teachers remember a whole range of thinking, analysis, or questioning that underlies the artifact.

4C
LEARNING-FOCUSED DATA

Sources of learning-focused data include the following:

- Grading
- Progress reporting
- Performance on formative assessments
- Feedback on student work
- Achievement data
- Student surveys
- Classroom interviews

Sources in this section help you examine, define, and document the impact of instruction on student learning as you carry out a variety of supervisory functions. When you hold a post-observation conference, for example, include an examination of assessment data that lets you and the teacher study the impact of his/her effort. Include teachers' grading patterns and grading values in your discussions of results from standardized measures of student performance. Use student voices to help teams of teachers "hear" how students perceive the intent and values that lie behind instructional decisions.

As in the previous chapter, discussions of each data source include sample questions to use in examining the data and sample indicators of mediocre or poor performance.

GRADING

A teacher's electronic or physical grade book is an essential data source in understanding the variables that impact student learning. What teachers choose to grade and how they assign value reveals the knowledge, skills, and habits of mind they consider important for students to master. Examining grading practices powerfully illustrates the adage that "you inspect what you expect."

As with many alternative sources of data, use grade books cautiously, always accompanied with other sources of information. Avoid rushing to superficial judgments about completeness or neatness. Beware of jumping to conclusions. A skewed grading pattern with a high percentage of A and B grades could result either from grade inflation or from a teacher's success in moving students to mastery of the identified standards.

**Legal Note 4C.1
Grading Policies**

Do not use grading as a source of data for individual teachers without considering the school's grading policies and practices. It is the responsibility of the employer to make sure that grading and reporting practices have been developed by the employer and communicated as a uniform expectation for all employees. Be sure to review and understand the requirements of your state's laws regarding student records and ownership and control of such documents as student work products, physical grade books, or electronic records.

The questions listed in Figure 4C.1 assume that your district has made some effort to move toward standards-based grading. However, we also recognize that many schools still use traditional grading systems. Answers might differ depending on whether your school is using traditional grading, standards-based grading, or a hybrid mix.

Figure 4C.1 Examining Student Grades and Grade Distributions

Asterisks indicate the need for a conversation with the teacher.

1. *To what extent are the grades based on valid and varied assignments that assess core knowledge?
2. Do students receive zeroes? Why? Are zeroes averaged into grades?
3. How are assignments weighted?
   —Are trivial assessments like true-false quizzes given the same weight as demanding writing assignments?
   —Have electronic grading programs been used to average all assignments without regard to relative importance?
4. Is the grading system emphasizing worthwhile objectives aligned to district or state standards?
5. Are grades determined by comparing students (i.e., norm referenced) or by using criteria established in relation to an identified standard?
6. *Does grading show evidence of leniency error and grade inflation, i.e., the use of a subjective basket of qualities including cooperation, compliance, effort, work habits, and extra credit that contaminate assessments of academic proficiency?
7. Does grading show evidence of high failure rates resulting from severity error, i.e., ill-defined "high standards," and a value system that relies heavily on duplicating the bell curve?
8. What opportunities exist for re-doing work without penalty? To what extent was work made up?
9. What is the homework completion rate? What are the expectations about making up homework? What percent of the final grade is daily homework?
10. What—if any—role does extra credit play in grading?

Sample Indicators of Ineffective Practice

Grading practices

- Do not allow students opportunities to redo work in order to achieve mastery or earn higher grades on important learning tasks
- Rate performance as "Basic" without explanation or suggestions for how to achieve "Proficient"
- Rely exclusively on the use of a normal curve and adjust scores to meet that curve

- Are inconsistent or inequitable across course, grade level, or subject-area teams
- Average zeros into grade calculations for one or two pieces of work—making passing a course difficult or impossible

PROGRESS REPORTS

Progress reports may be written narratives that accompany grades, warning notices when students are in danger of failing, or statements chosen from a menu of electronic comments. Examining a teacher's progress reports can confirm and amplify what you learn from looking at grading data. To provide students and parents with useful feedback, progress reports should communicate information about the student's growth and should cite supporting data for any judgments made. They should also cite what the students need to do next. Figure 4C.2 contains questions to focus an examination of progress reports.

Figure 4C.2 Examining Progress Reports

1. Are the comments specific and data based?
2. Are comments aligned with recommendation(s) for improvement?
3. Are the impediments to high-quality performance clearly identified?
4. Is there a clear focus on where students should exert effort?
5. Is there an underlying message of belief in the student's capacity to learn?

Sample Indicators of Ineffective Practice

Progress reports

- Contain cliché-ridden phrases such as "Blissy is a pleasure to have in class" or "Not working up to potential"
- Rely heavily on comments that are judgment-rich and data-poor
- Do not include detailed information about what the student needs to do to improve
- Are dated or appear after struggling students have lost all opportunity to improve or make up work

PERFORMANCE ON FORMATIVE ASSESSMENTS

Formative assessments refer to strategies for data collection at the beginning of, during, and after instruction with the following primary purposes:

- Helping the teacher adjust what s/he plans to do next to ensure student mastery
- Helping the learner determine what next steps s/he has to take in order to meet a standard

Such strategies include

- Pre-assessments and activators (e.g., background knowledge probes, misconception check, Things I Know, Do Nows, Brainstorming)
- Checking questions, regular log entries, or brief mid-instruction quizzes that ask all students to show what they know or can do before instruction continues
- First drafts of essays, sketches, models of potential projects, lab reports, outlines, etc. that students assess using criteria checklists before proceeding to the next stage of work
- Closure activities that require students to summarize, answer or pose a question, or solve a new problem based on the day's learning

A particular task might function formatively—meaning the student and teacher use the information gained to improve the performance in another round of work—or summatively, meaning the task leads to a final judgment about mastery. Summative assessments that occur at the end of instruction in order to give a student a grade are a different data source and are not included here.

Leader Alert
Inspect What You Expect

The presence and skillful use of formative assessments plays an increasing important role in new teacher performance standards across the country. Because they have been underused, evaluators have rarely spent time on this data source despite its well-documented impact on student achievement. The absence of artifacts or evidence of formative assessment is important data. Do not give up asking for such evidence even if it is not present initially. Your inspection signals the seriousness of your expectations and may well lead to the adoption of new practices. ◆

Figure 4C.3 contains questions to use in determining the quality and utility of formative assessments.

Figure 4C.3 Examining Formative Assessments

1. How are the skills and content aligned with curriculum frameworks and state standards?
2. What content knowledge or skills are being assessed?
3. What cognitive skills are required to produce successful responses?
4. What prerequisite skills must students have already mastered?
5. What is the range of artifacts employed (e.g., writing tasks, weekly checkouts, lab reports, problem of the week, or student self-assessments)?
6. How will the results be used to modify the next steps of instruction?
7. What is the format for the formative assessment (short answer selected response, extended written response, performance tasks, or personal communication)?
8. Does the assessment measure the important learning or only the easier to measure information?

Sample Indicators of Ineffective Practice

Formative assessments

- Are rare or not present at all in weekly practice
- Rarely influence or result in adjustments to a teacher's daily planning
- Are too long or too cumbersome to enable the teacher to provide students with relevant, timely feedback on performance
- Do not align with or provide information about daily lesson objectives
- Check only superficial recall of facts or memorized information and do not provide opportunities for students to practice higher order thinking

FEEDBACK ON STUDENT WORK

Feedback is the information, not judgments, given to learners about their current performance in relation to a target performance. While definitions differ slightly, researchers using meta-analysis techniques have clearly linked standards-based feedback to improvements in student learning. Marzano cites feedback as one of his "Essential Nine" instructional strategies that show statistically significant improvement in student achievement across all content areas and grade levels (2001). Hattie ranks feedback as ninth in importance in a list of 138 "Zone of Desired Effects" or variables that impact learning (2009). Figure 4C.4 lists questions that can help you examine the quality of feedback on student work.

Figure 4C.4 Examining Feedback on Student Work

1. What is the balance of responses to student work ranging from information about progress (feedback) to guidance, suggestions, or evaluation that judges performance?
2. Is the feedback aligned with target standards and clear criteria for success?
3. Can students use the responses to improve their own performance?
4. Does the teacher seek feedback from the students to help identify learning obstacles and make their thinking more visible?
5. Does the teacher structure opportunities for peers to give feedback to each other?

Sample Indicators of Ineffective Practice

Oral or written comments on student work

- Provide little or no information about performance in relation to standards and criteria or advice about how to improve.
- Routinely feature inexplicit praise or judgments such as "awesome," "super," "good job," or "vague," "disorganized," "????" that would not help a student to repeat a strength or fix a problem
- Rely heavily on tangible rewards such as stickers depicting "happy faces" or thumbs ups and points for "showing up"
- Confuse feedback with grading
- Encourage without specific direction "Just keep working on it"

ACHIEVEMENT DATA

For the purpose of clarity, we will designate *achievement data* as results from measures that have been standardized in some way—as opposed to data from classroom assessments designed and administered by a single teacher. Several different kinds of data fall into this category, including results from the following tests:

- State and locally mandated testing
- National testing programs such as the PSAT, ACT, or SAT
- Benchmark exams that are part of adopted programs in reading, math, science, etc.
- Common assessments designed by teams of teachers to measure essential curriculum objectives

In our current era of high-stakes accountability, achievement data from a mix of sources must serve several major purposes:

1. Provide individual teachers and teams of teachers with information that will enable them to make decisions about their instruction that will improve student learning
2. Provide school and district leaders with the information they need to make decisions about resources, structures, and strategies that will lead to improvements in student learning
3. Enable supervisors and evaluators to meet newly adopted requirements to rate teachers' performance in providing high-impact instruction

For purposes one and two—making short-term and midterm decisions about instruction and resources—achievement data are most useful if they

- Come from measures that are aligned to the required curriculum of the district
- Can be analyzed item by item to reveal specific strengths and weaknesses for individual students and sub-groups of students
- Enable groups of teachers who are responsible for the same content to make timely adjustments to what they are doing
- Allow teachers and administrators to compare the performance of students longitudinally

As evaluation systems increasingly require the inclusion of achievement data, purpose three has become a particular source of teacher and leader concern. In many states supervisors are asked to base a percentage of a teacher's evaluation rating, ranging from 25 to 50 percent, on student growth on state assessments and locally selected measures. Achievement data to be used for rating should provide a longitudinal picture of the teachers' practice rather than simply reporting on the results for one year of instruction. Figure 4C.5 suggests questions to ask as you consider the achievement data you are currently using. Figure 4C.6 offers questions to ask of the data themselves.

Figure 4C.5 Considering the Usefulness of Achievement Data

1. Do our curriculum and instruction align with the standardized measures being used to assess student achievement? Are there deliberately determined alignment gaps we need to acknowledge and adjust for?
2. How might we use existing data controlled by teachers such as common chapter

and course examinations, major assignments and projects, and performance on locally adopted benchmark tests?

3. How much time and effort have teachers and supervisors spent examining and understanding the demands of the measures being used to track student achievement?

4. How many years of data on standardized tests do we need to form a judgment about the teacher's impact on learning?

5. How do we track, analyze, and account for students who are absent most of the year for illness or truancy?

Figure 4C.6 Examining Achievement Data

---

1. What patterns of student performance over the last two to three years are clearly revealed by these data? What questions about potential patterns need further investigation?

2. How does student performance compare among teachers over 2 to 3 years? Does what a student gets to learn depend on who s/he gets as a teacher?

3. Are there repeated differences between students' anticipated achievement or past record of performance and actual performance for certain teachers over a multi-year period?

4. Are there repeated differences in performance for subgroups for certain teachers over a multi-year period?

5. Do achievement data highlight required knowledge and skills that are not being adequately developed by current programs and practices across all teachers?

Sample Indicators of Ineffective Practice

Longitudinal data show

- Patterns of low student performance in particular subjects or grade levels or among colleagues teaching the same courses with roughly the same distribution of students
- Repeated differences in the performance of identified subgroups from teacher to teacher when the data are disaggregated
- Consistent gaps in student knowledge and skills despite analysis that identified what needed to be taught and/or curriculum and professional development aimed at closing those gaps
- Low or poor performance in distinct contrast to grades being given to students

Leader Alert
Correlate Test Results with Other Data Sources

Test results of any type should always be used in combination with several other data sources so that each corroborates, expands, or refines what you have learned from the others. For example, comparing results on common science assessments may suggest the need for diagnostic observations of one or two classrooms, comparisons of students' term grades and comments, and sampling of the classwork and homework assigned weekly to determine how the practices in the lower performing classroom differ from those in more successful sections. ◆

STUDENT SURVEYS

"We are the ones who observe teachers every day. Why don't they ask us for our opinions?" asked one of the high school students we interviewed. While many student-oriented teachers routinely use student surveys to inform their decisions, poor performers, perhaps fearful of the responses, rarely voluntarily seek feedback from their students. For this reason, we support the concept of requiring student surveys as part of your supervision and evaluation system. For example, Montgomery County Maryland secondary teachers are expected to give and analyze student surveys and to be ready to discuss how they will use the data to inform instruction. You can also use student surveys to compare and contrast patterns of instruction and curriculum implementation across courses and teachers. New Internet tools make the construction and administration of surveys much easier (consult www.zoomerang.com or www.surveymonkey.com). Questions to focus your examination of student surveys are listed in Figure 4C.7.

Figure 4C.7 Examining Student Surveys

1. Are individual students' identities protected from the teacher?
2. Are the data focused on comparing teachers' course and unit patterns?
3. Has everyone been informed regarding purpose and use of survey?
4. Has the survey been validated for the age of the students? (Manatt [1996] has developed forms for younger students, but young students may not respond with sufficient accuracy.)
5. Can the information gathered be used to change classroom practice?
6. Do the items require students to produce specific responses to questions rather than simple statements of preference or opinion (e.g., asking students to "Please give two examples of actions the teacher does that help you learn and two examples of actions you think are not helpful to you as a learner" is better than "Is the teacher fair?" or "How do other students feel about this teacher?" [Peterson 2000 110-113])?

Unless the subject of collecting data from students and parents has previously been bargained for with the teachers' union, any effort at implementation is likely to precipitate allegations of unilateral implementation, which might be considered a prohibited labor practice and/or a grievance and demand to bargain.

Legal Note 4C.2
Surveys of
Students and Parents

Sample Indicators of Ineffective Practice

Student surveys

- Are not administered
- Are administered if required by contract but not used as a source of feedback to modify teaching
- Focus exclusively on superficial or affective aspects of the classroom and do not allow students to comment on the impact of policies and practices
- Are poorly designed so that information gained will not help a teacher address student concerns
- Are set up so that student responses can be identified or will not be kept confidential

Leader Alert
Teacher Rating Websites

Internet rating sites, such as RateMyTeacher.com, provide outlets for complainers and invite stuffed ballot boxes and skewed responses. Their findings are not reliable indicators and should not be used in evaluation. In one case, a slew of positive ratings showed up toward the end of the semester for a teacher generally conceded to be a mediocre performer. No one could prove it, but colleagues thought the teacher might have contributed generously to the data! ◆

CLASSROOM INTERVIEWS

You can collect valuable data about the impact of teaching practices on student learning by questioning students during observations and walks. To make your data collection less random, select a few questions from Figure 4C.8 Classroom Interviews Question Bank. As an example you might ask, "What do you do when you are stuck or confused?" Take notes on the responses, which could vary from "I am never confused" to "Ask the teacher for help" to "Double check my work, reread the problem, review the steps in the directions." Contrasting answers such as these give you data about the student's perceived level of challenge and whether the learners can apply effective strategies.

Note that questions marked with an asterisk (*) below might require longer discussion with students and not work easily during classroom observations. These might require a focus group of students.

Figure 4C.8 Classroom Interviews Question Bank

Objectives and Standards
- What is the most important thing your teacher wants you to learn today? What does you teacher want you to be able to do by the end of this lesson?
- How will this activity you are working on help you to reach the learning objective?

- What skills or knowledge are you learning or have you learned in order to be successful on this work?

Assessment
- How will you know when you have learned the most important things?
- How will your teacher know when you have learned the most important things?

Getting Help
- What do you do when you are confused?
- How do you get help to succeed?

*Rigor
- Please tell me about something that you found difficult to learn today or over the last few weeks? Did you work through it? Were you successful? What accounts for your success (or failure)? What did you learn about yourself during this time?
- How does your teacher help you learn something difficult?
- Can you give an example of something you couldn't do before but now can do well?

Goal Setting
- Do you set goals for aspects of your work? Can you show me an example? Do you come back and evaluate how are you are doing?

*Feedback
- How does your teacher let you know how you are doing?
- Can you show me or tell me some examples of ideas for improvement given by your teacher?

Self-monitoring
- Are routines in place for you to keep track of your own learning?
- Do you maintain any journals, logs, notebooks, or portfolios?
- If so, does your teacher collect them and make comments? How are these products helping you learn?

Expectations
- What happens if you do not finish your work, your homework for example?
- How often does your teacher collect and comment on your journal or notebook?
- Does your teacher provide you with examples of actual work to help you understand the quality s/he expects? Please explain.

*Modifying Instruction Based on Data
- Does the teacher ever make a change in a lesson in the middle of class or at the beginning of the next day? Can you think of an example?
- Does your teacher ever refer to what s/he has learned about your learning from test results?

As with any other data sources described in this chapter, student answers should not be the sole source of information about an individual. Such answers provide one point of data that can be cross-referenced against other evidence to identify strengths that can be built upon and areas where improvement is needed.

The data sources in this chapter—from the informal (what students say) to the formal (results on standardized measures of performance)—help you establish and document the impact of teaching. Once you begin to ask for, examine, and discuss these data sources, you signal the shift away from traditional supervision and evaluation practices. That shift in emphasis will indeed help you meet the demands of new teacher evaluation systems. More important, however, it makes the reason for staying the course with a difficult evaluation—students' present and future learning—clear and compelling.

No one source provides enough information to make judgments about a teacher's body of work or future employment. In combination, however, they allow an evaluator to create a multi-faceted image of what is and is not working effectively and to identify the interventions teachers need.

4D
NONINSTRUCTIONAL DATA SOURCES

Because our major focus is ineffective or unsatisfactory *teaching*, previous sections have concentrated on data sources linked to the classroom. As part of evaluation reform efforts, however, states and districts increasingly include or expand standards related to professionalism. Evaluating professionalism requires you to collect and report on aspects of a teacher's work that take place outside the classroom.

Historically, "professionalism" dealt with the teacher's attendance, participation in (not use of) professional development, and fulfillment of routine duties or policy and contract requirements. Failure to meet such requirements could be easily documented. It led to an escalated series of interventions that were communicated to the teacher through meetings and memos. In extreme cases, failure to comply could result in dismissal on the grounds of insubordination (see Section 5G, Chapter 9, and Chapter 10).

Now teachers are expected to be contributing members of a grade-level or content-alike team or a "professional learning community." They are expected to demonstrate that they are continuous learners by developing and carrying out meaningful growth plans and to demonstrate cultural proficiency in their communication and partnerships with parents and community. Thus you and the teacher may find yourselves looking for data in previously unexamined places.

In general, collecting data in this noninstructional category requires taking advantage of existing records or documents such as:

- Professional growth plans and goals
- Meeting artifacts
- Attendance records
- Arrival and departure records
- Communications to students, families, colleagues, or community
- Student placement data
- Discipline referrals

It also means adding observations of events taking place outside the classroom to your repertoire of leadership activities. Keep these data in whatever combination of traditional desk or electronic desktop files helps you to remember what you have seen, give good feedback and guidance, and back up any ratings you must make on these noninstructional standards.

PROFESSIONAL GROWTH PLANS AND GOALS

Refer to Section 7C for additional information on goal setting, particularly Figures 7C.1 and 7C.5 and Example 7C.2.

Many states and districts now require teachers to develop professional growth plans and to include goals for student learning. Such plans may be one of the requirements for initial certification, for recertification, or for multi-year staff evaluation cycles. At their best, the professional growth plans provide opportunities for teachers to assess their own practice and set personal targets that are aligned with school and district goals. Your district may be a model site for such work. However, in most places we see, these plans are simply make-work. Poor initial training, limited aspirations, and an emphasis on low-level compliance yield lists of vague activities that overworked leaders simply sign off on at the end of the year. Ineffective performers rarely change as a result of goal setting in such places. Figure 4D.1 lists questions you might use to examine the quality of professional growth plans.

Figure 4D.1 Examining Professional Growth Plans

- **What is the student-learning problem that establishes the need for a teacher-learning goal?** A problem statement provides the context or rationale for the plan, e.g., "Based on the data examined, students are not able to answer open-ended questions. How can we modify our instruction to increase student skill in responding to open-ended questions?"

- **Does the plan limit the number of goals to two or three?** Goals should be limited so that teachers can concentrate their effort. It is difficult to implement or monitor more than three goals. Districts that require more than three goals should consider reducing the required number of goals.

- **Are the action steps logical and clearly aligned to the goal?** Steps should logically produce a good outcome rather than statements of an activity or program the teacher wanted to try regardless of its relation to the goal.

- **What data are going to be collected?** Are the goals stated in measurable terms (see Figure 7C.5)?

- **How will the plan affect the identified student learning gap?**

- **Does the plan help to promote collaborative efforts to improve learning among teachers?** Sometimes goals are truly individual. However, impact can be magnified when goals are structured to promote joint problem solving and action.

- **Can a plan lead to insights that are transferable or actions that might apply across a wide range of teaching contexts?** For example, "Ninth-grade students will increase their skill in responding to open-ended questions from 52 percent proficiency to 75 percent proficiency by May 2012."

> ### *Sample Indicators of Ineffective Practice*
>
> Goals or growth plans
>
> - Show little or no evidence that data has been used to identify worthwhile learning for students
> - Focus on completing activities and/or minimal compliance with procedures that should be part of regular daily work
> - Are either unrealistically ambitious or trivial
> - Focus on personal interests not aligned to school, district, or team goals
> - Attribute gaps in student achievement largely to factors outside of school

Leader Alert
Teacher Self-Evaluation

Teacher self-evaluation is often required for professional growth plans or teacher evaluations. Ineffective performers tend to rate their performance significantly higher than do supervisors, parents, or students; good teachers tend to be overly critical and give themselves poor ratings on self-evaluations. Therefore, teacher self-evaluation has limited validity as a source of data for reflection. However, occasionally mediocre performers know that their skills, expectations, or curriculum knowledge have slipped over time. In this context teacher self-evaluation serves admirably as a source of data when a leader is trying to diagnose an individual's capacity for setting appropriate goals and participating in the design of effective interventions. ◆

MEETING ARTIFACTS AND OBSERVATION NOTES

As the adage goes, if you *expect* teachers to collaborate, you need to *inspect* and give feedback on the quality of the collaboration. You can collect information about collaboration in a variety of ways:

- Through direct observation: observing and collecting data on a team or committee meeting
- By examining artifacts such as meeting notes, agendas, reports, or products such as common assessments, unit plans, support materials for students, or student work that results from decisions made by a team
- Through conferences: teachers' reports about and analysis of agreements made, actions taken as a result of collaboration and the impact on their teaching and students' learning

Figure 4D.2 suggests questions that can help you analyze teachers' collaborative work. See also questions in Section 5D under "Contributions as a Collaborative Member of the Faculty."

Figure 4D.2 Examining Observations and Artifacts of Collaboration

- Do the teacher's verbal contributions and actions demonstrate a belief that all students can learn? Is s/he willing to try new strategies, take risks, or engage in substantial efforts to help students make progress in meeting standards?
- Is the teacher able to put aside his or her sense of individual autonomy and individual preferences in order to honor commitments made by a team and to make good decisions in service of students' learning?
- Does the teacher assume ownership and responsibility for students' performance and the results of instruction?
- Does the teacher contribute effectively to good problem identification and problem solving so that collaborative effort gets expended on work that is likely to have a positive effect on student learning?
- Does the teacher display a commitment to and skills in using standards and data to improve student learning?
- Does the teacher deal effectively and productively with disagreements and conflict or engage in "parking lot behaviors" that undermine the team's effectiveness?
- Does the teacher monitor his or her own behaviors and contributions and honor norms established by community?

To extend your analysis of collaboration, please consult *The Skillful Leader II: Confronting Conditions that Undermine Learning* (2008).

Sample Indicators of Ineffective Practice

Observations and artifacts of collaboration

- Show that teachers are accepting debilitating comments about students' capacity to learn and/or blaming students when data reveal achievement gaps
- Reveal patterns of blocking behaviors such as dominating the group, dismissing all ideas or "naysaying," failing to participate, making distracting comments, telling off-task stories, and using adversarial nonverbal expressions
- Emphasize teacher autonomy over team commitments to actions that would address student learning gaps
- Reveal regular attention to low-level tasks and concerns such as scheduling, parent complaints, or production of materials rather than to improvements in instruction
- Do not correlate with classroom observations, thus suggesting that individuals are not implementing what the team has identified as high-priority improvements

ATTENDANCE RECORDS

Absenteeism is a sensitive issue. As a supervisor and concerned human being, you face the built-in competition between empathizing with or tolerating the personal circumstances of the teacher and worrying about the quality of instruction that children receive when their teacher is absent. It really does not make any difference why a teacher is absent (e.g., legitimate illness, family illness, personal day, professional day). That absence disrupts the workplace and diminishes the quality of instruction students receive. In examining attendance records, you face two key questions: (1) when does absenteeism need a response, and (2) when does it become excessive so that that the teacher is no longer effective or qualified to continue to hold his or her position?

Unions carefully monitor how leaders respond to absenteeism. Sick leave and personal day benefits are fiercely protected because every staff member may face a health or personal crisis requiring extensive leave at some point. Students and parents view the teacher's right to be absent quite differently. Unless the caliber of instruction provided by a substitute is better than that of the assigned teacher, parents know that each substitute day a child experiences is likely to equal a lost or reduced opportunity to learn. With caution then, attendance patterns can be collected and analyzed with special focus on the use of allotted sick days, especially Fridays and Mondays.

Figure 4D.3 suggests questions that can help you investigate teachers' attendance reports.

Legal Note 4D.1 Dealing with Absenteeism

Determining when absenteeism is excessive and actionable depends on the circumstances of each case. It requires thorough and accurate record keeping with respect to each employee's attendance. It also requires centralized record keeping so that patterns and practices can be scrutinized from a system-wide perspective and reacted to where appropriate. The issue is further complicated by the interaction between local policies, contract language, state and federal laws pertaining to disabilities (e.g., the Americans with Disabilities Act), and medical leave (e.g., the Family Medical Leave Act).

Until you have irrefutable evidence of abuse, all absenteeism should be approached with caution, compassion, and a positive frame of mind on how supervisory personnel can obtain valid information regarding the cause of the absenteeism and the impact it is having on the goals of the organization. Developing an appropriate response may be further complicated by the private nature of the reasons an employee may be absent and the constraints of various privacy laws relating to medical records. Counseling, employee assistance programs, formal investigations, warnings, progressive discipline, and, ultimately, if justified, dismissal are all options available to the employer. The facts of each case will ultimately determine the appropriateness and the legitimacy of the employer's action(s) in response to employee absenteeism.

Figure 4D.3 Examining Attendance Records

---

1. Does the record show a clear pattern of absences on Fridays, Mondays, and days before or after school holidays?
2. Are there patterns of absence around deadlines and reporting periods?

3. Are there patterns of absence that result from administrative demands or increased supervisory attention (see Platt et al. 2008)?
4. Are there patterns of using up every sick day each year?
5. Is there an explanation for the observed patterns?

Sample Indicators of Ineffective Practice

Attendance records show a pattern of

- Single-day absences around holidays, vacations, and weekends
- Deliberately scheduling non-urgent medical procedures or optional surgery during the school year
- Repeated absences on professional development or meeting days
- Absences on or near grade reporting deadlines or near key testing periods

ARRIVAL AND DEPARTURE RECORDS

Everyone occasionally misses a deadline, forgets recess coverage, or overlooks required meetings. Here we are concerned with recurring patterns of failure to implement a commonly understood school policy. Establishing a punch-clock mentality by rigorous attendance taking and recording of arrival and departures should not dominate your time and leadership focus. However, pay attention to this source of data when teachers' arrival and departure patterns regularly violate the contract (see Figure 4D.4).

Leader Alert
Communicate and Consistently Honor Start and End Times

Do not ignore repeated minor contractual breeches because they can become part of the tacit institutional agreement that violation will be tolerated. Inquire immediately when you notice regular lateness (more than twice in succession) to professional meetings. A quick oral worry "I have noticed that you have been 10 to 15 minutes late the last few weeks to the fifth-grade team meeting. Can you help me understand what is going on?" can set the stage for written reprimands later, if necessary. Do not assume teachers are familiar with policies and agreements. Set the stage for documenting lack of compliance by explicitly communicating the policies and agreements in writing and during early faculty meetings. Do this even if this communication is not mandated in your district contract. For more detail see Chapter 9. ◆

Figure 4D.4 Examining Arrival and Departure Data

1. Does the teacher routinely (three or more times) arrive late for:
   - The start of school or classes
   - Duties
   - Dropping off or picking up students in elementary school at special subjects such as physical education, art, or music
   - Faculty, team, or committee meetings
   - Parent conferences or other scheduled appointments
   - IEP meetings
2. Does the teacher frequently need to leave early from:
   - The last period of school when it is a prep or planning period
   - Faculty, team, or committee meetings
   - Professional development sessions
   - IEP meetings
   - School on days before holidays or long weekends
3. Do you or others frequently have difficulty finding a teacher at the beginning or end of school or on professional development days?
4. Do sign-in or sign-out sheets contain signatures in handwriting other than the teacher's or are there repeated patterns of "forgetting" to initial such records?

Sample Indicators of Ineffective Practice

Arrival and departure patterns coupled with notes re requests and teacher-provided "explanations" suggest that individuals

- Treat start times as approximate or secondary to their immediate needs by routinely scheduling personal appointments and obligations that infringe on contractually specified departure times
- Frequently blame problems that cause them to be late or depart early while others facing the same traffic, student demands, or backlog of paperwork manage to be on time
- Have trained colleagues to cover for them for being consistently 1 to 5 minutes late for most obligations
- Limit opportunities for spontaneous collaboration or quick communications about students by being the last one into the building and the first one out every day

Leader Alert
Arrival and Departure Norms

Arrival and departure may be a cultural problem in a school when leaders are always late. Examine your own messages and behavior and those of district personnel first to determine whether there are unspoken agreements about when events really start or whether certain players use late arrival as a device to signal their power or importance. Turning such a norm around requires more than identifying and speaking to individual violators. You will need to identify and name the pattern and the problems it creates, perhaps by using a focus group and sharing data on arrivals and departures of individuals (even without names). ◆

COMMUNICATIONS TO STUDENTS, FAMILIES, COLLEAGUES, AND COMMUNITY

Professionalism includes communication with colleagues, families, and the community. Written communication to families is a powerful source of data that reveals important messages about expectations, curriculum and student-performance standards, the teacher's availability for support, and the teacher's understanding of students' interests and culture. Communications directed to colleagues or in support of system initiatives often show a teacher's understanding of key concepts affecting curriculum, instruction, and assessment as well as how changes that would benefit students come about. Some of your information about teachers' professional communication will come from your observations. However, to create a full picture of teachers' work, consider asking faculty to assemble a communication portfolio from the following list:

- Newsletters
- Beginning of the year letter
- Back to school night handouts
- Friday memos
- Email and web page (see Section 4B)
- Parent meeting notes
- Permission slips
- Substitute plans
- Notes and emails to parents and counselors
- Records of individual tutoring sessions and study groups
- Phone log
- Referrals (documentation of referral data and use of IEPs)

Figure 4D.5 suggests ways to examine teachers' written communications.

Figure 4D.5 Examining Communication Artifacts

- What is the repertoire of different communication strategies used by the teacher? How appropriately are they matched to the needs of the audiences identified?
- Does the teacher initiate communication with families and respond to family requests in a timely way?
- What is the quality of communication with colleagues and with leaders at all levels of the system? Does the teacher initiate appropriate communication to help serve students effectively? Does the teacher respond to requests for information from colleagues or district personnel in a timely and appropriate way?
- What is the quality of language precision and grammar in the written material?
- Is there a need for assistance in translating information for second-language families?
- Does the teacher adhere to school policies and timelines for communication?

Sample Indicators of Ineffective Practice

Written communications

- Contain spelling mistakes, grammar errors, or inaccuracies
- Show problems with appropriate matching of tone or content or appropriate discretion
- Are garbled, jargon-laden, or meandering

STUDENT PLACEMENT DECISIONS

Any time students, parents, or teachers have opportunities to request or recommend placement, you get a valuable window on some of the hidden treaties and underground patterns of behavior going on in the school. Sources in this category include

- Letters, memos, or verbal requests by parents (or students in high school) to have certain teachers and not others
- End-of-year placement decisions where, for example, fourth-grade teachers may protect all their special education students from a fifth-grade teacher who refuses to honor educational plan modifications
- Recommendations by counselors to make sure that certain at-risk students are placed with some teachers and not others
- Transfer requests and recommendations in high school and middle school

Honoring these requests without tackling the root of the problem can lead to unequal class sizes, inequitable student loads, and unhappy parents and students. Work-around solutions combined with a habit of withholding data about why the work-around has been created protect mediocre performers and almost inevitably appear to be punishing others. Rather than hiding the data about student placement requests, present them to the affected teachers and to their supervisors if you suspect that enabling has been going on. Once these patterns are out in the open, you can then work with the teacher to identify the reasons for the negative perception and to design appropriate interventions. Figure 4D.6 suggests questions to ask about student placement decisions.

Figure 4D.6 Examining Student Placement Decisions

1. Is there any evidence of inequities in teacher assignments and student loads resulting from placement decisions?
2. Do placement patterns show that a certain group of students are never assigned to one or more teachers in the faculty?
3. Is there evidence that individuals making placement decisions are routinely tailoring classes to avoid parent complaints?
4. Is there evidence that "high maintenance" students are routinely transferred from certain classrooms without informing the teacher or as a favor to the teacher?

> ### *Sample Indicators of Ineffective Practice*
>
> Placement patterns suggest that some individuals
>
> - Avoid assignments they perceive to be difficult by becoming labeled as "the person who doesn't do or doesn't like such and such"
> - Have trained colleagues, counselors, or administrators to make "protective" placement assignments by persistently demonstrating their displeasure at having to work with certain types of students
> - Have deliberately cultivated myths about their expertise or the inadequacies of others that routinely cause parental upheaval when next year's course placements are being determined
> - Benefit from placement avoidance and tailoring by getting easier assignments, e.g., smaller classes or a select group of students

DISCIPLINE REFERRALS

Assistant principals often claim that student discipline problems should be attributed to particular teachers rather than to particular students. A handful of students can disrupt any classroom they find themselves in. More commonly, however, certain teachers can manage and inspire students and rarely need help with disciplinary issues. Others routinely clash with and kick out students who are perfectly well behaved and productive in colleagues' rooms. You can use the patterns of discipline referrals as a source of data to identify students who are being sent to the office and to make comparisons with the same students in classes taught by other teachers. Be careful to monitor new teachers for their referrals. If new teachers never send students out, they could be tolerating too much off-task behavior.

Before using data from referrals to document poor performance, you need to provide institutional support to teachers struggling with discipline. Such support might involve adopting schoolwide discipline practices, offering a mentor or counselor to support behavioral programs, or providing training and feedback to help an individual acquire new skills.

The questions in Figure 4D.7 can help you investigate patterns in teachers' discipline referrals. For additional questions see Section 5B.

Figure 4D.7 Examining Discipline Referrals

1. Do particular teachers or combinations of students and teachers show discernible referral patterns?
2. Do referral patterns suggest that certain students or readily identified groups of students are being singled out for particularly stringent discipline or no second chances?
3. Has the teacher clearly communicated the expectations for student behavior?
4. How does the teacher describe the cause of disruptive behavior that results in dismissal from class? How does that compare with the students' explanations?

5. Do both parties attribute discipline problems to factors beyond their control, e.g., the students' home life or family circumstance or the teacher's dislike or prejudice?
6. What is the teacher's repertoire of ways to eliminate disruptions and inattentive behavior?

Sample Indicators of Ineffective Practice

Discipline referrals and reasons for those referrals

- Show that particular teachers consistently choose to avoid dealing with even the most low-level misbehavior in their classes
- Suggest that teachers' expectations for behavior and consequences for misbehavior are inconsistent, poorly communicated, or not well understood
- Show that certain students or readily identified subgroups of students are singled out for punishment at greater rates than others
- Routinely attribute problems to factors outside of school such as students' home life or family circumstances

Existing records (attendance, placement recommendations, and discipline referrals) and readily accessible information (agendas, work products, and communication artifacts) become sources of data about aspects of a teacher's professional performance that are not directly connected to instruction. Your file notes indicating communications about fulfillment of professional responsibilities combined with notes you take from observations of the teachers' interactions and contributions outside of the classroom (in meetings and during duties) can provide a window on the conditions that affect both the teacher's and the students' success. Any concerns arising from these data sources should be communicated directly to the teacher. Use the continuum of responses described in Chapter 6 and be aware of the public record laws in your state.

Noninstructional data sources are most frequently used to evaluate teacher performance associated with professionalism. Your evaluation standards and criteria are likely to include categories such as attendance, arrival/departure times and meeting deadlines. Compliance with contractual requirements that fall into those categories often becomes critical when you are using progressive discipline (see Chapter 9), but they will not drive your school improvement effort. Whenever possible, collect data and give feedback on professional growth plans and team collaboration. Paying attention to these growth areas of professionalism will signal clearly where you expect teachers to put their time and effort.

CHAPTER 5

DIAGNOSING PROBLEMS

5A
OVERVIEW

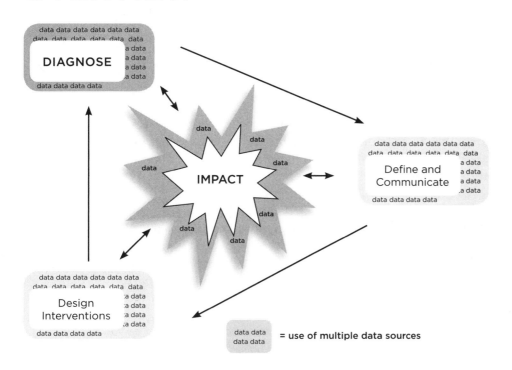

Figure 5A.1 The Diagnostic Step in the Action Cycle

To take appropriate and strategic action against ineffective instruction, you must be a diagnostician. Diagnosis is an essential process of problem identification and analysis that too many time-pressed administrators overlook. Don't skip this step in the cycle. It is the one that will help you make the most of your limited time, manage competing priorities, and survive the endless interruptions that threaten your focus on learning.

Diagnosis is primarily a growth-oriented function. In diagnostic mode, you are not abandoning your responsibilities as an evaluator. You are simply not waiting for or relying exclusively on an *evaluation system's* procedures and timetables to improve teaching and learning quality. You work flexibly and opportunistically with all the resources available to answer the following questions:

- Which teachers and students need help immediately, regardless of where they are in a formal cycle?
- Where should you and your team—coaches, specialists, other administrators, lead teachers, and counselors—invest improvement efforts to yield the maximum benefit for students?
- Which existing systems, such as those for professional development, goal setting, recertification, or research and accountability, can be aligned with evaluation to maximize the impact of individual interventions?

Ultimately, you want to determine where there are gaps between the standards all students should master and their current performance. You want to identify factors likely to be causing or influencing those gaps. You are a "problem namer" and a problem analyst at this stage, not a solution giver. Action at this step in the cycle therefore involves examining a range of data sources so that you can compile a complete picture detailing:

- How students are struggling
- What skills and content they have not yet mastered
- What is and is not happening in their classrooms and in the teams responsible for their learning
- What is not yet happening at the school level

Several key strategies, discussed below, will help you expand your diagnostic capabilities. They include differentiating between pervasive and individual problems, establishing shared frameworks for diagnosis, and developing a repertoire of diagnostic questions.

As Figure 5A.2 shows, skillful leaders distinguish between a *pervasive* problem in performance that occurs across many classrooms and a *particular* one in making their diagnoses.

Figure 5A.2 Diagnosing Where to Invest Effort

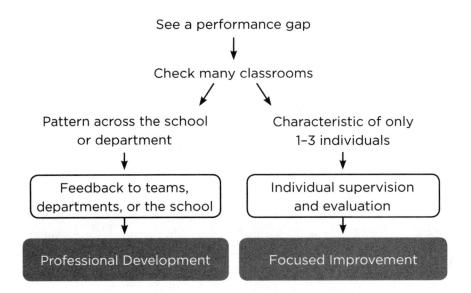

If many teachers are struggling with a new program or with helping students reach a benchmark, then the problem is pervasive. The arena for taking on a pervasive issue is not one-to-one supervisory interactions. For a widespread deficiency, you need approaches that make a problem public and that reach many people simultaneously. You might, for example,

- Report the data to a whole faculty and design in-depth professional development to close the gap you see
- Combine professional learning with collaborative work in teams
- Create cross-disciplinary study groups

Or, recognizing that nothing is more discouraging for high-performing teachers than to be subjected to blanket blame, you might choose to enlist the services of that group to teach and inspire others. The primary focus of this handbook is tackling the particular problems of individuals, but the frameworks and diagnostic questions in Sections 5B through 5G will help you gather and present data about gaps to groups of any size.

Establishing Shared Frameworks for Diagnosis

All school districts have evaluation instruments that identify performance standards for the different aspects of an educator's job: teaching, professional learning, and professional responsibilities. The format of the standards ranges from in-depth rubrics such as Marzano's Causal Teacher Evaluation Model (2011) and Danielson's Framework for Teaching (2011) to nonrubric descriptors such as the California Standards for the Teaching Profession (CSTP) or simple technical checklists with vague descriptors such as "Motivates students." Although many states are starting to adopt evaluation instruments that define levels of performance, the format for the tool you use is less important than the clarity and relevance of the content. Whatever instrument you adopt should provide you and your teachers with common language about professional capacities that is comprehensive, accessible, and based on research.

Diagnosing Classroom Responsibilities

To illustrate what we mean by a common language and framework, we have chosen to use the Map of Pedagogical Knowledge (Saphier et al. 2008), also known as the Skillful Teacher Pyramid (see Figure 5A.3). This map can be a companion to and resource for whatever evaluation system or set of performance standards your state or local district adopts. It is a compendium of research, a common language, and a concept system that can be used to explain or back up any evaluation instrument, provide substance for a diagnosis, and help you find intervention strategies.

The Skillful Teacher framework groups the tasks of teaching into four different functions: management, instruction, motivation, and curriculum planning. Each of the four functions has different areas of performance that teachers must master and apply. To motivate students, for example, a teacher must:

- Build good relationships with students
- Create a classroom climate that is inclusive and fosters student perseverance and confidence
- Communicate high positive standards and expectations through different arenas of classroom life from calling on students to offering help or dealing with errors

Each area of performance contains an extensive repertoire of research-based and empirically tested strategies teachers can select to match to their students, their goals, and the circumstances they face on any given day.

Figure 5A.3 Map of Pedagogical Knowledge

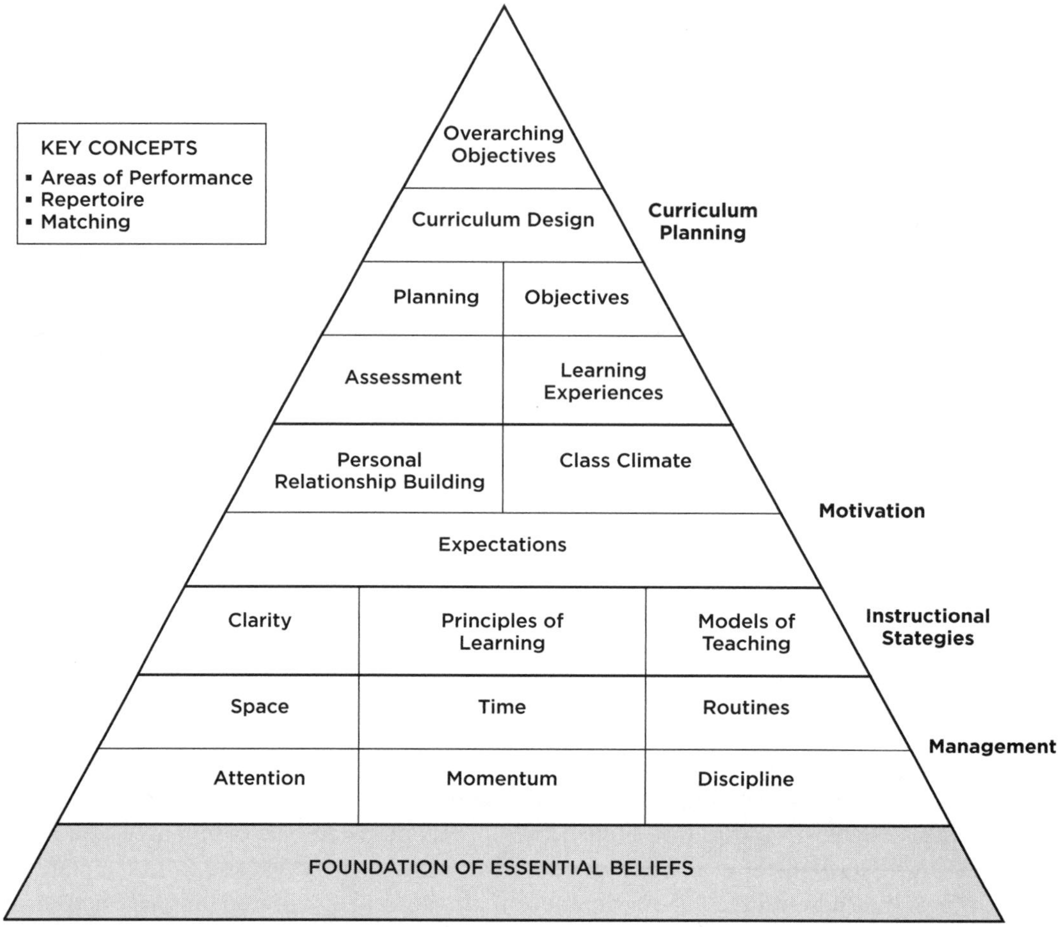

KEY CONCEPTS
- Areas of Performance
- Repertoire
- Matching

Overarching Objectives

Curriculum Design — **Curriculum Planning**

Planning | Objectives

Assessment | Learning Experiences

Personal Relationship Building | Class Climate

Expectations — **Motivation**

Clarity | Principles of Learning | Models of Teaching — **Instructional Stategies**

Space | Time | Routines

Attention | Momentum | Discipline — **Management**

FOUNDATION OF ESSENTIAL BELIEFS

Research for Better Teaching, Inc. · One Acton Place, Acton, MA 01720 · (978) 263-9449 · www.RBTeach.com

Diagnosing Professional Responsibilities Outside of the Classroom

The roles and obligations of teachers extend well beyond what goes on with students in a classroom. A number of different resources ranging from the Core Propositions of the National Board for Professional Teaching Standards to Danielson's Framework for Teaching (2011), Marzano's Causal Evaluation (2011), or Marshall's Teacher Evaluation Rubrics (2013) provide useful tools for breaking down and analyzing professional responsibilities outside of the classroom. With minor variations in wording, specificity, and emphasis, most evaluation standards seem to agree on a number of categories including: communicating and engaging with families and communities, collaborating effectively with colleagues to meet the needs of students and the school, growing and learning professionally (including reflecting on one's own teaching), and meeting obligations for record keeping, attendance, and punctuality.

Asking Diagnostic Questions

Carl Glickman coined the expression *cardiac assessment* to describe leaders who feel something in their heart but don't know exactly what the issue is or how to put their finger on it. You probably have had numerous situations where your gut tells you something is not right, but you don't have the data to prove it. Physicians and systems analysts often ask a series of diagnostic questions to pinpoint the likely causes when something is not functioning well. Sections 5B to 5G contain sample diagnostic questions to help you zero in on potential gaps in the teaching function being discussed. You can use the diagnostic questions to pinpoint problems when you are

- Trying to convert a general feeling or sense of unease into evidence that describes a specific weakness
- Doing a general check-up on school, grade level, or content area instruction
- Gathering data about specific areas of instruction that are the focus of school or grade-level improvement

As you examine the questions, note that some begin with a focus on learners to help you identify the positive and negative impacts of teaching and the consequences of teacher actions.

Content of the Diagnostic Section

Although your diagnostic work will undoubtedly require as much supervision as evaluation, ultimately you will have to match the data you collect and organize to the categories in your evaluation instrument. Most rubric-based instruments require examination and ratings in a large number of variously labeled "domains," "categories," "elements," or "indicators." That demand can be overwhelming when you are strapped for time. To help you with the task of matching the questions from the Skillful Teacher framework to your instrument's categories, we've organized the next six sections of this chapter by using the following labels:

- Management
- Instruction
- Expectations, personal relationship building, and classroom climate
- Planning
- Assessment
- Professionalism and collaboration

These categories seem to best represent the common content embedded in the major performance evaluation frameworks being used across the country.

Each section includes a short description of the function and its significance, the optimum context for concentrating on that category of performance, useful sources of data, and sample diagnostic questions to guide you in collecting data.

5B

DIAGNOSING PROBLEMS IN MANAGEMENT

Have you visited a classroom recently where students are off task, there are no routines, and no learning is apparent? Undoubtedly your diagnosis flew to poor classroom management. Management sets the table for the instructional meal to follow. It is a necessary but not sufficient condition for learning. Without good management, it is hard for students to stay focused and work productively. The academic energy of the classroom dissipates, and students sometimes report that they feel unsafe as well as untaught.

In the Skillful Teacher framework, management includes tasks such as:

- Getting, holding, or regaining attention
- Setting productive routines
- Preparing materials and keeping an orderly flow of events
- Arranging space
- Using time wisely
- Developing a repertoire for dealing with discipline issues

Other frameworks and standards may include tasks involved in creating an academically rigorous and welcoming classroom climate, conveying behavioral expectations, or motivating students.

Management problems are easily noted and documented. They frequently cause disruptions in school life that surface in complaints from colleagues, parents, or even students themselves. Every seasoned teacher with effective radar knows the difference between productive and unproductive noise billowing out a classroom door. But noise is an unreliable measure most of the time. Figure 5B.1 suggests some of the most useful data sources for examining day-to-day management and its impact on students.

Figure 5B.1 Sources of Data for Diagnosing Problems with Classroom Management

- **Classroom observations.** Visit classrooms for 15 to 30 minutes to determine whether basic routines and strategies for keeping students' attention are in place over time.
- **Walks that focus on class beginnings, transitions, and endings.** Drop in on multiple classrooms for 5 to 7 minutes to determine whether these powerful points in a lesson are ragged and full of wasted time or skillfully used for setting expectations, framing and connecting learning, and for lesson closure.
- **Discipline referrals.** Examine how frequently teachers send students to the office or counselors.
- **Set-up and use of space.** Look at whether furniture and resources are arranged

so that students can function independently and the teacher can circulate quickly and easily to monitor and respond to students.

- **Time allocation.** Construct a timeline for how teachers spend students' time (see Figure 5B.2).
- **Student interviews.** Ask a representative sample of students, "How would you describe the typical behavior of students in this classroom?" or "Would you describe students in this classroom as focused and on task?" Interviewing students directly offsets the skewed behavior an evaluator's presence sometimes causes.

Poor classroom management tends to be the diagnosis most likely to get a teacher labeled as incompetent. It can receive a disproportionate investment of supervisory effort relative to the resulting benefits for students. Before you settle on management as the primary reason for a teacher's problem or students' poor results, remember that other areas of performance can be the root cause for the surface symptoms you see, as in the following situations:

- The teacher has not set and communicated clear, attainable targets for learning and criteria for success [planning].
- The teacher holds and communicates low expectations for behavior [motivation].
- The teacher has no or poor relationships with students or has created an unhealthy climate for learning [motivation].
- Instruction is boring, confusing, or mismatched to the students' interests and level of development [instruction].

If these or other deficiencies like them are actually causing the off-task behavior, improvement in routines or disciplinary consequences alone will not produce the high-quality learning you seek for students. Select classroom management problems as a primary diagnosis when you see symptoms such as those listed in Figure 5B.2.

Figure 5B.2 When to Focus on Classroom Management

- Instructional time is regularly devoured by the 3 D's: downtime, delay, and distraction.
- Time is wasted and focus lost because of a lack of basic routines and work procedures for: start of class, getting supplies, making up work, and taking notes.
- A high percentage of time that should be allocated to challenging learning tasks is consumed by management routines, procedures, transitions, and directions.
- At least 30 percent of student-teacher interactions could be characterized as repeated nagging, reminding, or cajoling about management or behavioral issues.

If you find multiple deficiencies, you may want to determine whether a teacher is capable of learning and implementing basic routines and procedures before you move to more challenging issues. The sample questions in Figure 5B.3 illustrate the kinds of thinking that guides leaders when they focus on management. They are divided into the different areas of performance teachers must master for effective classroom management. These questions can serve as resources either for conducting a basic check on a teacher's management or for delving further into an issue when you suspect there is a problem.

Figure 5B.3 Diagnostic Questions for Management and Discipline

Attention
1. How do students respond to the teacher's attention repertoire—or lack thereof?
2. Is the teacher able to use a variety of techniques to gain, maintain, and regain student attention to task?
3. Does the teacher effectively use body language (facial expressions and posture) to set limits and expectations for attention?
4. How does the teacher use physical proximity to quash off-task behavior and send messages of accountability?

Momentum

Momentum, when used as a management term, means keeping events moving smoothly to avoid delays and distractions.
1. How does the teacher organize materials and set up workspace so that instructional time is not lost?
2. How does the teacher minimize the amount of downtime by giving notice of transitions, subdividing students when it is necessary for them to move, managing intrusions, and providing fillers when not all students are able to begin or end an activity at the same time?
3. How does the teacher anticipate blocks to momentum and take action to prevent or minimize them?
4. In what ways is the teacher able to monitor more than one activity at a time?

Discipline
1. When, how, and why do students display disruptive and inattentive behavior?
2. How do students understand and respond to the teacher's expectations for productive behavior, cooperation with the teacher and classmates, and self-discipline?
3. How does the teacher diagnose the cause of disruptive or inattentive behavior so that the solution can be matched to the problem?
4. How does the teacher identify and communicate high expectations for behavior and attention so that students are clear about what is required of them?
5. How well does the teacher handle the areas that often cause discipline problems such as personal relationship building, attention, and momentum?
6. How does the teacher work on building cooperation and self-discipline among students?
7. What is the teacher's repertoire of ways to eliminate disruptions and inattentive behavior?

Space
1. How can students use space and room arrangements to support or undermine effective effort and attention? (Are desks arranged in pairs, clusters, rows, circles, etc.?)
2. In what ways do students use the room and walls to support study habits, work procedures, and expectation messages?
3. How does the physical arrangement of the class match the lesson objectives and learning activities? When, how often, and in what ways is the physical arrangement changed?

4. How is the room arranged to put the least distance and fewest barriers between the teacher and any student in the class to help prevent or stop discipline problems?

Time

1. When, how, and why do students lose valuable learning time?
2. What percentage of student time is spent on: transitions and management routines? (Anything more than 15 percent to 20 percent is worrisome.)
3. How does the teacher allocate time for student learning, and how efficient is the teacher in ensuring that during this time students are actually working or attending to the lesson?

Routines

1. What work and housekeeping procedures do students follow independently and without prompting?
2. How does the presence or absence of routines affect the way students perform during instruction?
3. How does the teacher establish routines around work procedures and housekeeping?

Management problems are usually bounded and solvable if the teacher (1) is willing to work, (2) has reasonable personal relationship and organizational skills, and (3) will acknowledge that students' time and attention are valuable resources not to be squandered.

The third condition is the most challenging to obtain. Chronic mediocre classroom management—the willingness to waste instructional time for repeated intervals of 2 to 5 minutes during a period—thrives in numerous urban and suburban classrooms. We see teachers choosing to be inefficient most often at the secondary level. That choice shows itself in the following behaviors:

- Late arrivals to class, coffee in hand
- "Getting started" chats with students that bleed into 7 minutes
- The 4-minute "Do Now" that stretches into 9 minutes
- A search for materials accompanied by nagging, desk-banging, locker passes, and false starts
- The 5 minutes of downtime at the end of the period for lining up or starting homework

If the room is not chaotic, there are few discipline issues, and some students succeed in learning, such management issues often go unchallenged. When achievement results are uneven or poor, figure out whether there is a clear pattern of wasted time. If the answer is yes, taking action means

1. Determining how much is being wasted per month through sloppiness and lack of concern as opposed to lack of skill
2. Presenting the data to the offending teachers as a problem (see Chapter 6)
3. Making your expectations for improvement clear and, if necessary, helping the teacher figure out how to change (see Chapter 7)

5C
DIAGNOSING PROBLEMS IN INSTRUCTION

Because instruction is the core of teaching, all evaluation instruments include a category devoted to it. However, the content included under that heading can vary significantly from one set of standards to another. Instruction is enormously complex. The Skillful Teacher framework identifies three areas of performance that describe major components of instruction:

- **Clarity.** The repertoire teachers use to "make concepts and skills clear and accessible to students" (Saphier et al. 2008 161).
- **Principles of Learning.** Twenty-four, research-based practices teachers can use to "design more effective and efficient learning experiences" (Saphier et al. 220).
- **Models of Teaching.** The recognizable instructional patterns teachers use to develop students' habits of mind as well as to make content clear.

Clarity alone contains ten categories of teacher behavior organized in clusters and includes such familiar elements as communicating objectives, framing the learning, structuring engagement, providing processing and summarizing opportunities, selecting explanatory devices, dealing with student confusion, and asking different levels of questions.

In this section we can only deal with a small sample of potential data sources (Figure 5C.1) and questions for diagnosing instruction (Figure 5C.2). Fortunately, good resources abound to fill in the background research for both generic and content-specific instruction.

Figure 5C.1 Sources of Data for Diagnosing Problems with Instruction

- **Classroom Observations.** Visit when teachers are concentrating on certain key tasks such as: developing students' ability to apply concepts, surfacing and directly contradicting misconceptions, unscrambling confusion, or having students summarize. Collect data about the caliber of questions, questioning patterns, or the range of explanatory devices teachers use to connect to different types of learners.

- **Walks That Focus on Class Beginnings, Transitions, and Endings.** Drop in on multiple classrooms for 5 to 7 minutes to determine whether these powerful points in a lesson include the communication of objectives, agendas, and reasons for activities. Collect data about the way teachers make cognitive transitions between concepts or return to and reinforce objectives. Determine whether teachers are helping students anchor their learning by activating prior knowledge at the start of class or introduction of new content and by having students summarize at the end of a segment of instruction.

- **Lesson Plans.** Examine lesson plans to determine whether the teacher has identified strategies such as graphic organizers, concrete models, cooperative processing structures, manipulatives, or visuals that are likely to make the content clearer and more accessible to different types of learners.

- **Artifacts in Desks, Notebooks, or Portfolios.** Examine worksheets, practice tasks, homework and project assignments, resource materials and directions in centers, or lab materials. Assess how clear directions and materials are, what kind of prior knowledge or language facility might be necessary to complete them, and what level of work students are producing.

- **Artifacts on Walls.** Look at visual cues, reminder charts, criteria for success, or samples of student work.

- **Student Comments and Responses to Difficulty.** Interview students during a lesson and ask questions about what the learning targets/objectives are and what strategies they should be using. Design survey questions to give you data about how well students understand the value of what they are learning and what they do when content is difficult.

- **Assessments and Assessment Results.** Collect and analyze data from teacher-designed assessments as well as district benchmark assessments and state measures. These resources can all provide information on the impact of instructional choices.

Here we are using the term *instruction* to refer to all the strategies involved in the *delivery* of a high-quality lesson plan. As in the case of classroom management, problems that appear to be instructional may be caused by other deficiencies: poor or absent planning, lack of content knowledge, low or unclear standards for performance, or inadequate data about what is causing students difficulty. Choose instruction as a primary diagnosis when classroom management is effective, the environment is respectful and inclusive, the planning is adequate, but the conditions listed in Figure 5C.2 are present.

Figure 5C.2 When to Focus on Instruction

- Observations reveal that the teacher
  —Uses a narrow, unvarying repertoire of techniques without consideration of the results they produce
  —Uses confusing, inexplicit language and/or directions to explain concepts and introduce practice activities
  —Does not provide students with opportunities to learn and apply research-based strategies such as visual organizers, summarizing and note-taking, and comparing and contrasting (Marzano 2001)
- Students are unable to identify the underlying learning objective in completing a task.
- Students' work contains one or more uncorrected content misconceptions or inaccuracies.
- Students complain of boring, confusing, or inadequate instruction.
- A disproportionate numbers of students perform at basic or below basic levels on classroom assessments and common interim or benchmark assessments.

- Students make little or no pre-post test improvement.
- Trends and patterns of student performance on external assessments show little or no growth over time.

Figure 5C.3 offers sample questions to use when you examine the ways in which teachers make concepts and skills clear to students.

Figure 5C.3 Diagnostic Questions for Clarity

Framing the Learning

1. Do students understand—and can they explain to someone else—what they should know or be able to do at the end of a lesson?
2. Do students know why the work they are doing is important or how specific tasks fit into a larger context, e.g., the goals of a unit or potential responses to an essential question?
3. Do students have access to clear, appropriate criteria for success when they are asked to complete an important task? How do they use those criteria?
4. Do students show evidence that they can make connections between prior knowledge and skills and new learning?
5. In what ways does the teacher
   a. Communicate what students should know or be able to do at the end of the lesson and unit and help them see how the objectives are linked to larger contexts and ideas?
   b. Help students see the relevance of what they are learning by giving reasons for activities?
   c. Identify and communicate clear criteria for success?
6. How does the teacher
   a. Motivate students to be interested in the new topic and help them attach new information to what they already know, i.e., activate prior knowledge?
   b. Find out what students know or do not know in advance of instruction, i.e., pre-assess?
   c. Surface incorrect ideas and partial knowledge and anticipate misconceptions and confusions?

Presenting Information

1. Are all students able to make meaning of (i.e., interpret in their own words, connect to the objective, and apply in new situations) the different explanatory devices and language used by the teacher?
2. How does the teacher choose from a repertoire of explanatory devices (e.g., models, pictures, diagrams, cues, highlighting, and technology) according to the objectives of the lesson, demands of the content, and the needs of the students?
3. In what ways do the precision and caliber of the teacher's speech help or hinder students' understanding of the ideas and skills being taught?

Creating Mental Engagement

1. Are all students able to understand exactly what the teacher means by cues, questions, and references offered in explanations?
2. How well are students able to follow the directions given by the teacher without

asking numerous clarifying questions about language, necessary steps, or outcomes?

3. Are students able to make cognitive connections between new or current knowledge and past or future knowledge (i.e., show by oral or written links that they understand the resemblance between something new they are learning and something they have already encountered)?

4. In what ways are the necessary steps in directions communicated fully and precisely?

5. How does the teacher
   a. Make—or invite students to make—links that show the resemblance of new or current knowledge to past knowledge or foreshadow the ways in which current knowledge will be used in the future?
   b. Make clear transitions between ideas and use clear language to signal shifts in activity, pace, or level of challenge?
   c. Regularly ask students to compare and contrast concepts, content, skills, and processes?

Consolidating and Anchoring the Learning

1. Are students regularly and actively processing, taking ownership, and making meaning during lessons?

2. Do students demonstrate that they are able to summarize and understand the role of good summaries in helping them solidify their learning?

3. How does the teacher do the following:
   a. Break up teacher talk and direct instruction with periodic processing time to allow students to consolidate their understanding or develop ownership of information?
   b. End a lesson or major lesson segment by highlighting important points or causing students to do so?

Questioning

1. Does the behavior of all students demonstrate that they understand the language and purpose of the teacher's questions or that they are motivated to attempt to respond to challenging questions?

2. Are students being asked and responding to questions that require extended responses and higher level thinking?

3. How does the teacher
   a. Vary the purposes for which questions are used (e.g., to assess learning, instruct, promote cognitive engagement, manage the learning environment) in order to match instruction to the learning objectives and the needs of the students?
   b. Use invitational language in questioning so that students are encouraged to take intellectual risks?
   c. Avoid language patterns that send students miscues or limit the level of their thinking?

If you suspect that instruction is poor enough to be limiting students' opportunities to learn, remember to look for *patterns of deficiency,* not just the absence of a single move now and again.

Researchers can identify an extensive and varied repertoire of strategies for explaining, illustrating, organizing, and helping students hold onto concepts. However, struggling teachers often rely on default approaches (I lecture, you listen) regardless of context, objectives, or student results. They have little idea of how others accomplish certain functions, and try to seize on one or two activities they think will demonstrate compliance. As much as possible, describe problems in terms of the big areas of skill-deficit within instruction such as the need for visual supports and other explanatory devices that would improve conditions for many students quickly.

5D

DIAGNOSING PROBLEMS IN EXPECTATIONS, PERSONAL RELATIONSHIP BUILDING, AND CLASS CLIMATE

"You can't teach someone who isn't motivated" is probably the most common complaint of low-performing teachers. Underneath the lament, you hear a sense of helplessness (the charitable explanation) or an abandonment of all responsibility for what causes children to invest in school (the discouraging possibility). Despite abundant research highlighting the power of personal relationships and high positive expectations, some teachers have not accepted the idea that motivation can be nurtured and grown.

In the Skillful Teacher framework (Figure 5A.3) three key areas of performance are grouped together in recognition of their ability to influence student motivation and achievement:

1. **Expectations.** Teachers' ability to communicate key messages about students' ability to master important learning and their willingness to stick with students who struggle. ("This work is important. You can do it well. I won't give up on you.")
2. **Personal Relationship Building.** Teacher's repertoire for connecting with students and making them feel known and valued.
3. **Classroom Climate.** Teachers' repertoire and skills for creating classrooms where students feel known and included, confident, and safe enough to take academic risks in service of learning, and able to have choices and a sense of influence over what happens.

When students of all ages contrast their best teachers, the ones that transformed learning for them, with teachers they believe don't care, one or more of these three areas of performance almost always surfaces in what they say. Figure 5D.1 suggests places to find data that will reveal problems in teachers' motivation or expectations.

Figure 5D.1 Sources of Data for Diagnosing Problems with Motivation or Expectations

- **Classroom Observations.** Collect data on explicit communication of expectations in common arenas such as calling on students, responding to student answers, responding when students ask for help, or giving feedback. Look for evidence of practices that support or undermine students' ability to exert effective effort.

- **Data Conferences re Grading and Grade Records.** Listen for statements that stereotype children by presumed ability or background rather than current performance; listen to determine how grades are weighted and what role effort plays in success.

- **Discipline Records, Student Comments about the Reasons for Misbehavior, or Coaching Sessions with Students about Behavior.** Listen for statements about the student's belief that the teacher dislikes him/her, is unfair, does not care, is mean, etc. that may reveal difficulties with relationships and climate.

- **Weekly Lesson Plans.** Look for intentional planning of time for re-teaching and helping students who struggle.

- **Artifacts on Walls.** Look for posted criteria for success, exemplars of high-quality work, reminders of strategies for a variety of tasks, and confidence-building messages such as "When you do your best, you will be your best."

- **Formative Assessments.** Ask the teacher when and how s/he uses assessment; listen for beliefs about ability and achievement and about whether students should have second-chance opportunities on difficult tasks.

- **Feedback on Student Work.** Determine whether the teacher is giving smiley faces and nonspecific praise or useful information to assist students in reaching a higher level of performance.

- **Student Interviews.** Determine the extent to which students perceive effort to be the foundation for success.

Low-performing teachers frequently hold mindsets that assume student intelligence is fixed and student success is largely a result of native ability (Dweck 2006 7-11). High-performing teachers, on the other hand, tend to have a growth mindset. They believe a combination of enough intelligence plus effective effort, more than native ability alone, explains whether students meet high academic standards. In these rooms you are more likely to hear "You can do it" messages critical to many students' success. Converting an ineffective performer's mindset from a focus on student limitations to a focus on students' potential gives pause to even the most skillful leader. Generally, leaders seem to have more success by having teachers behave their way into new beliefs (Fullan 1993 15). The process of helping teachers come to new understandings through personal experience means that you may have to tackle problems of practice linked to instruction or assessment either before or in conjunction with tackling expectations. Adopting new, research-based strategies such as teaching students how to summarize their learning or providing opportunities to redo work will result in more effective effort and better learning for students. The development of the teacher's growth mindset can then follow a change in practice. However, there are times when leaders should make low or inconsistent expectations and negative messages to students a primary diagnosis. Select one or more of the areas involved in motivation when any of the conditions listed in Figure 5D.2 exist.

Figure 5D.2 When to Focus on Motivation (Expectations, Personal Relationship Building, and Class Climate)

- Students report that they feel unsafe, disliked, picked on, or left out in class.
- Students consistently report that the teacher does not like or care about them

as individuals or that the teacher hates or favors a particular group within the class.

- Teachers are unable or unwilling to use student names, cannot tell you anything about the students in their classes, or routinely confuse students belonging to particular subgroups both in conversation about them and in calling on them.
- Teachers are unwilling to allow students opportunities to influence any aspect of what goes on in class.
- Teachers' explanations for low student performance, misbehavior, or confusion blame students' innate ability or personal circumstances.
- Teachers communicate to students that making errors is a sign of being stupid rather than an opportunity for learning.
- Students can only play back rote facts and memorized information; they show no evidence of transferring skills to independent and nonroutine application because of low standards and teachers' messages about their capacity to learn.
- Teachers consistently jump in to rescue, speak for, or call on other students without giving them any opportunity to struggle with material or respond to cues.
- Teachers respond to individual students differently depending on their perceptions of the individuals' innate ability.
- Students give up easily in the face of difficult tasks.
- Students have unequal opportunities to respond to questions.
- Some students receive explicit debilitating messages implying, "You can't do this."
- Students are denied opportunities to learn specific skills to make effort more effective such as: summarizing, note taking, critical thinking skills, and use of nonlinguistic representations.

The three aspects of teacher performance that strongly influence student motivation can overlap. However, a teacher with good relationships and a friendly and welcoming climate can also have low expectations for students' behavior or academic performance. Therefore, we have separated the diagnostic questions to help you narrow your definition of the issue. Figure 5D.3 focuses on expectations. Figures 5D.4 and 5D.5 deal with personal relationship building and classroom climate.

Figure 5D.3 Questions for Diagnosing Low or Inconsistent Expectations

---

- Do students' behavior and comments show that they are convinced that their teacher
  —Believes they have enough innate ability to perform at high levels if they exert effective effort?
  —Will not give up on them and will be tenacious and persistent in getting them to work hard and make progress?
- Are students able to understand, explain to others, and apply principles of effective effort?
- How do students express and explain their teacher's standards and expectations for the quality of their work, their study habits, their interpersonal behavior, or the classroom routines?
- What evidence shows that the teacher believes that almost all children come to school with enough innate ability to achieve at a high level if we help them to have confidence in themselves as learners and to apply effective effort?

- Does the teacher have clear, high standards and the conviction that s/he has the right to expect that students will reach them?
- How does the teacher communicate the standards verbally and/or in writing to students and their parents?
- Does the teacher use a repertoire of strategies to enable all students to reach the standards?
- In what ways is the teacher communicating "What we're doing is important, you can do it, and I won't give up on you" messages through such arenas as: giving help, responding to students' answers, or grading and grouping students?

Figure 5D.4 Questions for Diagnosing Issues Involving Personal Relationship Building

---

1. How do students' behavior and comments show that they believe their teacher knows them, values them, likes them, and treats them with fairness and respect?
2. How does the teacher
   a. Make students feel noticed and acknowledged?
   b. Show students they are valued as individuals?
   c. Treat students with fairness and respect?
   d. Demonstrate "realness" through appropriate sharing of experiences, interests, and feelings?
   e. Use humor and fun to demonstrate enjoyment of students and teaching?

Figure 5D.5 Questions for Diagnosing Classroom Climate

---

1. How do students' behavior and comments show that they feel known as individuals, welcome and supported as members of the classroom community, and safe to take intellectual risks and tackle difficult work?
2. Do students show that they have a strong sense of ownership and responsibility for the work of the classroom?
3. How does the teacher work to create a climate that encourages risk-taking and builds students' confidence to tackle difficult work?
4. How does the teacher provide opportunities for students to develop a strong sense of ownership and responsibility for the work of the classroom?

Relationships and a sense of belonging are important to students' success. Your most difficult supervisory challenge, however, may come from individuals who focus all their attention on great relationships and warm climates and believe that raising academic expectations for all students conflicts with those priorities. Students often describe these teachers as "nice people" and then follow up by noting "but we don't learn much." Taking action to make motivation the problem that you focus on will often require that you (1) compare data about how students perform for effective and ineffective teachers and (2) listen to and compare students' explanations of their successes and failures from one classroom to another.

5E
DIAGNOSING PROBLEMS IN PLANNING

Planning is the act of translating curriculum into unit and daily lessons. The most abstract of all the functions a teacher undertakes, planning involves intricate, behind-the-scenes thinking, anticipating, and designing that make a high-impact lesson look seamless. Different evaluation frameworks emphasize different aspects of planning, including knowing academic content and content standards, designing curriculum sequences and alignment, and setting clear objectives for student learning.

Although unit plans provide the best information about a teacher's ability to sequence curriculum, daily or multi-day lesson plans provide the best source of data for teachers who seem to have routine planning problems.

Principals need to carefully implement practices (such as collecting lesson plans) that are consistent with district bargaining unit agreements. If different school sites in a district use consistently different practices, under arbitration, unions can employ the concept of *disparate practice* (see Chapter 10) to undermine a case. For example, if Principal A routinely collects lesson plans and Principal B never collects them, that fact could be used to rebut Principal A's case for disciplining or removing a teacher based partially on data from lesson plans. Arbitrators may not even seek to understand substantial evidence in support of poor performance if they can dismiss the case based on inequitable treatment.

Legal Note 5E.1 Collective Bargaining

Figure 5E.1 recommends specific places to find data to diagnose problems in planning.

Figure 5E.1 Sources of Data for Diagnosing Problems in Planning

- **Lesson and Unit Plans.** Use plans to determine whether the teacher has articulated worthwhile learning objectives or has simply listed topics to cover and activities to do. Analyze the intended alignment of the tasks and activities planned with the objective and determine whether the means of assessment is aligned and would produce useful data.

- **Classroom Observation.** Focus on the actual alignment of lesson segments with worthwhile objectives. Examine the use of transitions to reconnect to the objective and beginnings and endings as leverage points to focus the students on the learning goals.

- **Student Interviews.** Ask multiple students "What is the most important thing you are learning by doing this activity?" or "Why does your teacher want you to learn this?" Assess whether they can explain a learning goal in their own words or can only explain the activity they need to complete.

- **Observation of Common Planning Time or Team Meetings.** Keep a time log or review agendas to determine how time is actually spent on planning and the delivery of lessons.

- **Artifacts on Walls.** Determine the extent to which visual reminders include objectives, standards, and criteria for success or strategies to meet objectives, as opposed to focusing exclusively on directions and procedural information, such as agendas, due dates, and disciplinary expectations.

- **Artifacts in Desks, Notebooks, or Portfolios.** Examine project guidelines and grading criteria to determine the value assigned to different aspects of a task in relation to the objective values.

Poor planning, including the failure to identify rigorous, worthwhile learning objectives, is one of the most common underlying causes of ineffective performance. Beware of focusing your diagnosis on the symptoms rather than the problem. Outward manifestations of inadequate planning include: disruptive behavior or wasted time, disengaged students, and uneven performance on assessments. Before you eliminate poorly understood or poorly executed planning as a potential diagnosis, ask yourself whether the lesson on paper—or even in the teacher's head—reflected enough high-quality thinking and anticipation to have produced good results.

Focus on planning as a primary diagnosis when classroom routines and basic structures are in place, the classroom environment is inclusive and supportive, but the problems listed in Figure 5E.2 are evident.

Figure 5E.2 When to Focus on Planning

- Teachers cannot demonstrate that they have dug into the content for which they are responsible to identify critical concepts and ideas, themes, essential questions, or important understandings.
- Teachers focus their preparation on activities to do rather than outcomes or purposes for learning.
- Teachers report that the primary purpose of their lesson is covering a topic or doing an activity.
- Questions to focus students on key concepts or help them apply ideas are not designed in advance; teachers rely primarily on rapid-fire, low-level recall questions to check students' understanding.
- Questioning is inexplicit and includes "run on" or poorly worded questions with confusing syntax or focus.
- Daily plans show no evidence that the teacher has thought about or built in time for students to process information or to apply their learning in a new context or with new material.
- Students spend far more time on busywork than on tasks that are directly linked to academic learning.
- Students are unable to

—Articulate what skill they are learning or explain concepts that are central to the content they should be mastering

—Explain the purpose of activities beyond doing, completing, or covering

—Cite the criteria for an excellent performance

—Connect what they are learning to larger themes of the curriculum

Additional questions to guide your diagnosis and coaching of planning are listed in Figure 5E.3.

Figure 5E.3 Questions for Diagnosing Issues with Planning

1. Can students explain what they are supposed to master (know and be able to apply) by the end of the lesson and why the skill or concept is important?

2. Are students able to see and explain how key tasks they are doing connect to worthwhile learning targets?

3. Do the teacher's lesson plans and instruction demonstrate that s/he has
   a. Identified a worthwhile target for student learning and expressed that target in terms of what students should know or be able to demonstrate they can do by the end of the lesson?
   b. Aligned activities, explanatory devices, time allocations, assessments, and key messages to that worthwhile target?

4. How do students describe their experiences in completing or participating in different kinds of activities?

5. Do students find learning activities relevant, significant, and well matched to their cultures? Do learning activities draw upon their preferred learning styles?

6. How do teachers differentiate learning experiences according to a variety of attributes such as relevance, degree of abstraction, or information complexity?

Inadequate planning explains—or is a major contributor to—the majority of cases of ineffective instruction. Failure to plan exacerbates other problems from weak management skills to students' beliefs about whether they can actually learn from a particular teacher. Lesson plans, lesson artifacts, teacher conferences, and observation notes will all help you with the first part of the diagnosis: has planning taken place at all? If so, was it adequate? The second question is the prerequisite for taking action—why the failure occurred. If your diagnosis is poor planning resulting from a lack of understanding and experience, your interventions will be quite different from a diagnosis that says the person is choosing not to plan. Planning skills can be taught. But building the will to do the hard work of daily planning may require you to expand your interventions. You will need to make individuals face the impact of their choices, by examining the data about which students succeed and how well they do when their teachers plan skillfully. The effort is worthwhile; improvements in planning will almost always affect other areas of performance and improve conditions for students.

Figure 5E.4 represents the kind of thinking that a highly effective teacher undertakes in preparation for a good lesson or lesson sequence. It also suggests entry points for diagnosing ineffective planning.

Figure 5E.4 Planning and Conference Guide

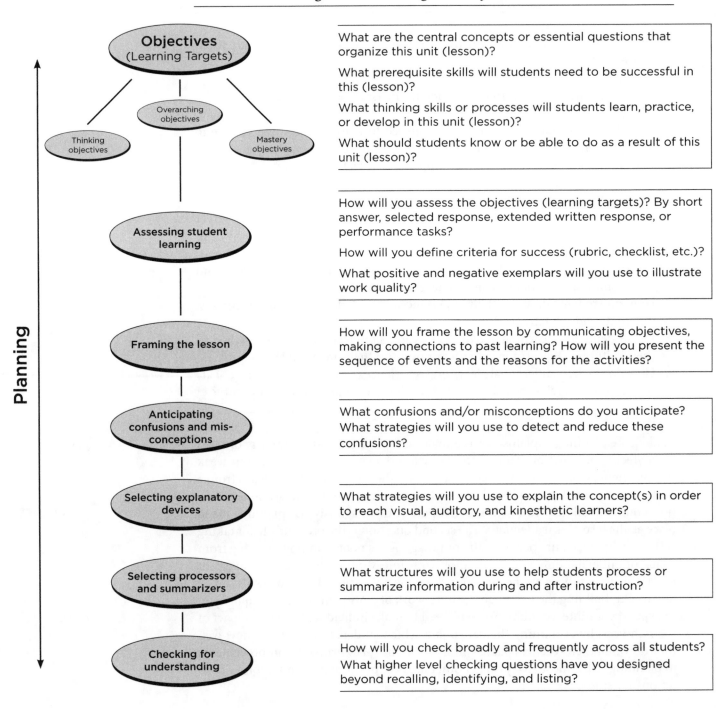

5F

DIAGNOSING PROBLEMS IN ASSESSMENT

Check your assessment literacy. To support your staff, could you successfully explain and give high-quality examples of the following: pre-assessments, formative assessments, benchmark assessments, common assessments, real-world assessments, summative assessments, assessments as learning, assessments for learning, norm-referenced measures, and criterion-referenced measures? Assessment with all its various definitions and sometimes competing purposes has great potential, often unseen or unacknowledged, to direct the route schools and teachers take to improvement.

The purposes of assessment range from "making summative statements about how well students have done overall in meeting course or unit objectives" to giving feedback to teachers and students or reporting progress to parents and the community (Saphier 2008 433). For our goal of improving ineffective instruction, we will concentrate on teachers' understanding of and ability to use classroom assessments—and particularly on teachers' competence in the function widely called *formative assessment*. Wiliam (2011 43) provides a valuable definition:

> An assessment functions formatively to the extent that evidence about student achievement is elicited, interpreted, and used by teachers, learners, or their peers, to make decisions about the next steps in instruction that are likely to be better, or better founded, than the decisions they would have made in the absence of that evidence.

Reformers and researchers seem to agree that this learning-focused commitment to collecting data on student progress and *using those data to adjust instruction* day to day is strongly linked to gains in student performance. Figure 5F.1 suggests ways to investigate whether teachers use formative data to adjust their instruction to their students' needs.

Figure 5F.1 Sources of Data for Diagnosing Problems with Classroom Assessment

- **Assessment Conferences with the Teacher.** Look for the frequency of assessment. Ask to see daily data-gathering tools and to be told how those tools affect what happens in subsequent days. Ask how the teacher uses homework, papers, and projects to make next-step decisions.
- **Artifacts That Are Labeled Formative Assessments or Data-Gathering Tools by the Teacher.** Look for appropriate alignment with curriculum and for the level of complex thinking required by assessment tasks. Analyze formative tasks for evidence of efficiency and timeliness of feedback, i.e., the ease with which the teacher could analyze the data and make changes to planned lessons.
- **Lesson Plans or Notes on Lesson Plans.** Look for evidence that the teacher plans thoughtful and challenging questions to check students' comprehension and ability to apply concepts as well as their recall of facts. Look for planned

opportunities for students to process information in ways that would give data about their individual understanding: one-question quizzes, journal entries, "do nows," nonlinguistic representations of concepts, or the use of challenge questions and whiteboards for simultaneous responses.

- **Quick "Decision Chats" or Discussions about Decisions Made after a Short Visit or Walk.** Ask the teacher how s/he decided on the day's focus and strategies. Listen for spontaneous offerings about data, previous performance, and students' difficulties and strengths in prior lessons. Ask specifically about when and how assessments were last used to make decisions about what to teach next.
- **Responses to Student Work.** Ask to see graded work samples to determine whether the teacher uses a range of responses from genuine academic feedback (nonjudgmental information about performance) to evaluation, advice, and praise (see Section 4C).
- **Materials on Walls, Charts, or Displays.** Look for and ask about guide charts, posted reminders, summaries, and criteria for success that would be evidence of instruction in response to performance as well as in anticipation of performance demands (see Section 4B).
- **Classroom Observation.** Focus on opportunities to collect information on student progress either seized or missed.

Leader Alert
Resist Blaming Individuals for Pervasive Problems

Because the use of good formative assessment is still relatively rare in the majority of American schools, evaluators could arguably rate the performance of a large portion of their faculty as basic or unsatisfactory on this standard. Poor understanding of assessment's power to affect student learning is an example of a pervasive problem. Be careful about blaming individuals by giving low ratings before you have provided all teachers with time and support to learn how to use good formative assessment. Once such training and support has been provided, you can then begin to evaluate formatively on an individual's *progress* toward becoming proficient. ◆

Poor assessment practices are so prevalent and so closely tied to poor planning that it is sometimes hard to determine where the root of a problem lies. Focus on assessment as a primary diagnosis when no problems with management or instructional strategies are obvious but regular and routinely accepted discrepancies show up in student performance among different classes of students or subgroups of students within classes. Figure 5F.2 suggests other indicators of poor assessment practices to watch for.

Figure 5F.2 When to Focus on Assessment

- Teachers report being overwhelmed by required curricula and unable to make choices about what to emphasize or when to reteach a concept.
- Teachers cannot explain how they determine what students need to do to make adequate progress before a summative assessment.
- Teachers do not use criteria for success, exemplars, rubrics, or other self-mon-

itoring tools to help students understand what is required for a "meets or exceeds standards" performance.

- Teachers cannot provide examples of how they have changed what they originally planned to do from day to day as a result of a quick formative assessment.
- Students cannot cite examples of how the teacher has reported back data on their performance to them, involved them in setting criteria for success or personal goals, or otherwise engaged them in monitoring their own progress.
- Both students and teachers primarily cite summative assessments such as: end-of-the-week tests, unit tests, or benchmark tests when they are asked to explain how they know about progress in meeting standards.
- Every Thursday is review-for-a-test day, and every Friday is take-a-test day.
- Both students and teachers report that there is no time to return to concepts that students have not understood after they have done poorly on an assessment.
- Multiyear data indicate that students are underperforming their peers.
- Grades are primarily based on narrow sources of assessment data such as short answer or multiple-choice tests.
- Assessments that have low cognitive demand are almost always recorded as final grades in the grade book.
- Teachers resist or ignore agreements about assessments made by their content-alike teams, sometimes by insisting on their "academic freedom" to decide "What's best for my kids."

Figure 5F.3 suggests diagnostic questions to determine whether teachers use formative assessment to shape their instruction.

Figure 5F.3 Diagnostic Questions for Assessment

1. Can students cite and explain standards and criteria for successful performance on an assessment task?
2. Do students report being able to demonstrate what they have learned in a variety of ways?
3. Do students report being able to assess their own work, make changes to improve that work, and set goals for personal growth?
4. Are students able to cite the ways in which a teacher assesses their learning beyond weekly tests and quizzes?
5. Do students have opportunities for frequent, relevant feedback about their performance prior to the end of a unit or a summative assessment?
6. Does the teacher demonstrate skill in using a variety of assessment strategies to
   a. Signal clearly what knowledge and skills students must master?
   b. Make instructional decisions including modifying plans and approaches as necessary?
   c. Give feedback to students?
   d. Provide summative statements re students' overall performance in meeting course or unit goals?
   e. Meet requirements for sorting, ranking, or comparing students for honors or placements?
7. Does the teacher use formative assessment frequently and in a variety of ways

to gain feedback about the effects of instruction and give students information about their current performance in relation to a target?

8. Does the teacher communicate clear standards and criteria for performance?
9. How often and in what ways are individual students able to show the teacher what they do and do not understand during a lesson?
10. What happens for students when they show they are confused during a lesson?
11. How often and in what ways does the teacher structure interactions with students so that they must explain their thought processes, assumptions, and questions verbally or in writing?

As districts adopt measures required by Race to the Top or public and private initiatives, assessment increasingly serves a purpose beyond giving students and teachers good information about progress and next steps. Most newly reformed teacher evaluation systems link a designated percentage of a teacher's performance rating directly to a variety of measures of student achievement. Some of these new evaluation systems rely on state tests or other externally designed tests; others are opting for a combination of external measures and locally designed or adopted assessments more closely tied to the curriculum of the district. Teachers who have not yet seen or understood the critical importance of good monitoring strategies and formative assessment for students will increasingly find themselves and their students at a disadvantage. Finally, high-quality assessment requires other key competencies to be in place. Therefore, investing your leadership effort in helping teachers build assessment competence can also yield improvements in planning, direct instruction, and expectations.

5G
DIAGNOSING PROBLEMS IN PROFESSIONALISM

Historically, performance evaluation has focused primarily on classroom responsibilities. To deal with duties outside of the classroom, state and local instruments included a catch-all category labeled *professionalism* or *fulfillment of professional duties* into which they put such disparate functions as "professional dress," "reliability and punctuality," "communicating with families," "reflective practice," "performance of routine responsibilities," and "professional growth." Unless a teacher displayed egregious behavior in any of these areas, evaluators rarely paid attention. Their time was limited, and the evidence of professionalism they collected was thin. Everyone who breathed, showed up at school with reasonable regularity, and could provide a list of one or two workshops attended (even if they were on school time) passed muster in this category.

Over the last decade, the criteria for professionalism and citations of its importance have evolved as researchers and reformers have studied the variables that affect school success. Teachers must now demonstrate that they are strong collaborators. They are routinely expected to work with other adults in their classrooms, to serve productively on teams and committees, and to be contributing members of their learning communities. These expectations and the challenges of creating high-performing professional communities are discussed at length in *The Skillful Leader II: Confronting Conditions that Undermine Learning*. Teachers are also expected to be culturally proficient: able to create and nurture a classroom and school environment that respects differences in language, gender, ethnicity, sexual orientation, and religion. As such expectations become more explicit, supervisors must learn how to diagnose, develop, and monitor these categories of professionalism.

Many experienced administrators report that they find evaluating professionalism challenging because it requires overcoming longstanding ideas about what supervisors can and cannot address. Like others, you may feel, that it is "not your place" to be observing, analyzing, and conferencing about adults' interactions with one another. You may also feel uncomfortable pointing out below-standard performance such as the following:

- Routinely violating norms of collaboration or failing to contribute effectively to the work of their grade-level groups or content-alike teams
- Deriding colleagues' efforts in public and private encounters
- Acting in ways that signal an implicit belief in the superiority of the dominant culture and a devaluing of the contributions of groups with different religious backgrounds, language, ethnicity, customs, or sexual orientation

However, diagnosing problems in these areas is critical in helping to remove obstacles to student learning. Figure 5G.1 lists useful sources of data for diagnosing and monitoring professionalism.

Leader Alert
Cultural Proficiency and Evaluation

Many evaluation instruments include aspects of cultural proficiency under building a supportive classroom environment. However, teachers must carry out a number of other tasks that require cultural proficiency, ranging from communication with families and community members to curriculum design and collaboration with colleagues from diverse backgrounds. Hence we have placed the topic under the broader heading of *professionalism.* ◆

Figure 5G.1 Sources of Data for Diagnosing Problems in Professionalism

- **Observations of meetings.** Take notes on and analyze the behavior of individuals as they are interacting with their content-alike teams or other professional communities. Look for the degree and quality of contributions to problem solving and evidence that both the individuals and the team are analyzing the impact of their instruction and designing ways to improve it. Pay particular attention to discussions about underachieving groups of students or individual students who are struggling.

- **Observations re implementation of team agreements.** Conduct brief visits to all the classes of teachers on a particular team after they have planned instruction or assessment together. Examine whether each teacher implements the agreements in ways that provide the same opportunities for students that colleagues are providing.

- **Student performance data and artifacts.** Compare products, performances, and achievement measures across a team to identify the degree to which collaboration is having a positive impact on student performance.

- **Unit and lesson plans and curriculum material.** Examine plans and materials to determine whether content and strategies support the diversity of the young people in the class.

- **Materials and messages displayed in the classroom and hallways.** Evaluate visuals and displays for evidence of cultural blindness or messages that inadvertently exclude some groups of students from the school community.

- **Teacher and school professional development plans.** Look for indications that individuals, teams, or whole faculties have included goals for improving cultural proficiency.

- **Communication logs and artifacts.** Look at newsletters, samples of letters home about programs and projects, records of calls and emails or, in some instances, notes about visits to families. Ask teachers to talk about a case or two in which communication between home and school helped a student improve performance. Look particularly for evidence of outreach to parents of English language learners.

- **Artifacts showing application of learning from professional development.** Examine logs, journals, or other artifacts that show how a teacher thought about and used ideas from professional development. Ask teachers to discuss how collaboration with their team affected their teaching decisions. Ask for evidence of modifications to instruction that resulted from the team's review of data.

Figure 5G.2 suggests some behaviors that indicate that professionalism, including collaboration and cultural proficiency, should be a primary diagnosis and focus for improvement.

Figure 5G.2 When to Focus on Professionalism

Select this area when the teacher

- Fails to meet obligations for or undermines the functioning of his/her team
- Fails to use the team as a support resource when required to do so by a recommendation or improvement plan
- Resists making or implementing team agreements about improvements in instruction
- Is producing results for his/her students but is reluctant to share ideas with colleagues
- Demonstrates insensitivity and lack of respect for cultural differences including:
  —Expecting and accepting differences in performance from certain groups or engaging in stereotyping
  —Making undermining statements about class, race, sexual orientation, or religious preferences
  —Routinely complaining about or blaming students from cultures other than his or her own

Figure 5G.3 provides sample diagnostic questions for assessing professionalism that are organized around categories commonly included in rubrics and evaluation instruments.

Figure 5G.3 Diagnostic Questions for Professionalism

Routine Administrative Duties

1. Does the teacher fulfill key management/contractual responsibilities by
   a. Arriving punctually to school and meetings?
   b. Reliably covering duties without reminders?
   c. Monitoring student interactions and anticipating problems during duties?
   d. Consistently upholding and carrying out school policies?
2. Does the teacher demonstrate high-quality record keeping and paperwork by
   a. Being accurate, legible, and complete in fulfilling paperwork or electronic requests?
   b. Submitting grades and reports punctually?
   c. Completing plans ranging from student educational plans to individual professional development plans thoroughly and with substance?
3. Does the teacher consistently uphold and carry out school policies?
4. How effectively does the teacher use support personnel and colleagues to benefit teaching and learning.

To address issues of failure to comply with policies and procedures, see Chapter 9.

Reflective Learner

1. Does the teacher demonstrate the characteristics of an analytical and reflective learner by
   a. Withholding initial judgments until s/he has adequate information?
   b. Defining problems before attempting solutions?
   c. Examining ideas and strategies from perspectives other than his/her own?
2. How does the teacher demonstrate that s/he is open to change and willing to experiment when evidence indicates that students need new approaches?
3. How does the teacher keep current in the field and apply new learning to his/her classroom practice?

Communication

1. Does the teacher communicate effectively with families, stakeholders, and the community by
   a. Initiating and following up on calls, emails, notes, or visits?
   b. Demonstrating cultural proficiency and caring when delivering difficult news about student performance or requesting support for the student?
   c. Providing high-quality written communications as appropriate?
   d. Seeking the help of translators and interpreters as needed to make sure information and meaning are clear to families?
   e. Seeking information and input from families and stakeholders?
2. Does the teacher demonstrate care and high professional standards when planning and carrying out activities such as open houses, back-to-school presentations, and reports on programs or curriculum for families and the community by
   a. Clearly communicating the overall goals?
   b. Presenting high-quality handouts or supporting materials?
   c. Handling questions with tact, respect, and clarity?
   d. Communicating how s/he will be available for families?
3. Does the teacher carry out responsibilities for reporting student progress and performance by
   a. Adhering to district policies for making up-to-date information about performance easily accessible to families and stakeholders?
   b. Providing students and families with specific feedback about students' strengths, and weaknesses?
   c. Avoiding generalities, clichés, or stereotyping in written or oral reports?
4. Does the teacher practice open, honest communication with colleagues and members of the broader school community?

Collaboration

1. Does the teacher maintain productive, respectful relationships with peers and act as an accountable team member by
   a. Frequently sharing materials and ideas to benefit students?
   b. Actively participating in data analysis and problem solving to improve student learning?
   c. Asking for assistance when necessary and providing assistance when asked?
   d. Participating in and contributing to collegial activities related to the improvement of teaching and learning such as study groups, lesson study, or peer observation?

2. Does the teacher demonstrate responsibility for and commitment to the well-being and learning of all students in the school by
   a. Assisting or mentoring new teachers?
   b. Assuming leadership or coordinating roles when needed?
   c. "Pitching in" during emergencies?
   d. Volunteering to cover for colleagues when student safety is involved or when colleagues face emergencies?
   e. Offering appropriate feedback and suggestions on ways to improve school functioning?
3. Does the teacher fulfill responsibilities for professional meetings by
   a. Regular, punctual attendance?
   b. Careful preparation?
   c. Substantive contributions?
   d. Respectful, civil, oral, and written dialogue?
   e. Monitoring body language and tone in response to others?
   f. Probing and clarifying information and assumptions?

Cultural Proficiency

1. To what extent can the teacher identify cultural differences and the need for multiple perspectives in the school or in his/her classroom?
2. What action has the teacher taken to incorporate the contributions of diverse communities into the curriculum?
3. In what ways has the teacher identified his/her own blind spots and deepened his/her learning about cultures represented by different students in the classroom?
4. In what ways has the teacher advocated for and supported programs and practices that would adjust instruction so that it is a good match for the learning needs of different groups of students within the classroom?
5. How does the teacher speak about and interact with others perceived as "different" within the school community?
6. What has the teacher done to learn about and teach students skills for dealing with conflict that may be caused by tensions due to cultural differences?

Source: Based on Randall B. Lindsey, Kikanza Nuri Robins, Raymond D. Terrell, *Cultural Proficiency: A Manual for School Leaders,* 2nd ed. (Corwin Press 2003).

Diagnosing the multiple facets of professionalism can be overwhelming. Select a focus criterion or a set of elements within a standard that, if mastered by all teachers, will help you meet school goals for student learning. Then communicate that focus to the faculty, your rationale for choosing it, and the rewards this aspect of professionalism offers in terms of improved learning for students and greater satisfaction for adults. Collaborate with faculty, or perhaps departments within a larger school, to identify the data sources you will use to assess growth and to establish evidence for interim and final evaluations.

If you find major deficits in planning, assessment, instruction, or management, you are likely to make professionalism a lower priority diagnosis. Do not ignore it entirely or decide to settle for less than proficiency if all the basics of classroom performance are in place. Teaching is so complex and intellectually demanding that trying to meet its challenges alone makes no sense, particularly for teachers whose performance is marginal and who need to learn from and be pushed by colleagues. Today's students need their teachers to be contributing to and learning from fully functioning and culturally sensitive teams who can pool their intelligence to produce the best possible outcomes for learners. If we expect effective adult collaboration to happen, we must establish the structures and find the time to protect it. We must create mechanisms for feedback and support. And finally, we have to evaluate professionalism as carefully and with the same demand for accountability and growth that we make in any other area.

CHAPTER 6

DEFINING AND
COMMUNICATING
THE PROBLEM

6A
OVERVIEW OF PROBLEM COMMUNICATION

Figure 6A.1 The Defining Phase of the Action Cycle

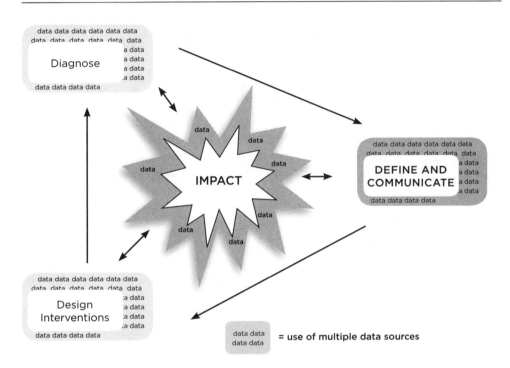

The defining and communicating a problem phase of the action cycle (see Figure 6A.1) can be a daunting prospect. Two parties—you and the teacher or the team—must end up with the same concrete picture of the difference between what is *presently* happening for students and what *should be* happening. Making a diagnosis and communicating the problem are tightly linked and sometimes occur almost simultaneously. For learning purposes, however, we have separated the two processes. Initially at least, each requires a different application of conviction, competence, and control. Communicating a problem starts with *conviction* about the importance of being an advocate for children, about the value of timely, focused feedback, and about adults' ability to improve if they are given the opportunity to do so. We have to believe that an individual or team can hear and think about difficult information if it is presented clearly and humanely. We also have to be convinced that individuals cannot change if we withhold the important information they need. *Competence*—having a repertoire of ways to present problems and knowing the pitfalls to avoid— reinforces conviction.

THE BASICS OF COMMUNICATING ABOUT INEFFECTIVE PERFORMANCE

When you encounter performance that should be rated as "not yet competent" (e.g., "Basic," "Developing," or "Unsatisfactory") and feel the tremendous pressure of limited time and competing priorities, it is easy to succumb to a number of unproductive temptations. You could

- Ignore the issue and hope it will go away
- Inflate the teacher's rating to avoid having a difficult conversation
- Dive right in with righteous intent and reel off lists of accusations and generalizations without supporting data
- Amass an overwhelming set of diagnostic data and bombard the recipient with everything that is wrong, every deficiency in multiple standards all at once

All of these behaviors undermine good communication. They can easily be avoided by paying attention to several basic principles.

Choose a Focus. If a diagnostic scan or an initial observation reveals numerous possible problem areas, pick one or two of the gaps to collect further data on and to define clearly. Resist the easy but not urgent issues and focus attention on what will have high leverage on student learning. Because problems overlap and interact, there may be no single "correct" starting place. And because problems overlap, so do solutions. Making a difference in one area often spills improvement into others. Choose a focus and go for depth over breadth.

Provide Substantive Evidence. Make sure all communication, whether verbal or written, contains specific, concrete examples of the missed opportunities or substandard performance that needs to be changed. Get the teacher's or students' exact words. Leaders sometimes worry that it is cruel or "devastating" to repeat the brutal facts. Remember that vague judgments such as "wastes too much time" or "classroom is disorganized" invite arguments rather than solutions. Detail the precise amount of time that elapsed or the examples of flustered searches for materials. The stronger the illustrative data, the easier it is to visualize both the problem and the steps to fix it.

Pay Attention to Impact on Students. Collect specific data about—and communicate—what happens to the students in the classroom as a result of ineffective choices or limited repertoire. Examine the student work on desks and in folders. Ask students to explain concepts, report how they arrived at solutions to problems, show their prior work, or explain what happens to a paper after they write it. Look at the tasks students are asked to do; consider how challenging they are and whether they are aligned to and support the lesson objectives. Keeping discussions focused on mutual commitments to meeting student needs helps to mitigate defensiveness and arguments.

Build a Repertoire and Match Your Strategy to the Situation. Jon Saphier (2008) first introduced us to the idea that skillful teaching involves constant decision making, i.e., the matching of strategies from an extended repertoire to the needs of the students and to content and context. We think the same principle applies to leadership. After watching skilled—and not so skilled—leaders at work over the years, we have noted a repertoire of ways to communicate about problems. This repertoire can be arrayed along a continuum (see Figure 6A.2).

Figure 6A.2 Continuum of Problem Documentation and Description

	Formative Assessment			Summative Assessment	
Low Documentation	"Early Worry"	"Concern"	Problem	Problem	High Documentation
	Brief oral or written feedback from single event such as a short classroom visit or meeting observation	Written statement of worry or concern with supporting evidence	Written description of a problem resulting from interim observations and other data	Written definition of problem that occurs after a negative rating on a summative evaluation	

Avoidance behaviors and ineffectual responses do not appear on the continuum. These behaviors, although never recommended, are often default responses in districts that lack the necessary conviction or skills to take on mediocrity. Ineffectual responses include sugar-coated communication, mixed messages, obscure references to something the teacher "might want to consider," imperatives not supported by any references to student needs or standards, and a general tendency to make accusations unsupported by data.

The high-intensity, high-documentation end of the continuum includes the detailed explications of sub-standard performance required by many contracts as a precursor to improvement plans. The more commonly used strategies for defining and communicating a problem fall somewhere in the middle of the continuum. All involve the use of formative assessments supported by data and a clearly stated expectation that practice will improve. They can be useful actions to take before you face the requirements for elaborate improvement plans and will resolve most performance problems. In choosing how you will communicate a problem, consider the following:

- The severity of the issue
- The variety and substance of the data you have available
- The time of year
- The recipient's prior history of problem-solving and self-directed improvement

OPTIONS FOR COMMUNICATING PERFORMANCE GAPS

In the remaining sections of this chapter, we will consider different options for communicating that learner and teacher performance is not what it needs to be. Section 6B illustrates a type of problem presentation we've called *communicating early worries*. A strategy for surfacing an issue or question in a relatively low-key exchange, it alerts teachers that they need to take a critical look at how students are doing or the impact of certain choices they are making. You might use this approach when you are following up on a first awareness of something bothersome from a *single data source* (e.g., a short visit, an observation of a single lesson or meeting, or an email from a parent). As its name implies, an early worry may prove to be unfounded. Examples 6B.1 through 6B.5 show supervisors communicating about worries that range from problems with management to questions of professionalism.

Section 6C presents guidelines and examples for communicating *concerns*. These problem presentations assume that leaders have appropriate evidence, drawn from multiple sources, of a performance gap that needs to be addressed immediately. Communication of concerns does not depend on whether a teacher is due to be evaluated or not—or even whether a team has asked for help. If the teacher or team responds effectively and the problem is solved, such communication may simply be part of a leader's desk file or memory aid and never appear in a formal record of performance. However, if a problem is difficult or persistent, communication of concerns is the first step in documentation. Examples in this chapter illustrate concerns about instruction, expectations, climate, and planning.

Section 6D provides models and examples of more formal *problem definition* for teachers whose performance on a particular standard has been rated as needing improvement or unsatisfactory either in a formative assessment or a summative evaluation. In such cases the assessor has found a pattern over time or across data sources that needs to be changed in order to improve conditions for students. For the samples in this section, we selected six areas of classroom performance from the Map of Pedagogical Knowledge (see Figure 5A.3). These functions are embedded in the content of virtually every credible set of performance standards or rubrics and should be transferable to your evaluation instrument. We have also included a sample from standards dealing with professional responsibility to highlight the importance of teachers as contributing members of collaborative learning communities.

Leader Alert
Communicating Problems to Teams

Most often you define and communicate problems to individual teachers. As you increase your supervision of professional learning communities, however, the audience for your communication may shift. We have included two problem definitions directed to groups of teachers (Examples 6B.4 and 6C.2), but other examples targeted to individuals can be readily modified if the issue is one that needs to be addressed by a team. ◆

Finally, as you think about expanding your competence in communicating clearly and setting expectations for change when instruction is ineffective, keep the following tips in mind:

1. Get and analyze the diagnostic data before you talk or write. Have it with you when you conference and put the data into your writing.
2. Keep the focus squarely on your mutual interest in students' learning and well-being. Include specific concrete evidence about the impact on learners of the choices the teacher or team makes and the actions taken or not taken.

3. Plan your oral communication ahead at least the first few times especially if you expect resistance.

4. Rehearse oral communication with a colleague, your administrative team, your mirror, or your pet. Ask someone you trust whether you have a tendency to talk in circles, sugarcoat messages, resort to jargon, or get too intense when you are nervous. Then check your practice communication for those issues.

5. Have someone read your first written attempts for the same issues detailed above.

6. Build and use a repertoire of problem communication strategies and match your strategy to the individual, the severity of the problem, and the quality of your data.

6B

COMMUNICATING EARLY WORRIES

Figure 6B.1 Early Worries on the Continuum of Problem Documentation and Description

	Formative Assessment			*Summative Assessment*	
Low **Documentation**	**"Early Worry"**	**"Concern"**	**Problem**	**Problem**	**High** **Documentation**
	Brief oral or written feedback from single event such as a short classroom visit or meeting observation.	Written statement of worry or concern with supporting evidence	Written description of a problem resulting from interim observations and other data	Written definition of problem that occurs after a negative rating on a summative evaluation	

As Figure 6 B.1 illustrates, "early worries" require talk and inquiry but not heavy documentation. They are tentative, preliminary identifications of something that does not appear to be working for learners. These worries often emerge from what you recognize to be limited sources of data: one observation, a single document, or a complaint. Taking action by communicating such worries before you have a fully developed pattern is an awareness strategy. It allows you to:

- Indicate your respect for the teacher's skill or capacity to look critically at his or her own practice
- Signal the school's culture of continuous examination and reflection
- Enlist teachers in formative conversations to improve conditions for students when issues first arise
- Provide a "heads up" opportunity for a teacher to make changes *if necessary*

You would not use this strategy if you have already had multiple interactions on the same performance issues with an individual or team or if you had sufficient data from several sources to signal that a serious problem exists. Choose to communicate something as an early worry if some combination of the conditions in Figure 6B.2 is present:

Figure 6B.2 When to Start with an Early Worry

- You do not know the individual's practice well.
- You have no prior pattern of data or history suggesting a problem.
- What you saw seems incongruous with past performance.

- You realize that new standards and expectations are changing what the school or district accepts as good practice.
- You realize you have seen the practice multiple times before without raising a question because you were preoccupied—or because you now know more.
- You believe the individual has sufficient knowledge and skill to make changes independently.
- You have good reason to think simply raising the question will cause the recipient to make changes.

Most often this communication is oral. It occurs almost immediately after a potential problem catches your attention. You begin with an open mind about whether this issue is a one-time event, an aberration, or symptomatic of something more substantial. You're curious, and your tone is invitational. Focus on the outcomes both of you want *for students* and on the data that suggest those outcomes are not yet being achieved. Avoid vague generalizations such as "students not engaged," expressions of feeling or belief, or personal injunctions such as "I would like you to. . . ." Figure 6B.3 gives some pointers on how to communicate early worries.

Figure 6B.3 How to Communicate Early Worries

- Include the data prompting the inquiry.
- Establish the student-centered reason for the worry.
- Establish (if appropriate) the agreed-upon objectives for instruction, for a program, or for a meeting.
- Signal your positive presupposition that the individual cares about the students and is open enough to consider whether a problem exists.
- Be explicit in inviting the recipient to offer additional or contradictory data and ideas for next steps or further investigation.
- Listen more than you talk.
- Pose a question rather than a suggestion after a brief visit.

The following examples illustrate typical "worry-level" exchanges triggered by a leader's noting—or being alerted to—potentially negative consequences for students' learning.

Examples

6B.1 **Management:** Students off task
6B.2 **Purpose for Learning:** Lesson objectives not communicated
6B.3 **Climate:** Parent complaints about student discomfort
6B.4 **Student Performance:** Poor results on interim assessments
6B.5 **Professionalism:** Department agreements not implemented

Leader Alert
When in Doubt, Write

There is always the question about when to put something in writing. Busy administrators often prefer communicating orally, at least initially. Or they decide that the recipient will be able to "hear" the invitation better if it is not in writing as some of our examples suggest. Giving people a "heads up" off the record is fine. However, when an accumulated body of data points to clear underperformance, it is critical to communicate in writing. ◆

In Example 6B.1, Department Director Reed noticed that a group of sophomores in the back row of Ms. Langue's Spanish II class were quietly off task during the entire 10 minutes he was in the class. He saw the teacher in the hall a few periods later and delivered a "slight worry" message.

Example 6B.1 Management: Students off task

Ms. Langue, when I stopped by during second period, I watched three sophomores in the back row who did not participate at all in the lesson and were off task throughout the 7 or 8 minutes you were conducting the recitation. A. L. was texting under her desk. The two males—I think one was T. J. and am not sure about the other—were working on Social Studies homework. I don't know if you dealt with them after I left or if this was typical, but I thought you might want these data as you look at seating and performance for this group.

Example 6B.2 shows oral communication of a worry that arises from a "learning walk" through the four sections of second grade at School Street Elementary. Conducted by Vice Principal Maureen Jones, two literacy specialists, and the grade 2 lead teacher, the walk focused on implementation of agreements made during summer professional development for the new reading program. The group wanted data on whether students were connecting the task assigned for seatwork to a worthwhile reading objective. In each class, Ms. Jones asked three to six students: "What is the most important thing you are learning by doing this worksheet exercise?" In three of the classes, the students were able to connect the task to the instructional objective. However, in Penny Lame's class, students' responses were consistently about "getting our packet done" and "filling in the worksheet." They had no frame for their learning or purpose for the task. Ms. Jones decided it was important to give feedback and present her worry about students' sense of purpose and understanding of the learning goals to the teacher. She could have sent an email but decided it would be a better match to talk to Penny after school.

Example 6B.2 Purpose for Learning: Lesson objectives not communicated

Penny, this week the reading team has been focusing on how all of us are (1) communicating learning goals and (2) communicating and helping students make connections between the "Habits of Good Readers" and the practice sheets. I'm worried that your students may not be clear about the purposes for the worksheets and seat work that go along with the new reading program. When I visited today, I randomly asked a half-dozen students, "What is the most important thing you are learning by doing this worksheet exercise?" This is what I got back:

1. "These are our worksheets we're doing; you have to have all your work done by lunch or you can't go out."
2. "We are learning about ah . . . not sure. Maybe something to do with reading."
3. "This is reading work so we can go over stuff while the teacher has the group at the table."
4. "How to practice stuff like dictionary work and spelling."
5. (From a student reading her own book) "We have worksheets all the time. She wants us to be quiet when the other kids are at group. I finished in, like, 5 minutes, so I can read what I want."
6. "You have to learn about things like spelling and plot and how to look up words."

This kind of response is what we all worried about in August: that students would not be able to connect the seatwork exercises to development of important reading competencies—and consequently that they might not be able to transfer what they were doing on a worksheet to other reading challenges. If these answers are typical of the current level of understanding, it would be important to get at the issue now while kids are still forming their ideas. What do you think might help them make better connections? I'm going to keep this as an interview focus when I talk to kids for the next few weeks so we can get ongoing data.

Example 6B.3 revisits Coach Frank Steel, an old friend whose profile appeared in *Confronting Mediocre Teaching*. After enrollment shifts caused cuts at the high school, Frank ended up at the new middle school in town. During the second week of October, his principal, Stan Dard, received several clearly coordinated parent emails about the "negative feeling" and "poor climate" in Mr. Steel's classroom. Dard decided to drop by the class randomly for a few minutes at three different times. He observed differential treatment of girls and boys and wanted to bring these data to the teacher. Given Steel's history of occasional truculence, Dard decided to put the data in writing.

For a more complete profile of Frank Steel, see *The Skillful Leader: Confronting Mediocre Teaching*, (Platt, Tripp, Fraser, and Ogden 2000 45-47).

Example 6B.3 Climate: Parent complaints about student discomfort

To: Frank Steel
From: Stan Dard
Date: 10/7
Frank, I received three different emails from parents commenting on the "negative feelings" and "poor climate" in your fourth-period classroom last

week. I was surprised since I know you care about making students feel welcome, so I wanted you to be aware of a potential problem. I did visit your seventh-grade classes briefly several times this week to try to understand what might be contributing to these families' perceptions. In each case, my notes show you posed more questions to boys than to girls while I was there. You also tended to stick with boys longer. I'm wondering whether you think these observed events are really patterns—and, if so, what unintended messages students may be getting. All three families who wrote have female students. Let's talk about your current strategy for balancing questioning and opportunities to respond and what else you might want to try.

Example 6B.4 illustrates a worry and invitation to improve directed to a team, the sixth grade Math PLC at Midtown Middle School. Benchmark results for the first eight weeks of school showed that the grade 6 math scores were worrisome. Three out of the four teachers had between 40 percent and 60 percent of their students scoring at the Basic level on geometry and problem solving. The remaining teacher had 25 percent of students in the Basic range. The K-8 math coordinator decided to visit the PLC meeting and to raise the issue with the entire team.

Example 6B.4 Student Performance: Poor results on interim assessments

As you know we had some disappointing results from the fall benchmark tests. I'm worried that students may have some gaps in background we hadn't anticipated. Let's work together to figure out the most likely causes and develop a team action plan so students can show improvement in the winter testing. We'll start with an error analysis to see exactly where students are going wrong and see if we can figure out what they are thinking or where the holes are before we start planning the re-teaching. I'll make sure I'm with you for all the team meetings over the next couple of weeks to support you.

Leader Alert
Teams Need Oversight

Note that in Example 6B.4, the worry about the gap in student achievement is presented to a team rather than an individual. The spirit is invitational and supportive. The supervisor is not simply *hoping* something will get better and leaving the group alone to muddle along. Instead she has data that suggest the team may not know how to proceed and has matched her response to that situation by stepping in to guide the effort. Beware of unwarranted confidence in a group's ability to collaborate effectively. Leaders who have created teams or professional learning communities need to check early and often to diagnose those teams' demonstrated skills and commitment. ◆

Example 6B.5 is about professionalism. After considerable deliberation and discussions with their respective departments, the high school Instructional Leadership Team (ILT) decided that it would adopt a common agreement that all teachers post and communicate their instructional objectives for each lesson and have students revisit the objectives as part of routine closure. Over a one-month period, directors conducted regular brief observations of beginnings and endings of classes. They talked to students, and helped teachers who were struggling or reminded forgetful members about the agreement. At the six-week mark, Director Hughes found that all department members except Ben Beenaround had settled into a consistent pattern of defining and posting objectives. They were also making good progress on designing closure activities. Hughes decided to have a quick, face-to-face meeting with Ben in his classroom after school one day. He chose to pose the worry as a question in order to learn more about Ben's thinking.

> ### Example 6B.5 Professionalism: Department agreements not implemented
>
> Ben, I know you are aware of the common agreement that was adopted by the ILT to post and communicate objectives and to make sure students came back to the objectives during the closure activity. We're making great progress as a department, and now I'm worried about the discrepancies I'm noting. I haven't seen or heard evidence of the learning objective either at the beginning or the end of class in the last three visits to your sections. Kids can tell me what the topic is and which chapter they're on, but only one or two have been able to say anything about what they should have mastered about the topic. Today all I heard were variations on "We have to know this for the test on Friday." Where are you on implementing this agreement?

Communicating worries is an action against ineffective instruction, but it is a gentle one. By communicating worries you signal a positive assumption, expressed not as a hope but as a conviction, that teachers can and will take appropriate action to close gaps before they become fully developed problems. In a culture of consistent feedback and learning-focused evaluation, this type of communication is simply an invitation to think through an issue and a promise to stay interested in the results of the discussion. However, beware of the temptation to linger at the worry level. Watch out for unwarranted hope that improvement will come or misplaced judgment that you will take care of the problem on the final evaluation. Worries either increase or diminish over time as more data are collected. If you do not see action or have evidence that the teacher is "on the case" after one or two discussions, move to communication of a concern, addressed in Section 6C.

6C
COMMUNICATING CONCERNS

Leaders have frequently used the term *concern* as a warning signal that current performance is problematic. Think of worries as intermittent whiffs of something burning and concerns as easily visible streams of smoke in the air. Neither should be ignored. You need to take some kind of action and get that action on the record. As Figure 6C.1 indicates, concerns are more serious and need to be better documented than worries. They may be escalations in intensity after an individual has not responded adequately to an invitation to rethink practice, or they may be the first interaction about a particular problem.

Figure 6C.1 Concerns on the Continuum of Problem Documentation and Description

	Formative Assessment			Summative Assessment	
Low Documentation	**"Early Worry"**	**"Concern"**	**Problem**	**Problem**	High Documentation
	Brief oral or written feedback from single event such as a short classroom visit or meeting observation.	**Written statement of worry or concern with supporting evidence**	Written description of a problem resulting from interim observations and other data	Written definition of problem that occurs after a negative rating on a summative evaluation	

Concerns should be raised as soon as they are noted so that there are no secrets between supervisor and teacher. They need to be communicated whether the individual is "on the list" to be formally evaluated or not. The recipient of a message of concern should usually be able to take action to improve well before any formal rating needs to be given or discipline applied. Choose to communicate something first as a concern if you have seen several examples of a particular problem or have data from at least two different sources indicating that a potential problem exists. Generally some combination of the conditions in Figure 6C.2 is present.

Figure 6C.2 When to Start at the Concern Level

- The issue is potentially explosive or likely to mushroom without immediate attention.
- You do not want the recipient to be blindsided or surprised by a low rating later in the year.
- You are several months into the academic year and want to make sure students' time and opportunities to learn are not being wasted.

- The potential recipient becomes uncomfortable with open-ended questions and shuts down when s/he is not clear about what exactly is expected.
- The personality type, learning style, or past responses of the recipient suggest that s/he will ignore a more subtle approach.
- You believe that the individual has sufficient skill and will be able to make changes independently if s/he is convinced that you and others view the problem as a serious one.

Unlike the worry level, the concern level is almost always expressed in writing and always involves citing multiple pieces of evidence and making a clear request for change. Figure 6C.3 shows how to communicate concerns.

Figure 6C.3 How to Communicate Concerns

- Present the specific data from multiple sources that indicate a problem exists.
- Establish the costs to students as the driving reason for raising the issue.
- Restate the objectives for students and the teaching standards, policies, or procedures that are not yet being met.
- Signal your positive presupposition that the individual would want to rectify the situation immediately.
- Be explicit in asking the recipient to offer additional or contradictory data and ideas for further investigation.
- Ask the teacher to specify what s/he will do to fix the problem.
- State your intention to follow up for further discussion and assessment and your willingness to provide support.

The examples that follow illustrate initial communication of a problem as a concern (Examples 6C.1, 6C.2, and 6C.3) and escalated responses after something that was presented first as a worry did not get resolved satisfactorily (Examples 6C.4 and 6C.5).

Examples

6C.1 **Instruction:** No visuals or explanatory devices
6C.2 **Expectations:** Low expectations for Special Education students
6C.3 **Planning:** Curriculum standards not being used
6C.4 **Instruction:** Purposes for learning not identified or communicated
6C.5 **Climate:** Disrespectful treatment of students

Example 6C.1 illustrates a concern uncovered by a high school administrative team during a round of diagnostic observations. The principal wanted to examine how the work of small content-alike teams was affecting day-to-day instruction. Pairs of administrators spent 15 minutes each in the six sections of freshman English during the first two days of the persuasive writing unit. Unlike other rooms, Sarah Blank's whiteboards and bulletin boards contained no charts with criteria for success, no graphic organizers or organizing templates, and no key vocabulary or concept reminders. In stark contrast to students in other sections, many of Sarah's had not even started to draft or were staring into space or doodling when she was not looking at them. No one was using notebooks or pre-writing exercises; no one could show observers any handouts that had been given to support students' learning. Students told the observers Sarah "mostly tells us stuff" and "she puts slides and things on the SMART Board™." Four of the six students who were staring into space and had no work in front of them offered variations on "I wait for her 'til she comes and helps me." The observation led AP Terrell Burley to compare the number of students with C's or below in Sarah's class with those of the other heterogeneous sections and then write to Sarah.

Example 6C.1 Instruction: No visuals or explanatory devices

Sarah,

When the administrative team observed how the persuasive writing unit was going in all the English I sections on Monday and Tuesday, we noted that at least half of your students had written nothing yet. Five or six were disengaged (staring or doodling), and others were writing one or two lines and then crossing them out and waiting for you to come and guide them to the next step. Your classroom was the only one of the six we observed that had no visual aids to support students in remembering and applying the key concepts necessary for good persuasive writing. Students did not have the criteria for success sheets, blank graphic organizers, pre-writing template, or any of the other tools I know your team identified as being important scaffolds for this unit. Thus many students could not go on to draft until they had talked with you. I know that you feel strongly about the value of working with students individually and making personal contact as they write. However, I am concerned that relying exclusively on oral directions, PowerPoint slides that students do not have copies of, and one-to-one conferences is negatively affecting your class's ability to meet writing standards. The number of students with grades of C or below for first quarter suggests this is a concern we should take very seriously. Let's talk before next Monday about how to increase the number of visual cues and aids in your classroom. I'm sure we can successfully mesh your commitment to individual conferences with the tools the team has developed. Let me know what time works for you.

Example 6C.2 shows how a director communicates a concern to a team in order to raise awareness and stimulate problem solving. After Central Elementary went to a full inclusion model, Special Education Director Gloria Worth repeatedly heard that her department was not providing adequate in-classroom support for students in grades 4 and 6. Central already had one more paraprofessional than other K-6 schools for a similar caseload. Gloria decided to observe mainstreamed classes with her special education team leader to see if she could diagnose what the issues were. After two rounds of observations in all of the classes, Gloria's data showed that mainstreamed students in grades 4 and 6 were rarely if ever allowed to try something on their own before "help" was provided. Often support staff swooped in before children had even picked up a pencil to begin. Gloria speculated that the unsolicited help was setting up a cycle of dependency that was directly counter to what the department was trying to achieve. She decided to raise the concern at a fourth-grade team meeting first. She knew the team had several members who had changed grade levels and that the special education staff member was a newcomer to the school. Gloria presented her concern in a memo so that people would have a chance to think about the issue in advance.

Example 6C.2 Expectations: Low expectations for Special Education students

To: Grade 4 Mainstream Team
From: Gloria Worth
Re: Tackling the challenge of helping students become more independent

Many of you have raised the issue of additional classroom support. I know that you do so out of your commitment to students' development—hence the purpose of our upcoming (10/27) meeting. To get a sense of your population and how they are responding, Corinne and I spent approximately 5 hours total in grade four classrooms over the past 13 school days. We focused our data gathering on two arenas: (1) our standards and expectations for study habits and perseverance and (2) offering unsolicited help. These are arenas we really haven't had a chance to dig into together, but they are clearly related to your doubts about whether students are willing and able to work on their own.

Take a look at the raw data we collected below. The letters across the top of the matrix are codes for your classes. The fractions represent the total number of times something happened out of the possible opportunities we recorded in the 13 days.

Classroom	A	B	C	D
Team study habits/procedural expectations for good independent work posted	✓	✓	✓	✓
Teachers referred regular ed. students to study habit charts when students not following them	7/8	5/7	4/5	7/7
Teachers referred special needs students to study habit charts when students not following them	2/9	1/8	3/10	3/8
Teachers offered students without education plans unsolicited help before students started assigned seatwork	3/50+	4/50+	2/50+	0/50+
Paraprofessionals offered special needs students unsolicited help before students started assigned seatwork	17/19	22/22	16/19	18/19
Special needs students with moderate disabilities not starting work unless an adult redirected or coached	6/6	4/5	3/5	2/6

Corrine and I are concerned that we all may have set up a pattern of rushing in to rescue our mainstreamed students instead of expecting that they should begin independently and show persistence. I am looking forward to your thoughts about next steps as you pull apart the data and reflect on the way we started the year. See you Wednesday.

Example 6C.3 shows a concern raised with Arnetta Wishom, a veteran kindergarten teacher who believes her students are "missing out on all the fun of childhood" as a result of mandates for more rigorous curriculum over the last four years. Arnetta has found it difficult to let go of her favorite activities. She frequently asserts that the new Common Core Standards are inappropriate for her groups and that she does not have time for all the new math that has been "crammed into" her day. Tonya George, the Early Childhood Director, has been working with Mrs. Wishom to plan lessons based on core math standards. They completed the first unit together. Ms. George then asked Arnetta to apply what she had learned by planning for the first week of the new measurement unit on her own. The resulting plans were a compendium of games, workbook exercises, and learning station activities that had little or no connection to the standard. Ms. George decided that she needed to escalate from cheerful support to a more straightforward expression of a gap to be closed. She put her concerns into an email.

Example 6C.3 Planning: Curriculum standards not being used

Dear Arnetta,

I have reviewed your plans for the measurement and data unit the kindergarteners will be beginning February 1 and have some concerns:

1. None of the six lessons refers to the standard that you are teaching to and that students must master.
2. Our planning template asks you to list the "big math ideas" that you will communicate to the students both initially and throughout the lesson. Those ideas can be found in the Common Core Standards as well as in our handbook. On three of the plans, you listed nothing. On the remaining lessons, you listed "Measuring is important," which is too vague and does not reflect any of our agreed-upon big ideas.
3. A number of activities listed for Lessons 2, 3, and 4 (e.g., coloring pictures of different measuring tools, "making a paper model of me," or making a height line-up do not refer to the specific standard and the core ideas of this first unit. You may have the connections in your head, but the plans do not reveal your understanding of and connection to the standards.
4. Several of the activities you listed, such as making paper models, will consume large amounts of time without significantly adding to students' understanding of the key measurement concepts we discussed. They will contribute to your sense that you never have enough time to do math as the curriculum is designed.

I am not sure what happened between the time that we co-planned the first unit and this set of lessons, but they do not demonstrate that you have a solid grounding in mapping backwards from the standards. If you are not sure what the important competencies are and how to get to them, your students are not likely to get the solid grounding they need.

Let's talk again on Thursday during your planning period.

Tonya

Example 6C.4 shows a response when a leader's initial assessment, raised as a worry after program-monitoring walks, is confirmed with further data. Vice Principal Maureen Jones initially talked to Penny Lame, inviting her to address an issue quickly and make changes (see Example 6B.2). Ms. Jones made a quick note of the date and what they talked about in her desk calendar and then checked in with the second-grade sections periodically over a 6-week period. Within that time she saw a widening gap in what students understood and could take ownership for in Penny Lame's classes versus all the other second grades. Therefore, Ms. Jones escalated the communication with a summary email to signal the seriousness of the issue.

Example 6C.4 Instruction: Purposes for learning not identified or communicated

---

Penny,

I am concerned that little has changed since we met briefly in October to talk about how you could help students (1) understand the purpose of the seatwork tasks in the new ELA program and (2) connect those tasks to becoming better readers and writers. During follow-up visits on 11/5 and 11/8, I collected additional data. Lesson goals and relevant standards were not posted on either day, so students had no visual references. The skills chart we discussed was still on your back table. On 11/5 your plan book listed only "Go over lesson 3.4" which is not a learning goal. On 11/8 all I found was lists of reading groups and tasks. I asked five to eight students the same question we agreed upon in the summer: What is the most important thing you are learning by doing this worksheet exercise? Answers included:

C.R.: "It's part of our ELA program. This is our independent work, and we're learning to finish on time."

J.K.: "We are practicing—ah…" (turns to a partner). "What are we learning?"

L.P. (partner) "Vocabulary words."

T.M: "We are learning to connect reading and writing. She told us we would need this for next week's story work."

P.W.: "I think this is so we can get good at the tests we have to take because they ask us questions like this."

J.V.: "This is our packet that we do by the end of the week, and you have to, like, read the story again three times … and then she calls you up to her table."

It is clear from this data that many students are not connecting the activities with larger purposes and frames of meaning and instead are focusing on completing disconnected tasks. Entries in the Reflection Journals were equally discouraging: "I learned that writing is hard." "I learned that I can ask a friend for help." "I learned that the smarter kids know all the answers." I recognize that this is a new curriculum for you, and you are struggling with all the management challenges associated with survival. However, managing the materials and also communicating the purposes for learning are not mutually exclusive. I know you can do both with a bit of advance planning and the use of structures already provided by the program. We need to get some clear commitments re steps you will take consistently over the next month to help students understand what they should know and be able to do—and why. Let me know what you plan to focus on and whether you'd like to work with the reading coach or a colleague on strategies to close this gap.

In Example 6C.5 Principal Dard follows up on his first memo communicating parental complaints about classroom climate to coach and Social Studies teacher Frank Steel (see Example 6B.3). As he and Frank had agreed, Mr. Dard focused on getting data about Frank's responses to students so both parties could understand why students were uncomfortable. He made three unannounced, 10-minute observations as he could find the time over approximately five weeks. Looking at his notes, Stan began to notice patterns in Frank's responses to student answers that would be likely to have a negative effect on the learning environment. After the first two visits, Stan left Frank the raw data and brief feedback, and the two talked informally about what to pay attention to. The incident described below caused Principal Dard to elevate his response to a serious concern.

Example 6C.5 Climate: Disrespectful treatment of students

To: Frank Steel
From: Stan Dard
Re: Continuing attention to classroom environment
Date: 12/9

This memo is a follow-up to our October 7 discussion about classroom climate and balancing opportunities to respond so that many students of both genders would receive positive expectation messages and feel comfortable enough to participate. As we agreed, I've collected and left data on calling patterns for you during my last three visits (10/27, 11/13, 12/8). You and I have both noted that the balance between males and females answering questions has improved.

Toward our shared goal of success for all students, we need to tackle another essential aspect of building a safe and respectful environment: making sure that your comments and responses to students consistently demonstrate respect for their diverse cultural identities. (See the Massachusetts Standards for Effective Teaching Practices Indicator IIC "Cultural Proficiency: Actively creates and maintains an environment in which students' diverse background, identities, strength and challenges are respected.") We discussed my concerns about your making off-the-cuff jokes about students in November. Yesterday the issue arose again. You called on Salvador to respond to the question "Why are Mexicans likely to want to come to the United States?" He fumbled for an answer. You said, "Well, I figured you would know," then chuckled and called on Larry K. Given Salvador's Puerto Rican heritage, your sidebar remark could be interpreted an insulting comment whether you intended it to be so or not. The impact was immediate. Several students snickered. A male in the back murmured, "He should ask his f--- mother."

This disrespectful remark was audible to all. It got no reaction from you. There was no apparent consequence for such disrespect. Salvador looked down, got up and took the bathroom pass, walked out, and was gone for 7 minutes. I doubt he will make any attempt to participate in class again soon.

I am very concerned that, were an assessment to be made at this point in the year, the climate in your classroom would be rated Unsatisfactory, based on the standard "Establishes an environment in which students demonstrate limited respect for individual differences." The situation is salvageable right now, and we want all your students to be able to say that you respect them and care about their success. Let me know what steps you plan to take and what kind of data you want collected next.

Defining and communicating worries or concerns is the first action step toward changing the ineffective instruction. Teachers cannot improve or resolve an issue if they are unaware of—or allowed to ignore—practices that are creating obstacles to student learning. Obviously, all of our preceding examples require something more than simply putting a teacher on notice that a gap exists. The next steps—figuring out when and how to help a teacher change and checking for sustained improvement—are equally critical. Notice how each communication is followed by a request for action: a subsequent meeting, notice of plans, or further communication to refine what the issues are.

A skillful leader may choose to speak about a concern first but will always follow up in writing. These communications hold detailed evidence that can be referenced in a final evaluation. They are part of the documentation to illustrate and defend a low rating if improvement does not follow or cannot be sustained. In the unlikely case you need to move to discipline or dismissal, these articulations of concern will constitute essential evidence that the teacher had adequate notice well in advance of any subsequent, more serious job action.

6D

DEVELOPING FORMAL PROBLEM DESCRIPTIONS

Figure 6D.1 Continuum of Problem Documentation and Description

	Formative Assessment			*Summative Assessment*	
Low Documentation	**"Early Worry"**	**"Concern"**	**Problem**	**Problem**	High Documentation
	Brief oral or written feedback from single event such as a short classroom visit or meeting observation.	Written statement of worry or concern with supporting evidence	**Written description of a problem resulting from interim observations and other data**	**Written definition of problem that occurs after a negative rating on a summative evaluation**	

Taking action against ineffective practice can begin with early, honest communication of worries and concerns. However, such informal and semiformal strategies are not always an appropriate choice. If a stronger response is called for, you will need the high documentation end of the continuum (illustrated in Figure 6D.1). You will have to craft and communicate a straightforward accounting of the standards the teacher is not meeting and the impact of that ineffective practice on student performance: that is, a *problem description*.

Your district may simply refer to the process of describing and communicating a problem as giving someone a negative evaluation. Problem descriptions appear in different locations. They may be negative paragraphs that are

- Part of an observation report
- Documentation under a low rating checked off on a rubric
- Part of an interim assessment or disciplinary memo
- Documentation on a summative evaluation

We use problem description to mean any written communication, discussed with the teacher, that does the following:

- Refers to and specifically names a performance standard not currently being met
- Provides an explicit explanation of a rating that indicates a standard is not being met
- Provides detailed evidence to support the existence of the discrepancy between the standard and current performance—thus helping the teacher understand when and how the problem occurs
- Establishes the negative impact of the discrepancy on students or the school
- Informs the recipient that change must take place

Note that this set of criteria does not include specifying what to do about the performance issue. Identifying and communicating the problem is the first part of taking action. You deal with the past, with what has or has not happened. Designing ways to solve the problem is the second part of your response. It takes place after the teacher has had time to absorb the message. At that stage, discussed in Chapter 7, you focus together on the future and what can be done.

The statement of the existence of a problem is nonnegotiable. Your critical first task is to get the teacher to understand and accept *what* the issue is exactly and *why* you are raising it. Concentrating on crafting and communicating the description first forces you to be sure you have adequate, clear, and compelling evidence and have linked that evidence to teacher performance standards. Talking to teachers about the problem before discussion of next steps reduces the likelihood that they will be distracted by the recommendations or assume a "Just tell me what to do" stance. Because the problem description may be difficult to receive, you can expect many teachers to push back or subside into silence even when you deliver the message as respectfully as possible. Only in rare cases are teachers ready to discuss solutions immediately. Reserving discussion of next steps allows you to structure a future-oriented second meeting where you engage the teacher in figuring out how to fix the problem. In the follow-up meeting, you invite the teacher to take ownership of the strategies and to make choices from a repertoire of options. Document the agreements from your negotiations along with a clear indication that the teacher has participated in their design.

Leader Alert
When to Combine Problem Descriptions and Specified Next Steps

Your contract or evaluation procedures may require you to provide recommendations for action on your official forms any time you give a negative evaluation or rate performance as substandard. In such cases, follow the two-part process above: write the problem description and meet with the teacher to discuss the rating and the issues. If you are pressed for time and must limit yourself to one conference, bring a separate document listing ideas for next steps that is clearly labeled "draft." After you have discussed the problem, engage the teacher in considering ways to tackle it. Record your joint agreements plus any additions you want to make and have informed the teacher about. Do not simply hand the teacher the finished product, action steps and all, and tell her to read and sign. ◆

Choose to communicate about an issue using a formal problem description when any of the characteristics listed in Figure 6D.2 are present.

Figure 6D.2 When to Use a Formal Problem Description

- Significant improvement does not occur within a period of weeks of the first communication of a worry or concern.
- Your worry or concern has not translated into their worry or concern.
- The individual does not demonstrate sufficient skills, background knowledge, or motivation to make changes independently.

- The problem is longstanding, as in inexplicit speech or repeated grammatical errors, and gentler approaches have not worked.
- The problem is acute and dramatic, as in a sharp decline in mental faculties or a series of harsh outbursts with colleagues, students, or parents.
- The "problem" is actually a number of complicated, interwoven issues that will need to be divided into manageable pieces and addressed by a series of interventions.
- The recipient of the feedback has trouble with auditory or language processing, has a track record of "not hearing" feedback, or consistently misrepresents ideas.
- The individual needs time to make sense of an issue before s/he can respond without extreme defensiveness.

Getting the description, the documentation, and the communication as crisp and clear as possible is a stumbling block for many leaders. When the defining and communicating stage is not handled well, both teachers and supervisors can invest hours of effort on follow-up activities that bear little connection to the root causes of students' difficulty. Thus this stage deserves sufficient attention as well as practice with the techniques of effective documentation.

Balanced Analysis and Components of a Problem Description

To prepare good problem descriptions, we rely on a technique called balanced analysis, introduced by Jon Saphier and used to support a wide variety of evaluation systems, coaching tools, and mentoring programs. Balanced analysis is a method of communicating about teaching either orally or in writing. It involves four key elements:

1. **Claims.** Statements that name a particular teaching skill or pattern that is either present or absent from instruction
2. **Evidence.** Data such as literal quotes, precise descriptions, examples from artifacts that caused the speaker or writer to make the generalized claim and that support and illustrate the claim
3. **Impact.** Statements and data that demonstrate the observed or likely effect of the instruction on students
4. **Judgment.** A rating statement that tells the teacher where her performance is in relation to an agreed-upon standard, given the current evidence

As Figure 6D.3 illustrates, evidence is at the heart of this kind of communication. Analysts look at multiple sources of data to determine what they have evidence of. They use that diagnosis to make a claim about teacher performance. They also use evidence to determine the actual impact on students or to predict what the likely impact will be if a gap in instruction persists.

Figure 6D.3 Relationship of Elements in Balanced Analysis

Examples 6D.1 through 6D.8 illustrate formal problem descriptions from different documents to serve as starting points or templates. These examples can be easily adapted to fit your district evaluation instrument and performance standards.

Example 6D.1 Classroom Management: Ineffective procedures and routines [observation report]

Example 6D.2 Instruction: Ineffective questioning and discussion strategies [interim assessment]

Example 6D.3 Assessment: Failure to provide timely and effective feedback [memo of concern]

Example 6D.4 Learning Environment: Negative relationships with students [interim evaluation]

Example 6D.5 Expectations: Low Standards and Expectations for Students [memo of concern following a midyear conference]

Example 6D.6 Curriculum: Ineffective Planning [final evaluation]

Example 6D.7 Assessment: Data not collected or used to modify instruction [final evaluation]

Example 6D.8 Professional Responsibilities: Poor collaboration [final evaluation]

To give you more model paragraphs to work from, most of these samples contain several claims. Your problem descriptions might be shorter but would still need a minimum of three pieces of evidence and a statement of impact to support the claim about a performance issue.

Observation Report: Klem Kayos

Example 6D.1 illustrates a midyear observation report for Klem Kayos, a teacher with classroom management problems. Note that we have labeled the elements of balanced analysis in this and the following example to show how balanced analysis is used for explicit problem description and communication. The claims are drawn from Marshall's Teacher Evaluation Rubrics (2012). Before she wrote this report, the evaluator had visited Mr. Kayos's classroom a number of times, expressed her concerns, and made suggestions for changes that were not implemented. The evaluator now puts the teacher on notice that he has a serious problem to fix by entering two claims under the relevant standard on her reporting form.

Example 6D.1 Classroom Management: Ineffective procedures and routines [observation report]

Mr. Kayos has not identified and reinforced procedures and expectations for being prepared with materials.

Claim that names a specific deficit using language from a standard

- Minutes into the period, only 6 of 26 students present had texts or notebooks ready despite 2 minutes of teacher prompting *"Let's get ready now folks."*

- Mr. K. had to individually instruct 14 different students re what they needed to have on their desktops initially "Kaylee, book and notebook," "Damien, where's your notebook? You know you need it every day." "Terese, notebook." It took 4 minutes before students were ready to work.

Specific evidence is bulleted. Each concrete example will later help both parties figure out what the teacher needs to learn to do differently.

- When he transitioned to the work packet, he went through the same process of repeating instructions with at least 12 individuals. The transition took more than 5 minutes before all students were on task.

- Mr. K. provided no consequences or feedback to five students who had forgotten materials and spent from 1-3 minutes banging cupboard doors, wandering along the shelves in the back, and being disruptive while "looking for" extra copies of books and worksheets.

As a result, students lost more than a third of available instructional time to materials issues.

Statement of the impact on learners—the reason that the teaching needs to change

Mr. K. has not identified and reinforced procedures and expectations for handling homework and classwork.

Claim related to the standard the teacher is not meeting

- Mr. K. checked approximately half the homework at the start of class, was distracted by a student outburst, and never returned to or instructed the remaining students on what to do. In the midst of the lesson, individuals began to call out questions like: "Yo, you want this or not?" and "I did my work; how come you didn't check it?"
There was no procedure for turning in completed packets or checking for missed work, despite agreements by the grade 7 team to establish a consistent process.
When half of the students could not find their "weekly homework sheet" and were yelling questions to one another re what they were supposed to do, Mr. K. responded "Well, maybe you should figure out a better place to keep it. Write this down somewhere."

Bulleted evidence that provides a specific picture of when and how the problem occurs

As a result, students report that they are unsure of what the teacher wants them to do. Typical comments from interviews include: "It seems he changes everything"; "The class is just disorganized; it's no good trying cause he's always on you"; "I used to like science, but now it's just a waste of our time"; "I'm not learning anything."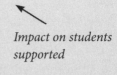

Impact on students supported

In Mr. K.'s case, the evaluator has seen several different manifestations of absent procedures and routines. She breaks the problem definition down into two claims plus evidence to make it easier for the teacher to understand. She avoids including recommendations prematurely but clearly establishes the groundwork for designing follow-up steps with the teacher. For follow-up recommendation for Mr. Kaos, see Example 7D.2.

Evaluation systems differ widely from state to state and district to district. Almost all good systems, however, require that an individual who rates a teacher's performance as needing improvement must provide the teacher with a rationale or evidence. Note the concrete examples provided to Mr. Kaos. Leaders who are new to the work of confronting ineffective instruction sometimes shrink from recording and reporting such "brutal facts." However, it is such specific, carefully documented interactions coupled with the costs to students that convince the teacher, union representatives, colleagues, coaches, and, if necessary, arbitrators, that leaders are not being arbitrary and capricious in their judgments.

Leader Alert
Negative Ratings and Problem Focus

Many districts have adopted comprehensive rubric-based instruments with large numbers of "categories" (e.g., standards, criteria, indicators, elements). You may wonder how many problems to identify and document when teachers clearly have deficiencies in multiple areas. In such instances, use negative ratings for all of the substandard or problem areas and provide the necessary raw data or evidence. However, develop only one or two detailed problem descriptions such as those we illustrate initially. This approach will help focus the teacher's work. It will also prevent later claims of harassment if you cite new problems after progress has been made on the first issue. Whenever you can, try to put your first effort into documenting and describing a "power gap," an issue that—if fixed—has the potential to close other performance gaps as well. ◆

Interim Assessment: Sally Friendly

Example 6D.2 is an interim assessment excerpt on Sally Friendly, the prototypical ineffective performer introduced in our first volume, *Confronting Mediocre Teaching* (2000). Sally has excellent routines, relates well to students, and contributes to building a strong school climate. (She brings cookies to meetings.) However, over a three-year period, her students' achievement scores and work samples have been mediocre to poor and compare unfavorably to those of her colleagues. The number of parents requesting that their children not be placed in Sally's section has increased for the last two years. Her evaluator has diagnosed several performance problems including low expectations, an inability to set substantive objectives for learning, and an over-reliance on activity-level planning. Those areas—like the failure to use effective questioning and discussion strategies communicated below—have all been rated as "unsatisfactory" or "needs improvement." Sally's principal chooses to focus first on effective questioning techniques because she knows improvements in that area are likely to require improvements in setting substantive learning objectives. The district has adopted the New York State United Teachers (NYSUT) performance standards and rubrics: usny.nysed.gov 2013.

Example 6D.2 Instruction: Ineffective questioning and discussion strategies [interim assessment]

Mrs. Friendly's questions do not invite a thoughtful response or further discussion. She consistently poses closed-end questions of low cognitive challenge during discussions and recitations.	*Claim that names a particular deficit within the standard*
• "Go over Hawaii questions" (plan for Social Studies 9/27), no focus question or objective for science 10/21, "Check re main characters" (plan book 12/12), no focus question or purpose for reading "Okay, who wants to read the first paragraph?" (obs. 11/6). • "What did Hawaiians eat? Is a mango a fruit? What does breadfruit grow on? I love sweet potatoes. Do you? Give me another thing they ate" (obs. 9/27). • "Name a main character. Okay name another one. Who is his brother? Now let's talk about setting. Where is this set? Right. What is the date? Right. How many years have gone by? Okay, who wants to start us off on the next part?" (obs. 12/12). • 12 of 16 questions during a 10-minute visit required low-level recall, 2 questions began with why, 2 questions were rhetorical and answered by Mrs. Friendly. This pattern was noted after three sessions of working with the literacy coach (obs. 12/12).	*Evidence drawn from multiple data sources to support and illustrate the second sub-claim*
As a result, students have had limited opportunities to practice the kinds of explanations and connections required to meet literacy standards. In contrast to patterns in other sections where 65%-77% of students showed growth between the first two benchmark assessments of explanation and argument construction, only 22% of Mrs. Friendly's students showed growth.	*Impact illustrated by providing specific data when such data are relevant and appropriate*
Mrs. Friendly allows students to respond to questions with single-word answers and does not invite or require them to elaborate upon or explain what they know or how they know it.	*Second sub-claim that names a particular deficit within the standard or specifies a gap closely related to the standard*

- 17 of 20 responses to questions consisted of one or two words; only one response was in a full sentence; no feedback or encouragement was given to students who did not respond fully (obs. 10/21).
- Mrs. Friendly instructed students to "explain your thinking" in math and then allowed all 7 students called upon to answer in single words or to give the number for the answer without explanation (obs. 11/6).
- Students who responded to comprehension questions in their reading journals or workbooks with one or two words rather than the expected constructed response had "Great job" or "Super work" at the top of their pages weeks after the literacy coach had worked with Mrs. Friendly on getting students to extend their language (artifact conf 1/9).

Evidence drawn from multiple data sources to support/ illustrate the claim

As a result, ELL students who need maximum practice in speaking and students whose writing strongly benefits from oral practice with concepts have not developed the kind of fluency and skill they need to demonstrate what they know.

Impact on students

For follow-up action for Mrs. Friendly, see Section 8C.

Memo of Concern: Dr. Lila Belated

Example 6D.3 is a memo summarizing a meeting between Lila Belated, a high school chemistry teacher, and Rose Mitchell, her department head, about a performance problem. After midterm grades were issued, Ms. Mitchell fielded three calls from irate parents claiming that their children had had no warning they were doing poorly. All insisted that the chemistry teacher had not returned any papers or quizzes during the marking period despite students' repeated requests. Parents reported that Dr. Belated had promised students they would get work back, then had been absent for three days in a row, and finally returned graded work only the day before the midyear exam. The parents all said they had not been sent midterm progress reports indicating a problem. In addition, two students requested transfers to other teachers' sections. Both said that Dr. Belated was "absent a lot" and they "never got tests or quizzes back." The busy department head was vaguely aware that Dr. B. had been out "several times" during the marking period. When she checked the records, she was surprised to discover that Dr. B. had been absent a total of seven days for the marking period and ten total for the first semester. There were indeed no progress reports for the three students whose parents had called. Since Dr. Belated was not due to be formerly evaluated that year, the department head summarized her findings and definition of the problem in a memo for the file. Notice that Ms. Mitchell deliberately made the consequences or impact of absenteeism clear in case that aspect of the teacher's problem needed to be addressed later or through progressive discipline (see Chapter 9).

Example 6D.3 Assessment: Failure to provide timely and effective feedback [memo of concern]

To: Dr. Lila Belated

From: Dr. Rose Mitchell

Re: Follow-up to our conversations about providing adequate and timely feedback on performance to students in Chem I and II

This communication is a summary of our meetings of Thursday, 1/26, and Tuesday, 2/2, at which time we discussed your problems in providing students with adequate and timely feedback during the first semester of this year. We reviewed the following issues that surfaced from three separate parental complaints, two student transfer requests, my examination of attendance records, and your explanation of students' lab folders and entries in your grade book for the second marking period:

1. Lab reports assigned from mid–November through to the week before the mid-semester exam were not graded and returned to students before the mid-semester. Thus students had no information that their understanding of concepts was inaccurate or incomplete and no warning that they needed extra help or an opportunity to correct misconceptions.

2. You did not grade, examine in detail, or return five of the seven worksheets that you asked your substitutes to administer and that you described as "worthwhile practice." You stated that you "looked over" some of the papers but were unable to tell me which students in your classes had difficulty with this practice work.

3. Because you had "fallen behind" in your grading and "did not realize" that particular students were struggling, you did not send midyear progress reports to 11 of the 15 students who had D's in Chem I. As a result, these students were not aware that they had incomplete mastery of concepts or were not meeting standards at the B level or better and that they needed further help.

4. You did not follow department policy for returning quizzes within two school days so that students could seek extra help and clarification if they were confused. As you agreed, all entries for quizzes in your grade book for the second semester were made from January 17-19, during which time you were absent from school. You stated that you "took some time off to catch up" and thus were able to return all second-term quizzes on January 20, one day before the midyear. You also stated that students "should not have been surprised" since you usually went over the right answers in class after the quiz. However, you could not remember whether you had ever followed up with students who reported being confused.

We also discussed your ten absences in the first 4.5 months of school. They have denied students opportunities not only for high-quality instruction by a certified professional but also for adequate and appropriate feedback about their level of understanding and ability to meet curriculum standards in Chemistry. Moreover, choosing to add three days out of school for "catching up on grading because of health issues" further compounded the problem. We agreed to meet again on Thursday, February 4, to map out ways to resolve this issue quickly.

For follow-up recommendation for Dr. Belated, see Example 7D.3.

Interim Evaluation: Clammy Kolds

Example 6D.4 is an interim evaluation for Clammy Kolds whose problem is negative relationships with students. Note how a leader can use the same categories and language that will be required on the final evaluation to label and organize evidence for an interim evaluation or midyear observation report. During September and early October, Dr. Gonzales, the new principal of Central Middle School spent as much time as possible going in and out of classrooms to encourage and monitor implementation of the just-adopted "Classroom Climate Change" Program. Using data from her walks, wall artifacts, and dozens of informal conversations with students plus discipline referrals, Dr. Gonzales found that almost all teachers were making genuine progress at building positive environments for learning. Clammy Kolds, an experienced seventh-grade teacher, was a clear exception. Kolds's growing numbers of referrals to counseling, requests for special education assessments, and assignments to after-school suspension stood in distinct contrast to those of her colleagues. Students frequently labeled her as "mean" or reported that she "did not like kids." Before the situation got any worse, Dr. Gonzales decided to conduct an interim evaluation and formally document the problem. In this case the district uses *The Thoughtful Classroom Teacher Effectiveness Framework* (Silver Strong and Associates 2011).

Example 6D.4 Learning Environment: Negative relationships with students [interim evaluation]

INTERIM ASSESSMENT   November 17
Standard 2: Dimension Two: Positive relationships

Interim Rating: Novice

Ms. Kolds is currently not creating a healthy climate that supports high student learning. She is not meeting the following criteria that the faculty agreed to make their primary focus for the first marking period:

2.2 Getting to know students and incorporating their interests, aspirations, and backgrounds into the curriculum
Ms. Kolds does not know or use students' names during recitations or instruction, nor does she demonstrate behaviors that show she is aware of students' backgrounds or interests.

- 9/26 (4.5 weeks into the year) No names used during a 15-minute visit; points to students to answer eight times; calls on "gent in the back, no not you, Mr. Sweatshirt," and "the lady in front here."
- 9/27 (conference) Lesson plans and assignments for weeks 3-5 show no evidence of connecting curriculum to backgrounds of the 60% of students who are Latino and no use of materials developed during summer workshops. Ms. Kolds reports that she will "be getting to that stuff soon" but that "it is not that relevant to my curriculum."

- 10/13 Calls on "Laura-Lauren-what's your name." Student frowns and responds "Lenora." Two minutes later calls same student Laura. Students in back snigger. Uses no male names during 10-minute recitation observed; instead says, "You" or points.
- 11/8 (artifact conference) Lesson plans, tasks, instructional examples show no evidence of modification to include students' interests or backgrounds. Ms. Kolds reports that she "does not understand how using student interests would help them get their homework done when they are unmotivated."

As a result, students get the message that Ms. Kolds does not like them or care enough about them to get to know them individually or to help them see connections between their lives and background and the materials they are using.

2.4 Building a classroom community that insists on respect and mutual support for each student's learning and provides opportunities for students to become familiar with each other

- 9/18 Two students making audible comments about the "b- - - - in back." Ms. Kolds did not respond, thus signaling that such remarks are permitted in her room.
- 10/1 Students ejected from class for "being disruptive during a discussion" report that they were responding to ethnic slurs and that they perceive that Ms. Kolds "doesn't care if people insult you" and that they feel that "rich kids just want to put us down." Ms. Kolds responds that she is unaware of any tension in the class and that "people who do their work when they are supposed to shouldn't have any problem with anyone in the class."
- September faculty meeting. Principal asked all teachers to bring a class community builder that they have used to foster tolerance. Ms. Kolds was the only teacher in the Middle School not to bring something to share.
- 10/13 Students do not know one another's names; random sampling of a dozen students all report variations on not liking to work with other students they do not know. This finding is in direct contrast to results of sampling in other seventh- or eighth-grade Science classrooms.

As a result of the disrespectful climate, students' learning is undermined; they cannot use each other as resources and do not feel safe to take academic risks.

For follow-up recommendation for Ms. Kolds, see Example 7D.4.

Memo of Concern: Donna D. Limits

Example 6D.5 shows a memo of concern that follows up on a midyear conference with a teacher. The inimitable Donna D. Limits, first introduced in *Confronting Mediocre Teaching*, has continued her self-appointed role as a champion for students she perceives as facing socio-economic and cultural challenges in an otherwise affluent and superficially homogeneous school population. Her championing activities frequently consist of urging colleagues to give "less fortunate" students a break on requirements such as homework and project completion or book selection. She provides elaborate explanations of all the outside variables that suggest certain students could not realistically be expected to perform at the same levels as others. When colleagues challenge her, she frequently becomes sarcastic and throws around scornful observations about their "limited world view" and "cultural egocentricity." Principal Yee has communicated his worries and concerns, but Limits ignores or misses the point about her low expectations. The principal recognizes it is time to raise the level of intensity. Since Donna is teaching in Dry Valley, California, the evaluation language used is from the California Standards for the Teaching Profession (CSTP 2009).

Example 6D.5 Expectations: Low Standards and Expectations for Students [memo of concern]

To: Donna D. Limits
From: R. W. Yee
Date: January 22, _____
This memo summarizes our conference of January 21, in which we reviewed several significant problems in your current performance on the following CSTP Standards:

2.4 Creating a rigorous learning environment with high expectations and appropriate support for all students

2.5 Developing, communicating, and maintaining high standards for individual and group behavior

6.3 Collaborating with colleagues and the broader professional community to support teacher and student learning

These problems are all connected and illustrate your ongoing struggles and confusion about what it means to establish high standards and expectations for all students.

1. CSTP 2.4/2.5 Your self-expressed desire to "understand and protect" students means that you consistently choose to lower standards and expect less of young people whose economic means you judge to be limited or whose family backgrounds you consider problematic. Examples of such choices in the last two months include

   - Insisting on substituting significantly revised criteria for success on the grade 4 essay for 6 students whom you—not the school—personally identified as "at risk" before the students had submitted any work or demonstrated that they were, in fact, unable to attempt the original assignment. This action was in direct contradiction to the advice of both the special education staff and the reading teacher, neither of whom recommended modifications for these students.
   - Informing AG's mother that you would not expect him to be able to complete the Social Studies project because "home was in such turmoil" and "Dad's difficulties were likely to mean he would not be able to concentrate."
   - Telling PK and TR that you knew they "wouldn't be able to practice their talks at home" and thus could just submit a PowerPoint or set of pictures instead of presenting an oral report to the class.

In each of these instances, the children and families involved got the message that you found them less capable. They were also deprived of the opportunity to meet the same rigorous standards as others in the class because you had predetermined their likely limited performance level in advance.

2. CSTP 6.3 Your definition of "protection" as not asking students to rise to challenges puts you in routine conflict with colleagues who are attempting to provide appropriate scaffolds while holding standards constant. Rather than being able to at least reflect on this alternate view, as Standard 6.3 would ask you to do, you default to attacking others with sarcastic comments. Recent examples include "Easy for you to say from your comfortable, middle class position" (faculty meeting 11/15) or "You really don't get what these kids' lives are like, but I do" (grade-level mtg 1/6). As we discussed, it is unprofessional to make such attributions rather than to focus your attention on what might be best for students. The impact of such exchanges is to limit effective communication and problem-solving in your grade-level team. When that happens, it is the very students you are trying to protect who are being harmed.

As we agreed, at our next meeting on January 23, we will lay out some action steps for helping you successfully meet the requirements for Standards 2 and 6.

For follow-up recommendation for Ms. Limits, see Example 7D.5.

Leader Alert
Citing Evidence from Prior Documents in Final Evaluations

Examples 6D.6 through 6D.8 all illustrate ways to write clear problem descriptions and documentation from multiple data sources when you must rate someone's performance as "needs improvement" or "unsatisfactory" (or whatever equivalent terminology your system uses). The most efficient way to handle the challenge is simply to cite the document name and date in which the detailed evidence—the quotes and data *previously discussed with the teacher* can be found. Examples 6D.7 and 6D.8 both use this method. Some contracts, however, require evaluators to reproduce evidence, thus creating a longer and more elaborate problem description such as the one shown in Example 6D.6. Clarify expectations for repeating evidence that can be found elsewhere with legal counsel if necessary and with your colleagues so that you all use the same system for indicating where the original quotes and supporting material can be found. ◆

Final Evaluation: Whim Winger

Example 6D.6 is an excerpt from the final evaluation of Whim Winger, the middle school science teacher from *Confronting Mediocre Teaching*. Whim prides himself on being "efficient, spontaneous, and fun" and having great relationships with his eighth-grade students. Spontaneity, however, substitutes for knowledge of subject matter and detailed lesson planning. He has his teaching "down to a science" with timesaving routines and grades based largely on what he calls "facty quizzes" and "worky sheets." While he is a pleasant presence on his team, whenever the work turns to curriculum planning, Whim consults closely with his SmartPhone. He works in a midwest district that has adopted the Danielson Framework for Teaching (2013).

Example 6D.6 Curriculum: Ineffective Planning [final evaluation]

Domain 1Planning: 1E Designing Coherent Instruction
Rating: Unsatisfactory

Mr. Winger does not design or carry out coherent lesson plans anchored in worthwhile learning targets. Instead he focuses on completing activities with low-level objectives.

Short Visit 10/5

1. Posted objective is inappropriate ("SWBAT complete our fun lab on friction.") and does not match curriculum and grade-level expectations. ("Demonstrate how forces, including friction, act upon an object to change its position over time in relation to a fixed point of reference.")

2. No lab sheet planned or used despite models available in the curriculum guide and department resource file. Item on the board mislabeled as a "Thinking Question" said "restate all the steps." It was Mr. Winger's interpretation of the required assessment question "What conclusion can you draw from your findings?" specified in the eighth-grade Science Curriculum Guide. All of the nine randomly selected students interviewed were unable to connect the activity they were doing to the key concepts about friction or to use vocabulary appropriately. Mr. Winger reported that he was "behind in the AM because of a parent meeting" and "did not have time to go through all the files to find a lab sheet or the curriculum guide."

Extended Observation (11/7)

1. No objective posted or communicated to students in first 25 minutes of class. Photocopied page from curriculum guide stuck in plan book has "Distinguish between rotation of Earth on its axis and its elliptical revolution around the Sun" circled.

2. Only evidence of planning under Methods section of plan book: "Ask questions & give quiz." No other documents available to provide evidence of planning.

3. Question content and sequence not pre-planned; questions were unconnected, low-level, and often confusing: "How long does it take for the earth to do its thing with the Sun? Can anyone remember anything about revolution? What is the most important thing to remember about the word axis?" As a result, students called out a series of random wrong answers, guesses, and single words that revealed misconceptions that were unaddressed, such as: "It's closer to the Earth in summer." In one representative sampling, 19/22 student responses had nothing to do with revolution and rotation.

4. "Practice task" (Sun and Moon worksheet downloaded from an Internet site and originally posted for grade 5) is low-challenge with no connection to key concepts in the circled objective. The five matching questions included nothing about the connection between rotation and revolution. Eight students reported they "just guessed" when completing the sheet. Two said they had "remembered" the information from elementary school.

Short visit beginning 25 minutes into a 50-minute period (1/09)
Planned series of learning experiences was not aligned with the intended/
posted statement taken from the exact wording of a science standard "Express mathematically how the mass of an object and the force acting on it
affect its acceleration." Students were reading articles on types of cars and
completing worksheet. When asked how worksheet connected to the posted
objective, they responded with variations of "This is what we do to get motivated." None were able to connect the activity to the objective or apply any
of the unit vocabulary and concepts to the task. Winger reported that this
was the "warm-up, fun part of the class" to "get the creative juices flowing
for a dry topic."

Artifact and data conference (2/10)
Focus was 17 students who failed the department assessment on Unit 6. No
written lesson plans available for 8 of the 12 days of the unit. Plan book
entries listed activities and lab numbers. No evidence of summary tasks being completed. Work samples show students completed only five of twelve
available practice exercises provided with unit material. No evidence of application tasks being used.

Conference re Science Assessment Results (4/9)
Mr. Winger's students showed significantly lower growth on the district-
developed grade 8 common assessment for Common Core Science Practice
#1: Asking Questions

Teacher	Percent Scoring Proficient or Advanced on Pre-Assessment	Percent Scoring Proficient or Advanced on Post-Assessment
A	32	80
B	26	85
Mr. Winger	35	56

As a result of inadequate planning and time wasted on misaligned learning
experiences, students are not progressing sequentially to worthwhile academic targets.

For follow-up action and a MiniPlan[sm] for Mr. Winger, see Section 7E.

Final Evaluation: Peter Passable

Example 6D.7 is a final evaluation for Peter Passable, our union activist from *Confronting Mediocre Teaching*. Peter does not use assessment data to inform or shape
his instruction. The evaluator has chosen to rate his performance as "Needs improvement" instead of "Unsatisfactory" for two reasons. First, he recognizes that
there are a number of teachers like Passable in the building who are still learning
to use assessments formatively. Second, he wants Peter to focus on growing and
expanding his existing repertoire rather than to argue about whether he possesses
a repertoire at all. Passable teaches in a district that use the Massachusetts Model
System for Teacher Evaluation (2012).

Leader Alert
Providing Adequate Training for Gaps That Are Pervasive

Before you select problems related to formative assessment for individuals, consider whether you have provided adequate training and support. Large numbers of teachers lack skill in formative assessment. And it may well be that this is a professional development issue rather than a supervisory or evaluation issue (refer to Figure 5A.2). Note that the Passable case focuses on failure to comply with assessment practices and policies. ◆

Example 6D.7 Assessment: Data not collected or used to modify instruction [final evaluation]

Element I-B. Assessment: Uses a variety of informal and formal methods of assessments to measure student learning, growth, and understanding; to develop differentiated and enhanced learning experiences; and to improve future instruction

Rating: Needs improvement

Mr. Passable's lesson planning and instruction have not shown appropriate use of good formative assessment procedures and principles. He has not yet been able to plan to incorporate formative assessment in his units and lessons or to use assessment results in designing future instruction. The evidence for this rating includes the following:

- Inadequate evidence of use of a variety of formative classroom assessments to monitor student progress (see observation reports 10/19, 12/3)
- Lessons not based on data drawn from pre-assessments or analysis of student needs (see feedback with questions from classroom visits 9/27, 11/1, 1/6; observation reports 10/19, 12/3; and email of 2/2)
- No modification of commercially prepared unit tests to reflect actual instruction, differences in terminology, or additions and emphases agreed upon by the Math Curriculum Team (memo of 11/18; email follow-up to parent complaints 3/1)
- Inconsistent, fragmentary implementation of strategies from professional development training and midyear coaching (assessment conference 11/5; student portfolios of pre-instructional probes and open-ended writing samples 4/27)
- Repeated difficulty in independently analyzing results of assessments and using analysis to differentiate or modify instruction as evidenced by coming to team meetings without analyses completed. No appropriate ideas for changing methods of instruction offered in three successive training sessions during February and March.

As a result, students have routinely missed opportunities to: (1) adequately represent what they do and do not know before they face summative examinations, (2) close gaps in their understanding through encounters with targeted re-teaching, or (3) be adequately prepared for high-stakes assessments. Thirty-seven percent of Passable's students' scored below 60% on midyear benchmark tests, as compared to 18% and 12% in comparable sections of heterogeneously grouped students. Spring benchmark assessments also showed a similar pattern: 35% of Passable's students were below Basic in their performance, and 27% were at the Basic level, as compared to comparable sections where 14% and 11% scored below Basic and 20% and 16% were at Basic.

For follow up recommendation for Mr. Passable, see Example 7D.6.

Final Evaluation: John Whiner Collabnot

Example 6D.8 moves away from instructional problems to provide a sample evaluation for John Whiner Collabnot. John will be familiar to readers of earlier Skillful Leader volumes. He is a traditional but capable classroom teacher who resents and tries to avoid requirements to work with his department to plan curriculum and create common assessments. Historically, barring egregious acts, teachers who performed well in the classroom escaped scrutiny in professional responsibilities. Expectations have changed. When teachers believe themselves to be "above" working with others or demonstrate they are unwilling to put in the time and effort required by collaboration, they often deny students opportunities to learn. Taking action to rate and document failure to collaborate after less formal efforts to communicate have failed is important. It protects both students and teams from the kind of erosion of possibility and energy that can happen when toxic behavior goes unchecked. Collabnot is in a district that has adopted Marshall's Teacher Evaluation Rubrics (2012).

Example 6D.8 Professional Responsibilities: Poor collaboration [final evaluation]

Standard F: Professional responsibilities
Rating: Ineffective

- **Criterion a. Attendance.** Mr. Collabnot does not meet standards for attendance at department and professional development meetings. He has been absent without excuse for 30% of the required department meetings (9/12, 11/14, 2/13) and has been more than 15 minutes late to an additional 30%. He has missed four data team sessions despite being present in school because he scheduled last-minute meetings with students and parents during those slots. This practice persisted several times after he was instructed not to do so (memo 12/4). During the times he is present in meetings, he rarely speaks unless it is to announce that the topic has nothing to do with his work or interests. Finally, he was absent for two of the three professional development days this year and thus has not yet adopted any of the text analysis strategies presented at those sessions.

- **Criterion g. Leadership.** Mr. Collabnot has routinely resisted becoming actively involved in and contributing to error analysis and re-teaching strategy sessions designed to help the department raise the performance of students in the college level sections. He either makes comments such as "These are not my kids; I have enough on my hands with the AP students without taking on the classes of others" (10/10) or sets himself apart and grades papers when others start to talk about how to teach a concept differently (12/4, 1/22). He has several times rebuffed the requests of younger colleagues to observe how he presents difficult concepts, in one instance saying publicly that "My kids don't look anything like what you are trying to deal with, so it wouldn't be relevant, really." (11/5). As a result, colleagues in the department have no access to the substantive knowledge and experience Mr. Collabnot could offer.

- **Criterion d. Professionalism.** Mr. Collabnot rarely honors faculty agreements to reinforce behavioral expectations by being present in hallways and providing feedback and guidance between classes and for the 7-minute transition period before and after school. He reports that his classes are not the problem in the halls and that he "does not feel it is his responsibility to take care of students who have not been appropriately guided by others." As a result, other faculty members must assume greater responsibility for monitoring hallways and for communicating expectations that should be Mr. Collabnot's work (obs. 9/10, 10/6; conf. re need to meet standard 2/1).

For follow-up recommendations for Mr. Collabnot, see Example 7D.7.

You only need to take action by moving to formal development of problems if communicating worries and concerns has not improved the performance. This stage requires you to adhere to rigorous principles of documentation. Avoid the temptation to jump to recommendations before the performance gap is clearly described. You will need to draw from multiple sources of data in order to provide sufficient evidence. Establish a professional tone by avoiding vague generalizations and minimizing value-laden or accusatory terms. As much as possible, include impact on learners and/or on the school to indicate why the problem is a consequential one that cannot be overlooked. When you have adequately defined the current problem, you are ready to involve the teacher in designing interventions. You are then ready for Chapter 7.

DESIGNING INTERVENTIONS

7A
OVERVIEW OF INTERVENTION DESIGN

Figure 7A.1 The Action Cycle

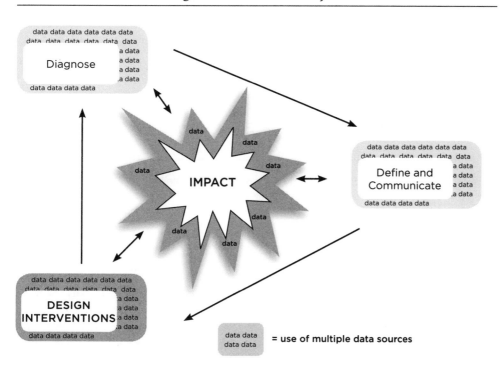

By this point in the action cycle (Figure 7A.1), you have diagnosed and documented the existence of ineffective teaching. You have communicated the problem to the teacher or team clearly and concisely. The next task is perhaps the most demanding: designing an intervention or interventions that will change the ineffective instruction and increase student learning.

Many well-intentioned efforts to confront problematic teaching fall apart at this stage. If your school system has not paid careful attention to learning-focused supervision, you may be facing the effects of years of fuzzy thinking, bad habits, and mediocre models. You and your colleagues may have been left to make your best try at filling in "Recommendation" sections on evaluation forms or completing one-size-fits-all improvement plans. In fact, if you are like many of the leaders we have met, you may have tried to do an improvement plan once and then avoided the experience ever after. Those time-consuming plans can become red flags for teachers and measures of last resort for evaluators on overload. Inevitably, they grow to be linked in the culture with documentation for dismissal rather than growth. Such an association undermines the purpose for which improvement plans were created in the first place.

Since we wrote *The Skillful Leader: Confronting Mediocre Teaching* (2000), our years working with site leaders have convinced us that there are a number of other ways to define, shape, guide, or require improvement before resorting to the formal plan laid out in Chapter 8.

USING A REPERTOIRE OF RESPONSES

We can identify a repertoire of intervention approaches and range them along an effort continuum illustrated by Figure 7A.2. All of the approaches are, or could easily be, a regular part of your supervisory practice. All share the same goal: to produce substantive changes and growth in instruction and, consequently, improvements in students' opportunities to learn.

Figure 7A.2 Repertoire of Intervention Approaches after a Problem Has Been Communicated

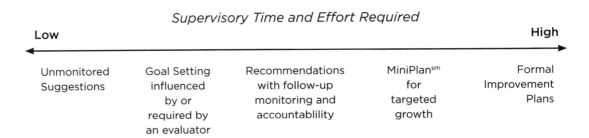

Supervisory Time and Effort Required

Low   High

| Unmonitored Suggestions | Goal Setting influenced by or required by an evaluator | Recommendations with follow-up monitoring and accountablility | MiniPlan^sm for targeted growth | Formal Improvement Plans |

Making suggestions that require little revisiting falls at the low-effort, low-impact end of the repertoire. Suppose the issue to be fixed emerges from an "early worry" (see Chapter 6) or is an easily addressed change such as minimizing teacher overuse of "OK" or establishing clear routines for keeping track of student work and materials in a classroom. In such cases, simple suggestions of alternatives might suffice. The teacher chooses which to follow. If progress is discernable, the supervisor may not raise the issue again. Leaders often resort to unmonitored suggestions at the end of observations or on final evaluations because they require little time or supervisory energy and can be soft-pedaled. However, they are the least successful responses for improving ineffective teaching.

Formal improvement plans anchor the high-complexity, high-effort end of the repertoire. This type of response signals that the teacher has multiple, overlapping deficits to address and needs tightly structured guidelines, clearly defined requirements, and support to carry out those requirements successfully. Although an improvement plan may ultimately be necessary, this level of response—with its contractual associations to dismissal procedures—is generally not a good *first* match for ineffective performance.

The approaches in the middle of the continuum—goal setting, recommendations, and MiniPlans^sm—represent ways to provide targeted and timely intervention when you diagnose subpar performance. Rarely or poorly used in the past, some of these vehicles are now appearing as required elements in a large number of redesigned teacher and administrator evaluation systems. Sections 7B, 7C, and 7D offer guidelines and examples to help you take full advantage of goal-setting strategies and contract requirements, craft good recommendations, and create MiniPlans^sm for improvement. But how do you decide which to use?

MATCHING THE RESPONSE TO THE SITUATION

In effective interventions, you align both the method of response and the intensity of response to the nature of the problem and to the current skills and stances of the teacher. Figure 7A.3 is a resource to assist you with this matching. Associate the green and red levels of response with standard go or stop colors. The rose pink is for limited intervention.

Figure 7A.3 Overview: Levels of Intensity

	Function/Audience	Characteristics of Interaction	Key Tools
GREEN LEVEL (Collaborative Interaction)	To promote awareness, reflection, self-assessment leading to self-directed change. Teachers who are engaged learners.	Invitational tone; communication based on data and nonjudgmental questions; optional suggestions. Teacher decides when/if to implement and follow up. Low accountability.	Data Collegial conferences Suggestions Summaries of next steps
ROSE LEVEL (Targeted Development)	To engage teachers in taking responsibility for and fixing a specific deficiency in instruction. For marginal performers who are willing to engage in their own improvement.	Administrator identifies standard not met and the data that have led to that rating. Teacher and administrator develop goals, select action steps, decide on data to collect, and identify indicators for success. Administrator determines whether standard has been met and next steps.	Data meetings Memos Recommendations Goal setting MiniPlan^sm
RED LEVEL Compliance	To mandate technical compliance with policies or procedures. For staff who need to be disciplined to adhere to expectations.	Administrator-driven. No choice. Escalated sequence of intervention includes clear accountability measures. May involve steps of progressive discipline and possible dismissal due to insubordination (see Chapters 9-10).	Data Meetings to clarify expectations Summary memos
Assignment to Formal Improvement Plan	To remediate performance using district-negotiated policies. For teachers with serious, unresolved problems.	Administrator driven with involvement of appropriate support systems/personnel and some teacher input. Failure to progress can lead to dismissal for incompetence.	Data Contractually designated forms and procedures Written feedback

Green is a "continue with what you're doing but consider fixing this specific issue" type of response. It is a good match for a teacher who simply needs to fine-tune proficient practice or be re-energized and who has demonstrated that she is capable of making high-quality adjustments given feedback and support. Unless an individual's performance has suddenly slipped from proficient to second rate, this level of response is rarely appropriate for ineffective teaching.

Rose is a middle-ground choice for problems whose scope or complexity requires that leaders provide a clear "not okay" judgment, a precise definition of the issues, moderate guidance on what to do and how to do it, and help in assessing the results. You clearly expect that the teacher will participate in parts of the process, ranging from selecting improvement action steps to helping to plan the data to be collected as part of evidence of success.

Red is high intensity and signals serious issues; it is the option for individuals with persistent, multi-faceted problems whose history shows little evidence that they have the knowledge, skills, or commitment to make the improvements independently. At this level the message is "stop that immediately and start doing this immediately." The design includes clear and stringent instructions for what to do and how to do it and close monitoring of implementation.

As we look at the different ways of intervening when practice is ineffective, we will use these two explanatory frames:

1. The choices along the time and effort continuum that let you match to the individual, problem, and context
2. The level of response (green-rose-red) "code words" that help you quickly think about the way your interactions should look and sound

Finally, remember you always want to maximize teacher participation in and ownership for the design of the intervention. You want teachers to take primary responsibility for gathering data about how well the intervention is working and to be active contributors to the discussions about how to modify or amplify original ideas and strategies. Moving from green to red levels of intensity reduces teacher choice about what to do and how to do it and increases the amount and specificity of direction you include in the design. However, do not assume total responsibility for spelling out all the particulars for action even in formal improvement plans.

7B
MAKING SUGGESTIONS

Unmonitored suggestions abound in evaluation documents. Because they are low effort (see Figure 7B.1), they are often the default but inappropriate response after an evaluator communicates negative information. If you are supervising a normally high-performing teacher in need of fine-tuning, beginning at the green level and offering suggestions could be a perfectly appropriate match. However, exercise caution and do not linger at this level with ineffective performers. Response and improvement should be rapid after you give suggestions. Otherwise, move on to the more focused approaches described in the sections that follow.

Figure 7B.1 Suggestions in the Repertoire of Intervention Approaches

Supervisory Time and Effort Required

Low				High
Unmonitored Suggestions	Goal Setting influenced by or required by an evaluator	Recommendations with follow-up monitoring and accountablility	MiniPlan[sm] for targeted growth	Formal Improvement Plans

In a green-level intervention, your goal is to provide the teacher with an opportunity to reflect on data. You assume s/he can and will assess her performance in relation to clearly defined standards and student outcomes. Begin the process with an open mind and a genuine willingness to let the teacher design and take the lead on large parts of the intervention. This stance does not require you to be a passive listener, however. Never give up your right to probe for specificity, worry aloud about business as usual, raise contradictory data, or otherwise elevate the level of thinking. Figure 7B.2 suggests contexts in which you might start with this vehicle and a green-level exchange.

Figure 7B.2 When to Choose the Green Level and Suggestions

Start at the green level and making suggestions if
- The individual is clearly motivated to improve
- The individual has sufficient background knowledge and skills to be able to identify worthwhile steps to take
- You are implementing a new curriculum or framework such as Common Core State Standards (CCSS)
- The individual has a track record of success, and the performance problem is relatively new
- No one in the school has received much in the way of feedback, coaching, or support over the last 2-3 years

- You are new to the site or the role and do not know people very well
- You have inherited someone who has been passed from building to building (a.k.a. the "dance of the lemons") and need to assess the individual's capabilities
- You are cleaning up from an ineffective or punitive predecessor and are focused on culture building

---

For the first few times you apply this kind of communication, use your commute to work to practice ahead of time so that you are sure your language conveys the belief that the teacher can be the primary problem-solver. You may subsequently consult, collaborate, provide feedback on request, or even be a cheerleader. However, the teacher will make decisions and be accountable for improvements without further directives and monitoring. Figure 7B.3 details the components of a green-level conference.

Figure 7B.3 How to Plan and Carry Out a Green-Level Conference

---

- Focus on the impact, i.e., the student learning need or performance target the school is trying to reach.
- Include available data about what the students are currently doing or producing in response to instruction.
- Ask open-ended, nonjudgmental questions to clarify the meaning of the data.
- Invite teacher reflections, e.g., hypotheses about causes, questions, further data to consider, ideas to try.
- Make concrete suggestions that might potentially help the teacher but do not consider them as mandates.
- Adopt invitational language such as "might" and "consider"; avoid directive language such as "ought," "must," and "should."

The components above can be presented in a different order, but all should be included in the conference or conferences about the problem. Example 7B.1 illustrates a green-level conference that starts with the gap in student performance. It offers an image of what *you* might say as a supervisor but does not capture the teacher's response. In a good conference, there would be long periods between your contributions where the teacher is talking and thinking aloud.

Example 7B.1 Green-Level Intervention Conference That Begins with Desired Student Learning Outcome

One of our goals for grade 4 this year is competence with fractions so that our students have the building blocks for upper level mathematics solidly in place. We said that by the end of February we wanted them to be able to solve word problems involving addition and subtraction of fractions.

This evaluator starts with a focus on students' needs, i.e., the impact, to establish the mutual goal.

When I was visiting your class on Tuesday, I noticed these five students were all passive or highly dependent on someone else to talk them through the problem solving during group work. In fact you noticed and went to Dan four different times, and he didn't try anything in between. That got me to thinking, so I looked up their performance on the last two quarterly assessments. I just pulled their math folders and journals yesterday.

She presents the data from several sources that illustrate the student performance gap.

See what I've noticed so far. All five had good solid scores last year, and they were okay through problem solving with whole numbers. Look at the difference in the quality of their work this last month.

Note that one of the data sources establishes that students are capable of meeting the target.

Do you have other assessments on addition and subtraction of fractions for them? What do you think might be going on?

The supervisor invites the teacher to provide more assessment data and reflect.

Okay, so you think some of this for Raphael and Sophie might be a matter of confidence and their discomfort with the unfamiliar. How could we check that out? Since it's so late in the year, it's hard to say we have to wait for them to mature. What have you tried in the past? And what about the other three? Have they shown you they have the basics?

Open-ended questions are offered in the spirit of clarifying what the data mean and helping to find useful next steps.

You've talked about some additional practice time and exercises and some positive expectations for Raphael and Sophie. One suggestion I have is to increase the amount of short-term checking for individual understanding so we get information much faster on who is floundering. Right now you just have a group sense. Maybe one timed challenge problem that each student has to do without help like a one-question quiz during the midpoint of the lesson or as a ticket to leave at the end of math time? Or would white boards help?

Eventually the conversation reveals that the teacher is not collecting much data about student understanding before the unit test. That helps the supervisor offer ideas to try.

Whatever you try will tie into Standard IV: Monitoring Learning and Adjusting Instruction. That's our big push this year. Let me know what you decide and how it goes.

The supervisor connects the potential intervention back to a teacher performance standard and offers an informal invitation to follow up.

In contrast to Example 7B.1, which started with a gap in student performance, Example 7B.2 first identifies the gap in teacher performance and then moves to impact on students. Again, the evaluator's goal is to stimulate the teacher's thinking and have him do most of the talking and planning.

Example 7B.2 Green-Level Intervention Conference That Begins with the Teacher Performance Standard

We've been focusing on really implementing Standard IV: Monitoring Learning and Adjusting Instruction in the Algebra I and II sections this year with the goal of closing the achievement gap in math for our 9th and 10th grade sub-groups. I've been collecting and looking at data about classroom assessments—what people use to monitor understanding and how the tools affect day-to-day planning—and I have some worries.

The department head here begins by reminding the teacher of the relevant performance standard and then adds a connection to students to establish the mutual goal.

The three examples of Friday quizzes that you submitted when we looked at tools would all be considered summative. You said that the results would go into students' grades but would not affect what you did on the following Monday. So that means some of the kids who failed, like Jason, Crystal, and Mariah, would never have a chance to make up the ground unless they came after school. That's an equity issue for those three particularly since they depend on riding the long route bus.

The data here come from an artifact collection, a meeting the department head attended, an informal discussion with the teacher, student grades, and student addresses—all sources that are readily available.

During that last tool discussion, your colleagues all had examples of how they used team-designed "challenge checks" during the midpoint of the block. They fed the results back to the students and modified their daily and weekly plans when kids were struggling. I didn't see or hear similar examples from you in that meeting, so I cross-checked to see if it was just because your students were performing better than the other groups. Take a look at this. Do you see the pattern for the subgroups here? What are your first thoughts?

I know you wish everyone would stay after, but they're not doing it. All the work you're doing after school with the kids who *can* stay is really paying off. They're making terrific progress. It's this set of kids from your three Algebra I sections—all of them from the East Side—that I'm worried about. They started out okay, but their grades have really dropped. What have you been noticing? What works with this group?

Here the evaluator acknowledges that some of the teacher's efforts are working and reminds him that he needs to stretch his repertoire.

What about formative assessments—just a quick one-question quiz instead of the elaborate "do now's" that you've been using? Then grab the kids who struggle for just a brief unscrambling session. Larry and Ann both say they've found their kids respond really well to regrouping for 10 minutes of focused re-teaching twice a week while everyone else works on challenge problems. They assign kids to "catch up group" but also let people who think their understanding is shaky nominate themselves. That's one thought. What else?

Not all ideas need to come from a supervisor. Those who teach the same level and content can be the best source of credible suggestions.

If the green level is a good choice for the two teachers in our examples, each of these exchanges above would lead the teachers to dig deeper into the identified problem, make subsequent changes in practice, and carefully monitor the results for students. While many skillful leaders will keep a mental note or a reminder in a file to follow up informally, they do not set up a formal structure for doing so as they would with rose- and red-level interventions.

Before you select a green-level approach as the best match for intervening where practice is not working, keep these ideas in mind:

- In the "collaborative green level," there is no formal accountability for implementation. The teacher decides whether to pursue follow-up. This makes it a poor match for most unsatisfactory performers but a possible match for some highly motivated, basic, or mediocre performers.
- The conditional language that is used to invite teacher thinking and problem solving in this approach rarely defines what steps the teacher should use to address gaps in performance systematically. If the recipient is not skilled at interpreting exactly what needs to change and monitoring his/her own implementation, invitational language will only be confusing.
- Suggestions that call for simple compliance ("Post the objectives") will not help a teacher to improve his or her practice.

7C
INFLUENCING GOAL SETTING

Figure 7C.1 Goal Setting on the Continuum of Intervention Approaches

---

Supervisory Time and Effort Required

Low   High

←——→

| Unmonitored Suggestions | **Goal Setting influenced by or required by an evaluator** | Recommendations with follow-up monitoring and accountablility | MiniPlan^{sm} for targeted growth | Formal Improvement Plans |

You may be surprised by our nomination of goal setting as a tool for taking action against ineffective instruction (see Figure 7C.1). If so, check whether your instinctive reaction reveals buried misconceptions about who is allowed to influence goals or how goals may be used. Do not fall prey to the "hands off" stance adopted by leaders who do not understand the focusing power of attainable goals. It makes little sense to have a teacher who is not yet meeting a standard of performance or whose students are lagging behind on achievement invest hours in pursuit of goals that are not connected to closing those gaps.

Goal setting tied to evaluation, as opposed to recertification or professional development, can be used as

- A primary intervention strategy to improve ineffective teaching in certain well-defined cases
- A component of a MiniPlan^{sm} or improvement plan for individuals who need help with multiple standards
- A required activity for all teachers who must demonstrate professional growth as part of their district's evaluation system

In this section, we are primarily interested in goal setting for the first two purposes. However, many of the fundamental steps for coaching and supporting the teacher are the same, no matter the purpose.

GOAL SETTING AS A PRIMARY INTERVENTION TO IMPROVE INEFFECTIVE TEACHING

Consider goal setting's underlying assumptions: that teachers believe in all students' ability to learn, are willing and able to analyze data, can make decisions based on their findings, and, if necessary, will abandon approaches that are not effective. Our experience says these assumptions do not hold true for most of the cases of below standard performance. However, goal setting can be an astute first intervention for a teacher who is aware that his or her performance has slipped from past, previously competent levels. It can also be appropriate for an individual who seems to have lost energy and focus because the school or department has offered little sense of challenge in past years. As a general rule, goal setting works best when you and the teacher:

- Have good data about a student learning problem
- Can define the problem clearly and in the same way
- Know you could easily capture data about the changes in student performance that are likely to result if the teacher changes practice

Consider using this approach when some combination of the positive factors indicated in Figure 7C.2 are present.

Figure 7C.2 When to Choose the Rose Level and Goal Setting

- The teacher is still a relative novice but learns quickly and has acknowledged the problem.
- The individual sees himself/herself as a leader within the school or department; s/he would be likely to respond well to an invitation to investigate a student learning issue.
- You have evidence that the individual can stay focused and direct his or her improvement efforts with minimum "hand-holding" from a supervisor.
- The performance problem has arisen as a result of new teacher performance standards and is likely be resolved with some concerted effort over the next year.
- High-performing colleagues are available who are interested in the same goals or outcomes and could provide stimulating professional collaboration.

For the individuals and circumstances identified above, goal-setting conferences bridge the green and rose levels. They are "rose" in nature because you, the supervisor, have defined the problem to be fixed (see Section 6D) and requested that the teacher set an improvement target and make a plan. They are green in nature because of the following characteristics:

- Your tone is invitational and collaborative.
- You intend that your major role will be coaching and facilitating.
- You have confidence that the teacher has enough background knowledge or willingness to learn to act independently.
- Both you and the teacher expect that s/he will do the bulk of the work in analyzing data, setting the target, and making decisions about actions necessary to reach the target.

We might, for example, use goal setting as an appropriate match for Mr. Passable, the veteran in Example 6D.7 who must learn how to use formative assessment or for Sally Friendly in Example 6D.2 who needs to improve her questioning techniques. It would also be a good choice for the Grade 4 team that needs to examine its procedures for helping special education students be more independent (see Example 6C.2). In these cases, the problem to be solved is well defined and bounded.

Before you hold a goal conference with the express purpose of helping a teacher set an improvement target in response to a problematic rating, do the same homework you would do for a problem conference. Collect and review the data and your problem statement. Make sure you know the relevant teacher and student performance standards. Spend some time thinking about what current assets the teacher could build upon. Try to identify some genuine strengths in this teacher's practice—perhaps high expectations, humor, or positive student relationships—that can be mobilized to tackle the student learning issue that is the focus of the goal. If you can't identify any, then goal setting is not likely to be a good intervention vehicle. Move on to something stronger and more directive, such as accountable recommendations (see Section 7D) or a MiniPlan^{sm} (see Section 7E).

Figure 7C.3 lists the typical steps you would take to help a teacher set a goal and make a plan for how to achieve that goal once a problem had been identified. Simply to show an overview of the process, we have listed them as if they could be accomplished in one conference. Realistically, refining a goal statement and making a decent plan with an individual who is confused or fearful about data might take several interactions. It is also possible that you will begin your conference with a teacher who has already drafted a goal or plan that is not yet acceptable so that you will need to help the teacher shape these early thoughts into a workable document.

Figure 7C.3 How to Conference with a Teacher about Setting a Goal after a Problem Has Been Identified

1. Open with the purpose of the goal setting, your mutual interest in solving a problem, and your conviction that the teacher can take action to resolve it.
    a. Review the specific language in the relevant teacher performance standard, indicators, and rubrics to identify what the standard requires and why that is important for students.
    b. Explicitly express with an action phrase such as "expand or build your repertoire" or "develop and implement a new set of . . ." or "revise and fine tune" or "learn how to and incorporate" the diagnosis you made about what type of work the teacher is facing in order to fix the problem.
    c. Present the teacher's genuine strengths, the assets already in place that can be used in service of the new learning and new practice.

2. Define the outcomes you want for all students—or for a designated group you have identified in the problem statement. Enlist the teacher in describing very specifically what all students in the class or in the target group would know, say, and do routinely if the teaching were sharpened, revised, or expanded.

3. Craft a goal statement that captures the end result you both want after specific actions have been taken. Note that steps 2 and 3 may merge or you may have to help the teacher select one or two target performances from the set you have both described.

4. Articulate the outcomes you want to achieve and map backward to the actions needed to achieve them. Together you need to
    a. Think about and define the kinds of actions the teacher would have to take for the students to perform in the particular ways you have described.
    b. Match those proposed teacher actions to the competencies identified in the standard named in your problem statement.

5. Identify the sequence of actions and the data to be collected in order to measure the effect of those actions.

6. Consider how the goal links to the work of the team or professional community with which the teacher is affiliated.

7. Establish a timetable for the plan and agree on checkpoints.

8. Identify interim indicators of success.

9. Review the data and information that the year-end goal summary will need to include to show how the teacher will be held accountable for the goal.

Leader Alert
Confront Misconceptions about the Use of Results in Goal Setting

---

Teachers in school districts that adopt goal setting involving measurable student outcomes often want to depress their aspirations and set low-level targets because they fear that they will lose their jobs if their students don't attain "the number" specified in their goal. As much as possible, confront the misconceptions, misinformation, or scare tactics by repeatedly stressing that the district is looking for serious and productive analysis and problem solving. If the teachers make genuine, well-thought-out attempts to improve practice without seeing the results they expected, focus on their analysis of what the data did show and what they will do next. ◆

GOAL SETTING COMBINED WITH OTHER INTERVENTIONS TO IMPROVE INEFFECTIVE INSTRUCTION

Subsequent sections of this chapter deal with recommendations and MiniPlans^sm as alternative approaches to intervening with an ineffective performer. Chapter 8 examines formal improvement plans. Designed to tackle increasingly complex or persistent problems, all of those approaches rely to a greater or lesser extent on variations of goal setting and plan monitoring. For example, if you have given a teacher a rating that indicates a need for improvement on a standard and followed that with a detailed recommendation, you would expect that the individual would use the recommendation to guide his or her plan of action. MiniPlans^sm and formal improvement plans also involve setting and pursuing worthwhile targets. Note that several conditions are essential for coherence and for helping teachers invest effort wisely:

• A strong problem statement backed by detailed evidence
• Alignment between the actions proposed and the outcomes needed
• Alignment of goals required for evaluation with systems affecting the teacher's work, such as recertification plans, a school improvement plan, or an individual professional learning requirement

The more work you have done initially to document and communicate the relevant teacher performance standard and the impact of poor performance on students, the clearer and more appropriate goals are likely to be.

GOAL SETTING AS AN EVALUATION REQUIREMENT FOR ALL TEACHERS

Setting goals occupies a central place in schools. We set district strategic goals. We create school or team goals, and we even ask students to set learning goals. Moreover, we talk endlessly about making all these goals SMART. You would think that this attention to goal setting would result in high-quality models that teachers could follow when they set growth goals as part of evaluation or professional development. Sadly, goal setting at all levels and in most places is replete with poor practices, weak implementation, and ineffective monitoring. It is easier to incorporate goal-setting requirements into policies than to carry them out well in practice.

If you are fortunate to be in the rare district that has already designed and implemented a set of effective goal-setting procedures, your coaching and oversight efforts will be substantially supported. But, more likely, you are on your own to carry out a negotiated set of goal-setting procedures that cause even high performers difficulty and highlight the limitations of low performers. As you wrestle with teacher submissions of goals, avoid the nine most common traps, listed in Figure 7C.4, that can undermine the quality of the goals and plans submitted.

Figure 7C.4 Traps That Undermine Effective Goal Setting

1. **Allowing vague, fluffy goals disconnected to student learning problems.** Statements such as "I will learn to be more responsive to learners" or "Students will learn about how ancient peoples lived" cannot be measured and do not refer back to identified gaps in student achievement.

2. **Modeling or accepting goals written as activities.** "My goal is to implement the new TERC math program." That statement names an action to be taken rather than a problem to be solved.

3. **Not providing a bank of exemplars for a range of targets and plans.** District committees often adopt goal-setting procedures but fold up their work without offering teachers (and administrators) a range of criteria-based exemplars that illustrate *high- and low-quality* plans. Such exemplars help teachers assess their own first efforts and make changes.

4. **Not expecting genuine professional learning.** Low-performing teachers tend to set low-aspiration objectives for both students and themselves. If leaders do not expect teachers to undertake additional professional training and do not set high expectations for what is to be accomplished, they cannot expect teachers to set quality goals for their own learning.

5. **Failure to build in monitoring systems or accountability.** Supervisors leave it to teachers to develop appropriate goals with little oversight. Goals are set in the fall and reported on in the spring with little midyear monitoring and adjustment. Reporting forms often do not call for serious data-based collection and reflection.

6. **Missing opportunities to encourage collaborative or team goals.** Rather than encouraging collaborative goal setting on problems that affect a large group of students, supervisors let teachers pursue goals in isolation with no expectation that learning will be disseminated.

7. **Equating success with carrying out steps in a plan rather than with seeing students make progress.** When goal setting is treated as a peripheral activity that has little to do with students' learning, districts often monitor by simply asking teachers whether they did what they said they would do. An emphasis on getting through all the steps can stop midpoint reflection about whether the actions being taken are even addressing the learning problem that was identified.

8. **Allowing personal goals to be disconnected from or potentially in conflict with school improvement goals.** Both parties fall into the trap of assuming that a teacher's personal interests should always be allowed to trump urgent needs that the school may have, thus causing teachers to feel pulled in multiple directions by multiple competing priorities.

9. **Equating having written a SMART goal with fully implementing it.** The potential impact of a strong goal can be undermined by unskilled implementation just as good lesson plans can collapse during actual instruction.

CONFRONTING INEFFECTIVE GOALS

Consider the typical "goals" that were submitted by teachers in Example 7C.1.

Example 7C.1 Ineffective Goals

1. I will implement the new math program to raise the achievement of students who score poorly on nonroutine problems.
2. My goal is to provide more opportunities for students to write so they do better on the benchmark test on literacy.

Ineffective goal 1 above is focused on program adoption. It has implied attention to student results but has not set a measurable target or qualified what key terms like "score poorly" or "raise achievement" mean to the teacher. Goal 2 is more of an intention than a goal. It is vague, not measurable, and not focused on student learning.

Proficient or low-performing teachers who create and submit these types of low-quality goals need training and support. To help all teachers meet the goal-setting requirements of your evaluation system—and actually bring about worthwhile changes—you need to be clear what a good goal looks like. Agree with colleagues on criteria for powerful goals and evaluate submissions thoughtfully and consistently. Figure 7C.5 lists some criteria to use when you are confronting ineffective goals. Example 7C.2 illustrates how to revise a poor goal.

Figure 7C.5 Criteria for Effective SMART Goals

- **Specific.** A goal must describe a precise outcome or behavior.
- **Measurable.** It must be possible to determine if a goal has been achieved. Being measurable implies that a standard or quality of excellence has been established and criteria for success have been set.
- **Aligned.** Effective goals are tied to an identified area of need such as school or district priorities, student academic progress, a stretch area from a teacher performance evaluation, or results of a self-assessment.
- **Results-oriented.** The focus is on ends and outcomes, not on processes. Goals should be separated from executing activities, programs, or instructional strategies.
- **Time and resource defined.** Timelines for pursuing goals and monitoring checkpoints should be laid out in months, not years.

Example 7C.2 Revising Ineffective Goals to Make Them SMART

Poor Goals	Better Goals
I will implement the new math program to raise the achievement of students who score poorly on nonroutine problems.	By the next math MAPS benchmark on Feb. 2, 20--, I will plan and deliver instruction that raises the achievement of the 33% of my students who initially scored at the Intensive or Strategic Levels on nonroutine math problems to the Benchmark or Advanced level.
My goal is to provide more opportunities for students to write so they do better on the benchmark test on literacy.	My target standard for this goal is CCSS.ELA-Literacy.W.8.2 "Write informative/explanatory texts to examine a topic and convey ideas." I am concerned that 58% of my 8th-grade students scored at basic or below standard on the fall writing assessment while my colleagues only had 26% scoring at that level. I will collaborate with my 8th-grade ELA colleagues to design units and re-teaching plans that will enable at least 85% of the target cohort to score at the proficient or advanced level on the spring assessment.

This section should help to rejuvenate goal-setting processes by steering you and your teachers away from lists of activities and projects that characterized pro-forma efforts in the past. As you develop your expertise at identifying worthwhile targets and helping teachers hammer first drafts into SMART goals with real potential, you will be aligning all of your improvement systems for maximum impact—not just taking action against ineffective instruction.

7D
DEVELOPING ACCOUNTABLE RECOMMENDATIONS

Figure 7D.1 Recommendations in the Repertoire of Intervention Approaches

Supervisory Time and Effort Required

Low ←—————————————————————————————→ High

| Unmonitored Suggestions | Goal Setting influenced by or required by an evaluator | **Recommendations with follow-up monitoring and accountablility** | MiniPlan^{sm} for targeted growth | Formal Improvement Plans |

Recommendations for action are an important part of an evaluator's intervention repertoire (see Figure 7D.1). They are, however, the most underused or misused tools in evaluation systems. When school districts do not provide their supervisors with training, calibration exercises, or opportunities to analyze cases and learn from one another, the recommendation box on any form becomes a repository for platitudes. Consider these classic examples culled from real documents:

> "Mrs. D. creates an exciting classroom for most of her students but should consider raising standards for her low-performing students."
> "In the future, it would be important to add to your repertoire of teaching strategies. Think about how to include a wide variety to meet the needs of all learning styles."
> "Please reorganize your teaching to focus on higher level thinking skills."

Vague recommendations leave the recipient clueless about what or how to improve. It is not clear whether any action *must* be taken or whether the supervisor will ever revisit the issue with support or a subsequent reassessment. No wonder ineffective performance persists.

Keep several points in mind as you read this section. We are not talking about the kind of generic summary statements, such as the previous examples, that districts sometimes accept as recommendations—and that nobody takes seriously. What we call *accountable recommendations* are rose-level interventions after a problem has been diagnosed and communicated to the teacher. They provide some specific guidance on what to do and how to do it. You expect to monitor implementation and return to assess progress periodically. Craft accountable recommendations if suggestions have had no effect or for one or more of the reasons listed in Figure 7D.2.

Figure 7D.2 When to Start with Recommendations

Choose to begin with a recommendation for any combination of the following reasons:

- Program implementation lags either because professional development has not stuck or the teacher is resisting making the required changes.
- The data collected show specific, well-defined performance problems that the teacher has not recognized independently.
- Discussions about the problem show that the individual is looking for guidance or does not yet have a clear picture of action to take.
- The individual has a pattern of being willing to take responsibility but dependent on authority to diagnose an issue initially.
- The school or district has adopted more stringent teacher performance standards or new programs that are in direct contrast to past expectations.

Teachers who receive ratings below "proficient" or "meets standards" should reasonably expect carefully crafted recommendations and follow-up from the evaluator. The contents of the recommendation should never be a surprise to the teacher. They should be discussed in a conference and then captured in writing. Come to the conference with a draft of recommendations but clearly indicate that you expect and will accommodate a teacher's valid contributions.

Recommendations begin with clear communication of a problem, as outlined in Chapter 6. That communication includes specific data. The more explicit the presentation of the student learning discrepancy or the unmet teacher performance standard and the supporting data, the easier it is for the teacher and the supervisor to imagine the steps that would close the gap. As Figure 7D.3 indicates, effective recommendations go beyond merely listing actions that the teacher must take.

Figure 7D.3 Criteria for Effective Recommendations

A written recommendation should contain the following:
- A clear statement of the problem that includes the teacher performance standard(s) not currently being met at an acceptable level and the gap between the desired versus present student performance and outcomes. Try to align your language to the language of the relevant indicators from your rubric.
- Several sample actions and strategies to implement including a balance of concrete quick fixes and approaches more likely to produce long-term, adaptive changes.
- Guidelines for kinds of data to be collected and analyzed by the teacher, such as how the teacher will monitor his/her own progress and that of the students.
- A timeline for implementation, formative checks, and next assessment.

Looking at Sample Recommendations

The remainder of this section contains examples of accountable recommendations that you can use as models and starting points for your own work. As you will see in the summary chart Figure 7D.4, all but one of the sample recommendations (Al Drained) follows up on a case and problem described in Chapter 6. Al Drained's case has been deliberately unpacked and annotated to demonstrate the kind of thinking that supports crafting an effective recommendation. Do not be discouraged by its length. As you scan each example, keep in mind that these recommendations follow a detailed discussion of the data that precipitated the problem description and the problem itself. Before the final recommendations were documented, the teacher should have participated in identifying next steps, making choices among options, and suggesting data to collect.

Figure 7D.4 Examples of Recommendations in Section 7D

Example	Reason for the Recommendation	When/Where Provided	Focus Standard
7D.1 Al Drained	Previous suggestions resulting from observations and analysis of student performance have not resulted in any teacher action to improve; standard has been rated as unsatisfactory.	During a review of the summative evaluation; on a summative evaluation form	Demonstrating knowledge of students; increasing student engagement in and ownership for learning
7D.2 Klem Kaos	Ineffective procedures and routines; classroom is often chaotic.	After multiple short visits and a midyear formal observation; provided as next steps after a poor rating	Classroom management
7D.3 Lila Belated	Parental complaints, artifact examination, and conferences with the teacher show she is not grading papers/tests and providing feedback to students.	After several meetings about the issues uncovered as a result of pursuing the complaints; in a summary memo	Using assessment strategies effectively; providing timely and appropriate feedback to students
7D.4 Clammy Kolds	Students perceive teacher does not like and care about them; teacher is allowing negative, disrespectful interactions between students.	Interim evaluation conference and report; appears in a box below the rating of "novice"	Building positive relationships with students and a positive climate for learning
7D.5 Donna D. Limits	Early diagnostic walks and other data sources revealed problems for a subgroup of students.	After a post-observation and data conference; on an observation form	Conveying consistent high expectations and creating a culture for learning
7D.6 Peter Passable	Teacher does not use formative assessment strategies and does not collect data to shape his planning.	On a final evaluation to detail work to be done in the next year	Lesson planning and assessment
7D.7 John W. Collabnot	Teacher does not meet team responsibilities or behave appropriately in meetings or situations that require working with colleagues.	Discussed and crafted after a final evaluation rating of unsatisfactory on the standard; recorded on the final evaluation form	Professionalism: collaborative practice and shared responsibility for students

Recommendations for Al Drained on a Summative Evaluation

Al Drained is a veteran high school teacher who began his career in Business Education but has found himself reassigned after his original department was eliminated. Over the past 15 years, Al has variously taught basic math classes, career education "modules" under the guidance department, and, finally, half-semester modules in Technology Education required for freshmen and students who need the course to meet graduation requirements.

This year Al has struggled. Never particularly dynamic or student centered to begin with, his instruction has increasingly consisted of rambling lectures delivered in a monotone and tightly controlled exercises and worksheets. These "activities" are largely busywork and do not acknowledge his students' background interests, level of skill, or hunger to experiment with tools and technology. Students describe Al as "mean," "disrespectful," or "stupid" and his classes as "boring" and "teaching nothing." Mr. Ramirez, Northern High's newest vice principal, noticed the high numbers of disciplinary referrals coming from Al's classes. He listened carefully to students' explanations for their behavior. He looked at Al's grades and noticed that students who were successful in all their other courses were getting C's and D's in tech ed. Alerted to the problem, Mr. Ramirez began dropping in on different sections and at different times of day and spending 10 to 15 minutes observing. More often than not, he saw students proceeding in lock-step through low-level procedural exercises while Al talked on and on. After each visit, he suggested strategies to increase student engagement and urged Al to find out more about students' backgrounds and interests and to link his content to purposes students could understand. Al always nodded in agreement, but nothing changed in practice. Therefore, Mr. Ramirez rated Al's performance as unsatisfactory on Danielson's Domain 1b Demonstrating Knowledge of Students.

Because this conference was to be an extension of the ongoing exchange he and Al had been having, Mr. Ramirez decided to combine presenting the problem statement and identifying next steps. Knowing that Al needed something visual to help him stay focused, he brought a draft they could work from. His plan involved the following steps:

1. Ask Al to read the problem statement and supporting data with the goal of being able to summarize exactly what part of his teaching needed work.
2. Present each component of the recommendation and link it back to the standard.
3. Ask Al to decide when and how he would like to carry out the steps or which of several options listed he would choose and why.
4. Involve Al in jointly indicating what data he would collect and analyze to monitor his own progress.

Example 7D.1 Recommendation re Increasing Student Engagement in and Ownership for Learning

Standard: Domain 1 Planning and Preparation; Component 1b Demonstrating Knowledge of Students

Rating: Unsatisfactory

Mr. Drained does not demonstrate and use an understanding of how students learn, students' current levels of background knowledge and skill, and student interests to plan lessons that engage students actively and intellectually.

Problem statement uses the language of the teacher performance standards.

Mr. Drained will carry out the following steps, identified and agreed upon in our 5/24/_ conference:

1. Enroll in and successfully complete by November 30, _ "Studying Skillful Teaching: Using Data Day to Day."

   a. Drawing from that course, incorporate at least two different activities that involve collecting data about students' background, interests, and current level of skills into the opening unit of each new technology section.

   b. Apply at least three new techniques from the course for getting all students actively participating in discussing and using technology beginning in September of the 201_____ academic year and continuing throughout the year.

   Data to collect and provide for 10/1: samples of collection activities and student responses, evidence of how information affected his instruction for that unit, i.e., what changes he made as a result of the findings.

2. Carefully organize lessons to increase student opportunities for active participation. During each period for the first month of school or until the pattern becomes habitual, use a timer, peer observers, student helpers, or other resources to consciously monitor teacher talk so that students are given an opportunity to summarize, discuss, or apply concepts after every 10 minutes of direct instruction.

   Data to collect and provide for December conference (date tbd): "detailed" lesson plans and log of time use (see attached model).

   Also per our agreements of 6/2, XYZ School District will reimburse Mr. Drained for the cost of course tuition upon successful completion of all requirements.

Note that the steps specify what should happen as a result of taking a course, not just that he participate.

Teacher and supervisor agree on the data that will constitute evidence the recommendation is being followed.

Note the listing of a resource to be provided. Because this individual is being <u>required</u> to take a course, the district's contract specifies that the district reimburse him for tuition.

Recommendations for Mr. Kaos after an Observation

Example 7D.2 is a recommendation for Mr. Kaos, the teacher who struggled with classroom management (see problem statement in Example 6D.1) It is provided as part of the follow-up to an observation. As a general rule, recommendations should be written as close to the data about the problem as your form permits. If they must be placed at the end of a report, it is useful to restate the standard that the recommendation addresses, as the evaluator does here.

In conferencing with Mr. Kaos, the evaluator plans to go back to the specific evidence in the report to help him see the kind of preparations and forethought that might have averted the difficulty. The evaluator will state the outcomes that have to be evident and help Kaos make some selections about how to get to those outcomes that match his personal style. Notice that the actions to be taken that result from their discussion are concrete, basic, and fairly prescriptive because of the nature of the problem and the teacher's failure to figure out what to do on his own.

Example 7D.2 Recommendation re Establishing Effective Procedures and Routines

Mr. Kaos has not established classroom procedures and routines that support student learning. We have agreed on the following action steps to be carried out by January 28, ____ . A follow-up observation and artifact review will be scheduled for the week of February 2.

1. Establish and consistently implement the following procedures to solve problems with materials at the beginning of class.
   a. Post a list of materials needed for your class each day by the end of homeroom period.
   b. Require students to write what they need to bring to class in their homework agendas.
   c. Greet students at the door; ask them to check re whether they are ready to go and give focused praise to those who come prepared until the expectation is clearly internalized.
   d. Establish a lending and points-lost system for forgotten materials (see Mr. D. or Ms. J. for ideas)
2. Consistently implement team agreements (see memo of 8/29) re established place and process for submitting homework and classwork in each room.
3. Devise and consistently use a public recording system that allows students to check on what work they owe and what homework is due (e.g., posters used by Ms. V., and Mr. L. or homework website being piloted by your team).

Recommendations for Lila Belated following a Memo of Concern

Lila Belated is the science teacher whose deficiencies in providing students with timely feedback and whose failure to grade and return student work triggered an investigation and memo of concern laying out the problem (see Example 6 D.3). Knowing that Dr. Belated was likely to be upset or defensive and to need some time to compose herself after the problem had been communicated, her department head Rose Mitchell told her they would have a strategy conference several days later. That conference would help Dr. B. identify the specific steps she would need to take. She asked Dr. B. to show her some samples of the assessments she used so that they could think about potential changes before they met. Not surprisingly, Belated's "assessments" were all elaborate multi-page tests or problem sets she called quizlets and longer documents she called weekly or biweekly tests.

In choosing what to do about the problem, Department Head Mitchell wanted Lila to see how improvements she made were not just a matter of "fixing complaints" but rather would help her to meet one of the teacher performance standards for the district. Mitchell's conference plan called for the following steps:

1. Review the relevant teacher performance standard(s) and the science department policies related to assessment and timely feedback to establish the "non-negotiables."
2. Ask Lila to reflect on the value of her sample assessments in generating useful information for her students.
3. Ask Lila to think about and offer suggestions re how to collect data re student understanding quickly and efficiently and to involve students in self-assessment.
4. Acknowledge the difficulty of providing feedback when a teacher is not present and remind Lila about the importance of minimizing absences.

After the conference, Mitchell summarized their agreements in a follow-up memo.

Example 7D.3 Recommendation re Assessment/ Feedback to Students

To: Dr. Lila Belated
From: Rose Mitchell
Re: Summary of Recommended Actions to Resolve Issues Discussed on 1/26 and 1/31

Below are the actions we agreed upon to ensure that students receive timely and appropriate feedback and that you are successfully meeting criteria for Domain 3, Component 3d Using Assessment in Instruction.

1. Choose and implement three different checking for understanding strategies that will allow you to determine how well students understand a concept before the next class period. We discussed one-question quizzes, concept probes, and learning logs as starting examples. You noted that you had other resources you could consult.
2. Implement your idea of publically posting charts with data from the checking at least once a week and having students discuss their progress. Invite me in to observe one of those discussions.
3. Reduce the length and complexity of quizzes to assess one to three essential aspects of the previous lessons and adhere to the departmental policy of returning all quizzes within 2 school days.
4. Provide feedback on problem-sets, lab reports, and practice sheets that allows students to self-correct and to seek extra help quickly when they need it. Per departmental agreement, if students have been required to spend 45 minutes or more on an assignment, that feedback must be provided within 5 days of the time of original instruction on the concept. We discussed experimenting with criteria checklists and self-assessment cards as a starting point. Keep a file and notes on what you try and find helpful so that we can think together again in early March.

Finally, we discussed policies governing attendance. Because your total absences have now reached ten for the year, please provide a doctor's note for all additional days out.

Recommendation for Clammy Kolds following an Interim Evaluation

Clammy Kolds' indifferent and disrespectful attitude towards students (see Example 6D.4) exemplified the kind of toxic behavior her new principal, Dr. Gonzales, had been trying to turn around. In contrast to her colleagues, Clammy resisted adopting a new program that would help change the climate and relationships in her room. After suggestions did not work in the first several months, Dr. Gonzales decided to indicate how seriously she took the problem by completing an interim evaluation and rating the veteran teacher's performance on the novice level on her district instrument. She presented the existence of the problem and the need to fix it as non-negotiable and then listened to Clammy vent about how she had "no time for and wasn't into touchy-feely stuff." Then she sent Clammy away with the charge to think about how both outcomes—implementing the program to improve the climate and avoiding what Clammy considered "touchy-feely"—could be accomplished in preparation for their next meeting. Example 7D.4 shows the agreements from that follow-up meeting recorded by the principal.

Example 7D.4 Recommendation re Building Positive Relationships and a Positive Climate for Learning

Ms. Kolds has not implemented a series of activities from the Class Climate Change (CCC) program that would enable her to get to know her students' names, backgrounds, and prior knowledge. As a result, students perceive that she does not like or care about them. In addition Kolds is not able to help them see connections between their lives and concepts or skills they are attempting to learn. After discussing alternative strategies that would be consistent with her teaching style, Ms. Kolds and I agreed that she would undertake the following actions to change the climate in her classroom over the next four weeks:

1. Administer and analyze the "All About Me" activity from the CCC program. Report the patterns identified to each class and use the results to plan clear connections to students' interests within the next 4 labs. Record the connection examples in the lesson plan book.
2. Learn students' names and use names when calling on students and as part of instructional examples.
3. Engage students in designing a class contract and norms to address and prevent the put-downs and name calling students have specifically cited as making them unwilling to participate in discussions.
4. Ask students to write anonymous reflections re the climate of the class and the factors that help them to see why the labs are important to their lives prior to our next meeting.

We will meet during the week of _____ to review Ms. Kolds' findings and planned next steps.

Recommendation for Donna D. Limits on an Observation Form

Because he noted disturbing evidence of reduced standards and expectations for certain groups of low socio-economic status students, Principal Yee had already had several discussions with Donna D. Limits and sent her a memo of concern (see Example 6D.5). On a walk through the 4th grades several weeks later, Yee noticed that students in Donna's room were rushing through worksheets, were off-task during independent time, and were giving up without making any sustained effort to review or edit their writing. Back in his office, he looked at data for first quarter Language Arts benchmark assessments and found that 12 of Donna's students were performing below the proficient level. He returned for an extended 30-minute observation during which he talked to students and looked through their portfolios. He found that many students—not just those who were struggling—were turning in sloppy, incomplete work and getting smiley faces and positive comments for little effort. In interviews students were not able to distinguish when they were putting in effective effort and when they were not. Thus they were not getting the opportunities to learn how to work hard and strategically, a major goal of the school.

Yee decided to focus his recommendation on closing a specific gap in Donna's practice that had been clearly evident in his drop-in visits and in the extended observation. He reasoned that changing some behaviors from negative to positive might ultimately help him chip away at Limits' negative beliefs as well.

Example 7D.5 Recommendation re Expectations for Student Performance

Ms. Limits does not clearly communicate her expectations for the procedures students are to follow or the quality of the work students are to produce. [CSTP 2] Ms. Limits has identified and will carry out the following steps by 12/15:

1. Review materials and agreements re teaching effective effort strategies from August 10__ workshops and team meetings; fully implement attribution retraining including lessons for students on how to invest hard work and use their strategies for writing.
2. Develop criteria for what effective effort would look like for at least three assignments per week. Communicate criteria in several ways and assess which works best for students.
3. Require all students to assess their effort against these criteria before submitting their work. Determine how to reward students whose assessments are on target and study the effect of the rewards.
4. Make an appointment with me for the week of _____. Bring artifacts, lesson plan notations, and records showing results on classroom assessments to illustrate the impact of these action steps on student performance thus far.

Recommendation for Peter Passable on a Final Evaluation

Peter Passable has earned a rating of Needs Improvement because he has thus far showed no signs of learning about or using formative assessment to shape his unit and daily planning (see Example 6D.7). He is a capable teacher who enjoys his students. However, as association president, Passable's interests have been elsewhere over the past two years. He tried to invest as little time as possible in his planning and did not keep up with his colleagues' experiments with formative assessment. Thus he has not shared their enthusiasm for the impact regular data gathering has had on student performance. Peter's principal knows they need a plan of action that Peter can buy into (without losing face if possible) and that he and Peter can monitor during the following year. Their back and forth discussion allows Peter to ask for resources such as district support for his attendance at a high-status conference and then to commit to investing his own time in return. Note that the principal and teacher agree to establish a "controlled experiment" of sorts that interests them both and will necessitate ongoing discussion. Finally, the stipulation that Peter experiment with assessment and present his findings is one he himself suggested and is consistent with his self-image as a leader.

Example 7D.6 Recommendation re Assessment and Planning

Mr. Passable has identified the following steps to improve his performance on using a variety of informal and formal methods of assessment to measure student learning and to use assessment results to improve future planning and instruction. [Element I-B]

1. Attend ASCD summer institute on formative assessment with support from the district conference fund. Use information from that institute to identify six different formative assessment techniques to put in place during the first semester of 201_.
2. Experiment weekly with using formative assessment to shape lesson planning in a minimum of two of his four World Civilization sections from September through December 1. Keep a detailed log of adjustments made to lessons and of the differences in student performance between the sections where formative assessment is being implemented and the "control" sections.
3. Collect data from students re their understanding of how access to formative assessment has affected their learning.
4. Present combined findings to department and/or faculty meetings during the January professional development day.

Recommendation for John W. Collabnot on a Final Evaluation

Mr. Collabnot's problem is described with detailed evidence in Example 6D.8. John has been resistant to change and is not willing to take ownership for the problem. Therefore, the recommendation that follows the rating on the summative evaluation, Example 7D.7, is highly prescriptive. In the conference about next steps, the evaluator takes a strong role in spelling out exactly what John would need to do to meet standards for professionalism and the data sources the two will consult to determine whether the recommendation has been carried out. Notice that this example does not include the language of mutual agreement found in many of the others. Here the evaluator's primary purpose is to make sure that she has documented the clear expectations for improvement in case intervention must be escalated to an improvement plan or progressive discipline.

Example 7D.7 Recommendation re Meeting Professionalism Standards for Collaborative Practice and Shared Responsibility for Students

Mr. Collabnot's actions and speech do not meet standards for Standard Professional Responsibilities. To resolve the problem, Mr. Collabnot will need to take the following actions for the 201__ academic year and onward and to provide the evidence of success indicated in brackets below:

1. Attend and arrive punctually at all professional meetings.
2. Come fully prepared with student work, requested background reading, etc. to all required department, team, and faculty meetings. [Artifacts of work]
3. Refrain from scheduling any activities or appointments that would conflict with meeting obligations and actively refrain from allowing informal, unscheduled exchanges to prevent being on time for meetings. Be present at the start of all department, team, and faculty meetings and attend for their entire duration. [Sign in sheet]
4. Actively and positively contribute to all error analysis, planning, and problem-solving sessions for the content team. [Artifacts contributed, list of suggestions made and pursued]
5. Be stationed at his door and actively monitoring the hallway during passing periods and the AM and PM transition periods per the *Faculty Agreements and Faculty Handbook,* 2013 version.

Crafting accountable recommendations is at the core of taking action against ineffective teaching. They certainly require more time than requesting vague action. You communicate your belief in the teachers' capacity to improve when you ask them to rise to a challenge and provide some structural support for them to do so. In many instances, evaluators and teachers report that the mere act of paying close attention to a single identified gap with a focused recommendation starts a larger improvement process. Remember that much of the work of designing what to do and all the primary experimentation, data collection, focused monitoring, and study should be done by the teacher. The degree to which you intervene to specify exactly what activities, language, and strategies will be used depends in large measure on how much background knowledge and motivation the teacher has. When in doubt, try to offer a choice between several approaches that might work in order to help the teacher feel a sense of ownership and control over the process. Finally, schedule short bursts of time to monitor progress on recommendations. The follow-up appointments, brief check-in conversations, or walk-through visits that you do are a critical part of ensuring that the recommendation has an impact on teaching and learning.

7E
CREATING SHORT-TERM
MiniPlans^{sm}

A MiniPlan^{sm}, is a small, lower profile cousin to a full-blown improvement plan. Think of it as a way to repair recognizable potholes or a washout in the road, not as a useful strategy for a road that needs to be completely repaved. It is a short-term strategy for naming and addressing a bounded and fixable performance problem that needs more formal attention and monitoring than a recommendation. Mini-Plans^{sm} let you tackle an issue with the teacher when it occurs and when you can make the most difference for students. You do not have to wait for some official point in the evaluation cycle.

Figure 7E.1 MiniPlans^{sm} in the Repertoire of Intervention Approaches

Supervisory Time and Effort Required

Low   **High**

| Unmonitored Suggestions | Goal Setting influenced by or required by an evaluator | Recommendations with follow-up monitoring and accountablility | **MiniPlan^{sm} for targeted growth** | Formal Improvement Plans |

As Figure 7E.1 indicates, MiniPlans^{sm} fall between the gentler rose responses of recommendations and goal setting and the red or high alert intervention of a formal improvement plan. They are more demanding and structured than accountable recommendations and require a more prescriptive stance from the supervisor. This type of intervention is a good match for individuals who have received basic or unsatisfactory ratings but can take responsibility for problem(s) identified. Mini-Plans^{sm} are also a good match for individuals who become easily overwhelmed by possibilities and distractions and seem to respond well to clear criteria and timelines. However, if you have already tried several other approaches without success, are meeting with resistance, and suspect that you are dealing with deeply entrenched behavior pass by MiniPlans^{sm} and go directly to Improvement Plans in Chapter 8.

Figure 7E.2 provides guidelines for choosing a MiniPlan^{sm} as an intervention strategy.

Figure 7E.2 When to Use a MiniPlan^sm

Begin with the MiniPlan^sm level when some combination of the following conditions is present:

- The teacher has not responded to lower level interventions such as goal setting and recommendations.
- The performance problem could reasonably be remedied with effective effort and some short-term coaching if you can call on resources such as mentor teachers or skilled colleagues.
- Discussions about the problem show that the individual does not yet have the knowledge or skills to be able to make the change without some guidance.
- The individual has a pattern of being willing to take responsibility but also of being unable to initiate changes successfully without support.
- You need a small-scale "test" to determine whether you should refer the teacher to a formal improvement plan for the following year.
- You need a scaled-down intervention for someone who is coming off of a successful improvement plan year.
- You need a strategy to help someone whose performance is rated as basic but not unsatisfactory.

Leader Alert
Contractual Obligations

Almost all districts have contractual obligations around improvement plans. A MiniPlan^sm is not a new vehicle that needs to be bargained or announced. You offer teachers the opportunity to participate in a short-term intervention consistent with recommendations that are allowed in all teacher evaluation instruments. Don't even use the name MiniPlan^sm if it will cause undue negative reaction. The approach is intended to be supportive and invitational, but if a teacher does not agree to participate, you always have the option of referring the teacher to the full improvement plan. ◆

Unlike year-long goal or improvement plans, MiniPlans^sm should be implemented and their success evaluated within one to two months. A MiniPlan^sm offers a struggling teacher significant support and guidance for a short period. You establish a high bar for what will constitute a successful demonstration of proficient performance. Insist that the teacher collect and analyze data about the impact of his/her efforts on student growth and do not settle for documentation of compliance ("I did what you said; what else do you want?"). Compliance-level responses only invite a return to ineffective performance as soon as attention goes elsewhere.

A MiniPlan^sm allows you to assess whether an individual can improve under favorable conditions but does not by itself measure how long the change is maintained. Lack of sustained progress tells you that more intensive intervention is needed and that you are dealing with entrenched, persistent issues of low performance—possibly incompetence. Figure 7E.3 defines the essential differences between MiniPlans^sm and formal improvement plans, which are discussed in Chapter 8.

Figure 7E.3 MiniPlan^sm vs. Formal Improvement Plan

	MiniPlan^sm	Formal Improvement Plan
Context for Selection of Approach	Serves as a voluntary pre-referral or step between a recommendation and an improvement plan. Evaluator has reasonable confidence that teacher can improve with support within 1-2 months. Evaluator does not see the defined problem as one that would jeopardize the teacher's continued employment *at this time.*	Evaluator sees the problems as complicated enough to require the work of a team and likely to result in referral for dismissal if they cannot be resolved. Previous efforts to intervene have not been successful or the teacher has been unable to sustain proficient performance over time. By contract, the district agrees to invest anywhere from 4-18 months in helping the teacher improve.
Impact on Students	Preliminary or short-term data show students not performing at target levels.	Multiple data sources show evidence of substantive negative impact on student learning over time.
Performance Level	Substandard performance noted in writing after interim or midyear evaluation.	Actual unsatisfactory ratings on summative evaluation. Potential incompetence or patterns of inefficiency.
Nature of the problem(s) to be addressed	Limited in scope and severity. Issues are able to be satisfactorily fixed and assessed in less than 3 months without calling in an assistance team.	Problems are complex, involve several standards or elements, and require significant time and resources to fix. Problems have persisted through previous attempted interventions.
Teacher Obligation	Teacher assumes large degree of responsibility and ownership for the problem and plan implementation.	Teacher may or may not assume ownership for the problem but must participate in required procedures.
Advantages for Supervisor	Small-scale, flexible, and evaluator-initiated way to trigger remedial action with limited commitment. Requires no negotiation or formal adoption. Aligns with existing evaluation procedures governing recommendations.	Governed by policy and/or negotiated agreement; therefore consistent throughout a district. Provides potential district resources to assist in formal intervention.
Disadvantages for Supervisor	Teacher has no contractual obligation to participate.	Tightly prescribed set of procedures. Missing steps could undermine entire plan.
Data Collection Responsibility	Most of the data (75%-80%) collected by the teacher.	Data collection shared by teacher and evaluator or team (50%-50%).
Determination of Appropriate Progress	Data analysis conducted by teacher and evaluator. Evaluator ultimately determines whether progress is appropriate.	Data analysis conducted by team. Evaluator—or team if so designated by contract—makes ultimate determination of appropriate progress.

The process of creating MiniPlans^sm involves certain now-familiar principles. You diagnose the problem using multiple data sources. You define and communicate the problem before any solutions are proposed and provide time for a teacher to respond before proceeding to jointly identifying goals and actions. Though a few districts provide a template to help supervisors and teachers work efficiently, a form is not essential. A well-designed MiniPlan^sm should meet the criteria listed in Figure 7E.4.

Figure 7E.4 Criteria for Effective MiniPlans^sm

An effective MiniPlan^sm should include

- A clear statement of the problem that spells out (1) the teacher performance standard(s) not currently being met at an acceptable level and (2) the gap between the desired versus present student performance and outcomes. Include appropriate language from the relevant teacher performance criteria or indicators as much as possible.

- Specific, sequenced actions that require the teacher to plan, apply his or her plan, evaluate, and reflect on its success. These actions should require the teacher to learn and use new behaviors.

- Data, to be collected and analyzed by the teacher and supervisor, that would show how the two parties intend to monitor progress and how the teacher will document his or her efforts.

- A clear set of criteria against which to measure success.

- A timeline for implementation and indications of when there will be formative check-ins and a next assessment.

Background on Whim Winger

For our sample MiniPlan^sm, we return to Whim Winger, the poor planner from Example 6D.6. Whim has not responded to less intensive intervention. He has shown no sign of applying the initial training provided to science teachers as his district has begun to implement Common Core State Standards (CCSS). The consequences of allowing Whim to continue with his low-quality, unfocused "planning" are glaringly apparent. As the school seeks to make instruction more rigorous, Principal Evans needs to make Whim understand the seriousness of the problem and recognize he must change. He decides to rate Whim's performance as unsatisfactory on the three elements of his district standards (adapted from Danielson 2013) related to planning and questioning that are listed in Example 7E.1.

Example 7E.1 Excerpt from Whim Winger's Problem Description

Mr. Winger does not regularly do the following:

1. Plan instruction by identifying worthwhile lesson objectives to help students meet district standards aligned with CCSS. [Ic Setting Instructional Outcomes]
2. Plan a sequence of activities to engage students in active intellectual activity. [Ie Designing Coherent Instruction]
3. Plan questions with high cognitive challenge. [III b Using Questioning and Discussion Techniques]

As a result, students spend substantial instructional time completing meaningless busywork or sitting passively listening to Mr. Winger's lectures and answering low-level questions.

Reasoning that Whim knows his subject, believes in kids, and is more whimsical than resistant, Evans decides a MiniPlan[sm] would be a good intervention match. It would be a quick, targeted test of whether Whim is capable of sharpening his practice. For additional leverage Evans also decides to include Practice 1 from Common Core Science Standards as the centerpiece of the MiniPlan[sm] but to let Whim choose the appropriate content standard from the district curriculum. In this way he hopes to elevate Whim's teaching fairly rapidly to the level of performance the school needs.

As you read Whim's plan in Example 7E.2, identify the criteria illustrated. Note that Whim assumes the majority of responsibility for collecting and reporting data. His plan

- Has a small, manageable scope: three to four lessons focused on producing student growth on clearly identified skills
- Includes three steps: planning, application, and evaluation/reflection
- Integrates Common Core State Standards with teacher performance standards
- Includes observation of and interviews with students as sources of data

Finally, note that successful completion of the plan requires more than simply checking off completion on a series of mandated activities, thus avoiding the "I did what you told me, and it didn't work" syndrome.

Example 7E.2 MiniPlan℠ for Whim Winger

Action Step	Description of Action	Data to Be Collected and Collection Method	Indicators for Success
1. Planning	By xx/xx/20xx, plan a series of 3-4 lessons that include: __ Objectives that specify what students will know/be able to do re (a) selected content and (b) target skill: determining relationships between dependent and independent variables (Practice 1) __ Activities and questions for students that are designed to develop target skill from Practice 1 (see above) __ Tasks that engage students in asking and answering questions re content concepts and target skill (see above) __ Pre- and post-assessments of students' mastery of selected content and ability to identify dependent and independent variable	Teacher submits written plans for 3-4 lessons to coach who examines them for criteria by xx/xx/20xx.	All criteria met without significant need for multiple revisions. Pre- and post- assessments require students to use targeted skill from Practice 1 with content of increasing challenge.
2. Application	Implement the lesson series including: __Communicating and making connections to the objectives initially and as each activity is introduced __Explicit instruction in the target skill of asking and answering questions (Practice 1) __ Presenting practice tasks that provide students with opportunities to answer and ask questions re dependent and independent variables __ Administering and scoring pre- and post-assessments and presenting students with feedback on performance	1. Mr. Winger collects __Data from pre-test and adjustments made during instruction __Actual vs. planned questions asked __ Data re performance on practice tasks __Data chart showing student pre-post results. 2. Mr. Evans observes final full lesson and collects data on teacher and student questions and other relevant student behaviors that demonstrate their ability to meet objectives	All steps of the lesson plans implemented with fidelity. Data from both observation and assessments show appropriate student growth on Practice 1 and content concepts.
3. Evaluation and Reflection	Evaluate the lessons' impact as follows: __ Plan vs. actual implementation and reasons for differences __ Learning from pre-test(s) and adjustments made __Questions and tasks that worked and didn't work and why __Post test results and implications for next steps __New practices to incorporate and why	Mr. Winger presents findings, reflections, and future commitments to principal, coach, and science department head	Written/oral reflections show understanding of: __Differences in practices used and results obtained before/after the focus on planning __ What students need in order to meet a CCSS.

Source: Next Generation Science Standards Science and Engineering Practices, Appendix F, 2013: nextgenscience.org

MiniPlans℠ provide another strategy in your intervention tool kit. In many ways a MiniPlan℠ resembles its more formal Improvement Plan cousin, but it is small-scale and short-term. By involving the teacher in the development of the plan, requiring agreement on its components, and mobilizing support, you create a laboratory to determine whether the teacher can make deep changes under ideal conditions. A MiniPlan^{sm} does not ensure long-term sustained growth but does tell you change is possible. If the plan works, it primes the pump so that a judicious combination of team collaboration, goal setting, and accountable recommendations can be used to continue the growth. If the MiniPlan^{sm} fails and students are still losing out, then turn to Chapter 8 for what to do next.

DESIGNING IMPROVEMENT
PLANS

8A
OVERVIEW

Figure 8A.1 Formal Improvement Plans in the Repertoire of Intervention Approaches

Supervisory Time and Effort Required

Low →→→→→→→→→→→→→→→→→→→→→→→→→→→→→→→→→→→→→→ High

| Unmonitored Suggestions | Goal Setting influenced by or required by an evaluator | Recommendations with follow-up monitoring and accountablility | MiniPlansm for targeted growth | **Formal Improvement Plans** |

In the continuum of intervention (Figure 8A.1), a formal improvement plan is what we have labeled a "red-level" intervention requiring substantial investment of your time and effort. Reduced to its essentials, a red-level exchange says, "Stop what you have been doing and start doing this immediately; your job is in jeopardy." There are two types of red-level intervention:

1. Referral to the contractually defined formal improvement strand of an evaluation system, best suited to dealing with instructional deficiencies
2. Referral to progressive discipline, best suited to issues of noncompliance with directives, policies, and established practices

Usually an improvement plan is your last resort in taking action against ineffective teaching prior to recommending dismissal. Most likely you have tried other approaches unsuccessfully and have rated the teacher's overall performance as unsatisfactory. At this point, you think that the teacher *may* be incompetent. Figure 8A.2 gives more specific criteria to identify when an improvement plan is needed.

Figure 8.A.2 When to Choose an Improvement Plan

This intervention is an appropriate match under some combination of the following conditions:

- Other appropriately documented interventions tried for a period of at least 6-12 weeks have not led to significant improvement.
- The causes for the poor performance are not deficiencies within the organization or problems of the specific supervisor, e.g., lack of expertise in supervision and evaluation or a clear personal bias.
- The problem is not a case of policy infractions or insubordination, i.e., "willful failure or refusal to obey reasonable orders of a superior" (Kennedy 2010 320). These issues are better handled through progressive discipline (see Chapter 9).

- Student performance data indicate that teaching deficiency is having a documented and deleterious impact on learning.
- The teacher has received at least one summative evaluation that contains one or more ratings of "Unsatisfactory" or "Does not meet standards."

Legal Note 8A.1 Harassment

> Expect that when you begin to take action against ineffective instruction through escalating interventions, the individual and/or the union may claim harassment. Harassment has direct legal implications if you specifically violate a prohibited practice such as discriminating on the basis of racial or ethnic identity. In the context of improvement planning and other interventions, harassment is more likely to be about other kinds of disparate treatment. Always have a well-reasoned and well-articulated basis for treating the individual differently from those who are performing the same or similar duties. If you have a reasonable basis for disparate treatment and provide a detailed explanation of the difference, you are not likely to be found harassing the teacher.

Referral to formal improvement demands the most extensive documentation and carries the greatest potential for procedural slip-ups that could undermine a case. Therefore you need thorough knowledge of evaluation regulations, contract provisions, and district policies. While the contents of a plan should not be subject to grievance, procedural issues are often grieved. Pay close attention to forms, timelines, and communication requirements. Make sure you have documented earlier efforts at intervention ranging from conference summaries to a MiniPlan^{sm}. Those initial efforts become part of the evidence to show that you have provided the teacher with opportunities and support for improvement.

Legal Note 8A.2 Specifying Expectations and Following Procedures

> Always remember that the plan becomes the primary document should it become necessary to seek termination or other disciplinary action. Specifying deficiencies together with clear expectations for what you want the teacher to do is paramount. The outcome of legal challenges to the evaluation process is frequently determined by the clarity of what is laid out for the teacher. There should be no ambiguity—no dispute as to what s/he had to do. Cases can also be lost if the union can argue that what you expect the teacher to do is arbitrary and unrealistic. Reasonable expectations combined with opportunities for remediation and periodic re-evaluation fulfill the ethical and legal requirements of fairness and due process. More often, dismissal efforts are undermined by evaluators' failure to follow procedures unrelated to the substantive arguments. Know and follow your procedures.

USING AN ASSISTANCE TEAM

Establishing an Assistance Team sets the stage for the additional structure and accountability required by an improvement plan. Creating a team accomplishes several things. First, it provides support for all parties. Different voices provide new ideas and energy. In addition, after several months of intervention, friction and frustration often exist between the primary evaluator and the teacher. Second, establishing a team clearly signals that the institution has a commitment to improvement that goes beyond the individual supervisor-supervisee relationship. Finally, convening the team signals a fair and fresh start at problem solving. The team's goal is to create the following conditions for success:

- Detailed action plans targeted to solving the identified problems and therefore improving practice
- Intensive intervention that includes, but is not limited to, frequent feedback, observations of different duration, and coaching
- A fair process for identifying the data needed to determine that the problem is solved and for formative (if not summative) assessment of progress

Leader Alert
What if Assistance Teams Are Not Required?

Keep in mind that all of the steps in the plan apply whether or not you convene a team. A few states and districts use peer assistance and review teams, but in many cases forming a team may not be required in your contract. As a time-starved, hassle-avoiding administrator, you may be overwhelmed by the call to organize an assistance team. This chapter proposes an ideal support scenario for a seriously underperforming teacher who has not responded to earlier levels of intervention. Even if it is not *required*, consider creating a small team including peers to support the improvement effort. In the absence of a formal assistance team, consider involving other qualified supervisors and/or consultants to assist in the development of improvement plans and to review your work to make sure that your plan is aligned with and supported by the problems identified in the final performance summary. ◆

Selecting Team Members

The pool of potential participants for Assistance Teams should include colleagues for the supervisor as well as for the faculty member since both sides need thought partners. Do not, however, fall into the trap of trying to represent a dozen different stakeholders. Keep the size manageable—generally somewhere between three to five members, including the identified teacher and supervising administrator. Groups above this number become cumbersome. Unions will want to have involvement in any improvement plan. In many cases it is helpful to have union representation even it is not required. However, in case of disagreements with the union or the assistance team, the principal and superintendent should preserve the final decision re the need for and content in a plan.

Typical rosters might include a subset of the following:
- A curriculum specialist or department head with expertise in an identified problem area
- A teacher union representative
- A trusted teacher colleague selected by the teacher
- A mentor teacher or coach
- An administrator from another school with strength in analyzing instruction
- An outside consultant or university professor with established expertise
- A central office representative from Human Resources, Curriculum and Instruction, or Data and Accountability

**Legal Note 8A.3
Union
Representation and
Weingarten**

Questions arise about when the union can be involved in matters of teacher evaluation. For communication about a performance evaluation, a union representative should typically not be present. You do not want the union to be involved in problem description and documentation. However, they will rightfully insist on being represented when you are conducting meetings about the development and implementation of an improvement plan requiring very different treatment. You will actually want them to be present. Even if they don't perfectly align with your school context, you should be aware of the following cases from Labor Relations. Under *Weingarten,* an employee's right to union representation on request is limited to situations in which the employee *reasonably believes* that the interview with the employer will result in *discipline.* The test is whether a reasonable person in the employee's situation would have believed that adverse action would follow *Amoco Chemical Corp.,* 237 NLRB 69, 99 LRRM 1017 (1978). The right to have a union representative present does not attach unless the meeting is *investigatory in nature.* Thus, where a meeting is not held to elicit information from an employee or to support a further decision to discipline an employee but is merely convened so that the employer can deliver a warning, Weingarten protections do not apply. *Baton Rouge Water Works,* 103 LRRM 1056 (1980); NLRB v. Certified Grocers of Calif., 587 F.2d 449, 100 LRRM 3029 (9th Cir. 1978).

Although you cannot control union representation, whenever possible choose assistance team members who have the following characteristics:

- Ability to support the teacher's improvement efforts with substantive ideas and feedback
- Competence in assessing data drawn from multiple sources
- Strong communication skills
- Conviction that all children deserve competent instruction
- A reputation for knowledge and fairness within the district
- Commitment to attend meetings and participate thoughtfully
- Certification in designated content areas or supervision

Enlisting Outside Expertise

Although outside consultants do not routinely serve on formal improvement teams, they can be valuable assets when districts lack internal expertise or when internal resource staff is not perceived to be credible by the teacher being supported. In some cases such as music, technical education, occupational therapy, or counseling where there are only a small number of colleagues in the district to consult or you face issues of confidentiality, you may need to seek advice outside the system. Outside consultants can be assigned to work with teachers or administrators as confidential helpers to the teacher, as advisors or facilitators for the planning process, or as supporters and monitors of the implementation of various strategies incorporated in the plan.

Structuring the Work of the Assistance Team

Many of the individuals you or the teacher recruit for an assistance team may not have served before and may be unfamiliar with the process and their responsibilities. Expect that some participants will come with misconceptions about what they can and cannot do. As a skillful leader, your first job is to structure the initial "organizing meeting" of the assistance team so that you lay all the important foundations and create the conditions for them to work effectively. Figure 8A.3 lists the key ideas that must be considered and communicated when you are focusing the work of an assistance team.

Figure 8A.3 How to Focus the Work of the Assistance Team

1. **Establish the purpose.** The primary charge should be to develop and support the implementation of an improvement plan and to provide formative feedback during the plan.

2. **Clearly establish evaluation responsibilities.** Unless the district has adopted a formal peer assistance process that gives evaluation authority to the team, the main purpose of the team is to assist the teacher in his or her improvement quest. The primary evaluator is still responsible for the ultimate evaluation of the success of the teacher in improving performance.

3. **Assign roles and responsibilities for each member of the assistance team.** It is important that supporting processes are separated from evaluation processes. In order to have an objective, neutral leader, have a evaluator other than the primary evaluator be chair. The job of taking notes and disseminating the minutes/agreements should be assigned to another member of the group.

4. **Review agreements on confidentiality.** Establish or check other norms if necessary.

5. **Decide which evaluation documents the primary evaluator should and can share.** Determine which can be read by the team in their original form and which need to be summarized.

6. **Decide on the duration of the plan.** Plan duration should be matched to the number and level of deficiencies and years of employment of the identified teacher. Some states allow plans as short as 30 days, but these would constitute documentation for egregious problems and significant loss of student learning rather than structured plans for genuine improvement (see Legal Note 8A.4). Typically, improvement plans run four to seven months but can sometimes be as long as two years.

7. **Establish agreements about the frequency of meetings and set a schedule.** Because the teacher needs appropriate time to carry out the action plan and assess its impact on students, teams generally meet every four to six weeks.

**Legal Note 8A.4
Plan Duration**

The duration of a plan must comply with any collective bargaining agreements or policies regarding such plans. Some agreements and/or policies will stipulate a minimum period of time during which the plan should be in effect. Ideally, as the employer you should retain the discretion to determine how much time the teacher should be given to improve. Unless otherwise prescribed by contract or policy, the length of an improvement plan should be determined by the seriousness of the problem.

Once you have focused the team on its task and established the governing agreements, the group will be ready to design the actual plan. Section 8B details all the steps involved in creating an improvement plan and includes suggestions for the number of meetings with estimates of the time. Section 8C illustrates those steps applied to a case and contains a model of a completed plan. Before you proceed to create a plan of your own, review Chapter 10 as well so that you understand the legal landmines to avoid.

Referral to the improvement plan process is a clear signal that there are several unresolved deficiencies and that you are giving the teacher a last chance to demonstrate improvement. Expect to shift to more formal documentation with a real prospect of dismissal should no improvement be forthcoming.

8B

STEPS IN DESIGNING AN IMPROVEMENT PLAN

We have already considered most of the steps needed to devise a formal improvement plan:

1. Clearly communicating a problem or problems tied to a standard of performance (see Section 6D)
2. Helping a teacher set effective goals (see Section 7C)
3. Recommending specific actions the teacher can take to learn new skills, improve his/her own performance, and ultimately improve student learning (see Section 7D)

If you have developed skill and fluency in the competencies involved in less stringent interventions, you will be well equipped to tackle this high-stakes level. The process outlined on the following pages should feel familiar and not overwhelming.

MASTERING THE 4-PHASE APPROACH TO IMPROVEMENT PLANS

An improvement plan needs to be structured to address two learning gaps:

1. The *teacher learning gap:* deficits in the teacher's knowledge of skills, concepts, or content that affect his or her ability to deliver quality instruction
2. The *student learning gap:* poor student performance that can be linked to or results from gaps in the teacher's learning

Designing and monitoring the implementation of a good improvement plan takes place in phases that build upon one another. The phases help you and the assistance team save time and energy and enable the team and teacher to be as productive as possible.

Phase 1: Analyze the Data and Focus the Work

The first phase of analyzing and focusing gets all parties on the same route with the same end points in mind. It involves three crucial tasks described in detail later in the chapter: (1) identifying the target problems, (2) developing teacher and student learning goals, and (3) verifying causes. They can be completed fairly quickly. The better the quality of the preliminary work done by the evaluator—from data collection to the formal problem statement—the more efficient the team can be.

Phase 2: Structure Teacher Self-Assessment and New Learning

The second phase of work involves designing what the teacher will do to take responsibility for improvement. The team identifies structures for self-assessment that include collecting baseline data on students' current opportunities to develop identified skills. We use this term *opportunities* deliberately to highlight inequities that result when some students have the bad luck to draw a teacher who cannot adequately help them. Struggling practitioners often blame students and their families for poor results, an attribution that only increases their sense of helplessness and gives them excuses to avoid taking any positive action. Focusing teachers on the number and quality of opportunities they provide emphasizes what is actually under their control and minimizes the blame game. It helps individuals start to "own" the idea that they can change their current results.

Phase 3: Structure Guided Application and Feedback

Phase 3 requires the teacher to apply what s/he learned in Phase 2. If the target problems have to do with instruction, Phase 3 immerses the individual in the plan-teach-assess-reflect, and then plan again cycle with built-in opportunities to get feedback and coaching from others, if needed. Strategies and actions often require the teacher to plan and deliver a series of three to five lessons that involve the newly learned practices and an assessment of their effect on students. At this point the focus widens to include attention to student learning as well as teacher learning. Therefore the individual also collects evidence that these lessons are having the desired impact on student performance.

Phase 4: Plan for Independent Application and Monitoring

Two types of low-performing individuals will not proceed beyond Phase 3:

1. Individuals who had a well-defined and bounded problem and "discovered" that they were capable of fixing it with good support and coaching
2. Individuals who floundered, stalled, or were unable or unwilling to do what was needed to show sufficient growth and new competence

The first type is rare; the second is more likely. Most often with long-term ineffective performers, some progress will be present. However, you and the team will not yet be convinced that the teacher can keep functioning at the new level of proficiency once the intense scrutiny and support has been removed. Thus, Phase 4 becomes critical—for the teacher, the students, and your sanity. *Sustainability* is the keyword for this phase. The team asks the teacher to continue to use all the techniques learned and applied in Phases 2 and 3 consistently, thoughtfully, and at a proficient level without others routinely present for a period of several months. Data sources are often random, unannounced visits, observations, or artifact checks combined with checks on how students are doing on meeting their performance goal(s).

Planning in phases lets you make a decision at several key points to stop the plan if it is producing no significant improvements in performance. Those decision points are shown in Figure 8B.1. Note that Phases 1 (goal setting) and 2 (self-assessment and new learning) combined could be considered to fulfill a contractual requirement for an improvement plan. If the teacher cannot successfully carry out the self-assessment strategies called for in Phase 2, there is little likelihood of success for the application and integration phases. As the flow chart indicates, you may choose to discontinue the extended planning at this point.

Figure 8B.1 Decision Points in the Planning Process

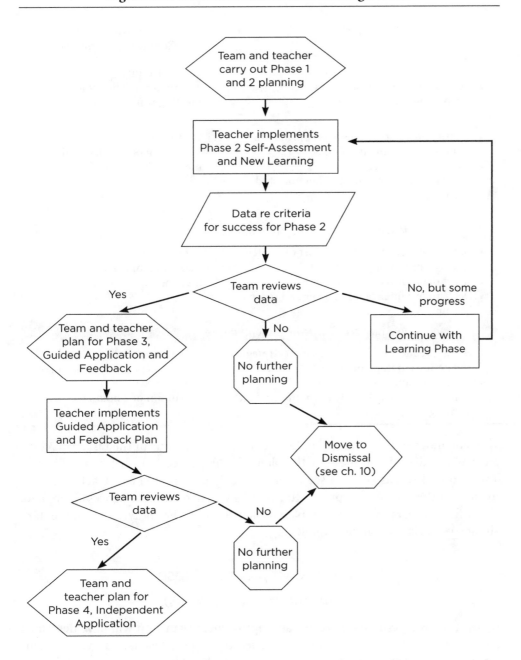

UNDERSTANDING THE CRUCIAL TASKS OF 4-PHASE PLANNING

Within each phase you will need to complete certain tasks. Figure 8B.2 summarizes the complete improvement plan process including these tasks. In most cases it will unfold over anywhere from 10 weeks to 8 months depending on the complexities of the problems chosen and the teacher's progress in rectifying the deficiencies. This chart also contains estimates of the actual meeting time required to help you plan and communicate with the team. Notice that the steps in Phases 2, 3, and 4 are almost identical. You undertake the same type of activity in these steps although your overall purpose for the step will be different.

Figure 8B.2 Overview of Improvement Planning and Monitoring

	Tasks	Estimate of Time Commitment for Team
Phase One **Analysis and focus.**	• Identify the target problems. • Develop teacher and student learning goals. • Verify causes for problem(s).	1 to 2 meetings Maximum of 2 hours total meeting time
Phase Two **Teacher self-assessment and new learning.**	• Identify broad **strategies** and appropriate **actions** to implement them. • Select **data sources**. • Determine **evidence** for teacher and student learning.	2-3 meetings Maximum of 3 hours total meeting time
Analyze data and decide whether to continue.		
Phase Three **Guided application and feedback.**	• Design, refine, or review next set of **strategies** and **actions** to implement. • Select **data sources**. • Determine **evidence** for teacher and student learning.	1-2 meetings Maximum of 2.5 hours of meeting time
Analyze data and decide whether to continue.		
Phase Four **Independent application and monitoring.**	• Design, refine, or review next set of **strategies** and **actions** to implement. • Select **data sources**. • Determine **evidence** for teacher and student learning.	1-2 meetings, which would include a review of phase three evidence Maximum of 2 hours

The remainder of this chapter contains detailed discussions of the tasks you complete as you design and monitor the plan. The first three tasks happen only once. The second three, as you can see in Figure 8B.2, are repeated as a teacher "passes the test" at the end of each phase. To help you visualize how the process is applied, you'll find an example of a completed plan for Mrs. Friendly and commentary about specific choices in Section 8C.

Tasks to Complete in Phase 1

Identify the Target Problem(s).

By the time you get to the need for an improvement plan, you will have described and communicated the problem(s) and tried to help the teacher address the deficiencies. All this preliminary work must be completed before a team assembles or you and the teacher start planning. There should be no surprises for the teacher and no new information from the evaluator(s) at this stage.

The primary evaluator summarizes the identified and communicated problem(s) for the team, who then share the challenging task of selecting a focus for the plan from the many possibilities. Do not tackle all the documented problem areas at once. Making too many commitments often undermines sustained practice with new techniques and good follow-up. Start by seeing whether the teacher is able to demonstrate sustained improvement in practice on one or two worthwhile targets. Because problems overlap and feed into one another, improvement in one domain often transfers to other areas. Think of the Pareto Principle: 80% of the problems can be solved by focusing on the "vital 20%" (Conzemius 2012 47).

Figure 8B.3 suggests criteria for selecting "power problems" that will likely have the most improvement leverage. Much of this will be familiar to readers of Chapters 6 and 7.

Figure 8B.3 Criteria for Selecting Problems

The target problem:
- Will lead to some immediately recognizable impact on students' opportunities to learn or actual performance in 3-8 months
- Will likely have a positive effect on other problem areas ("the vital 20%")
- Requires change that is more substantive than simple compliance with policies and procedures
- Is not caused primarily by the organization's failure to provide professional development, practice, feedback, and coaching
- Has the teacher's agreement as a first choice for effort, if possible.

Most districts are permitted to share data on a "need to know basis" with administrators and evaluators who interact with the teacher. Consult with your local school attorney about privacy rights of the teacher in relation to sharing evaluation data with a team of peers and evaluators or with any third parties.

**Legal Note 8B.1
Sharing
Confidential Data**

Develop Teacher and Student Learning Goals

This task requires skill and patience. Ownership of improvement is more likely when teachers have choices and develop a stake in monitoring their own goals. However, the inability to set and pursue effective goals is itself a symptom of ineffective performance. The team will need to be directive. Consider drafting several possibilities and letting the teacher have influence by choosing which makes the most sense. Most important, teams must set goals for the student growth that should result from teacher learning. The goals for students establish the moral purpose, not just the legal purpose, for improvement. Figure 8B.4 gives criteria to help in choosing effective goals for improvement plans (see also Section 7C).

Figure 8B.4 Criteria for High-Quality Goals

An effective teacher goal
- Is directly aligned to the identified problem and the relevant performance standard.
- Addresses only one problem or piece of a problem.
- Meets the standard for a SMART goal (see Figure 7C.5).
- Can be implemented in a specific context but is transferable to other curricula areas, e.g., skills in questioning to stimulate thinking in mathematics would be transferable to social studies and science
- Cannot be met by simply complying with policies or procedures but requires a complex change of practice

An effective student goal
- Focuses on a worthwhile outcome
- Is appropriately aligned to the identified problem and the relevant curriculum standard
- Meets the standard for a SMART goal
- Measures progress using district-adopted benchmarks or summative assessments

---

Verify Reported Causes of Problem(s)

Goals set the end learning points for the plan. However, they do not explain why the teacher has been unable to reach such targets in previous efforts. The actions to help the teacher reach a goal should signal what the planners recognize as the causes of the problem. It is likely that earlier intervention efforts will have surfaced at least some assumptions about why the problem exists. At this stage, stop and confirm the legitimacy of those assumptions or figure out the most likely causes of the problem if none have been offered thus far. Doing so allows everyone to anticipate potential impediments to improvement and to *choose strategies and actions that explicitly target those underlying causes.* Causes for performance deficiencies tend to fall into three general categories:

1. **Lack of expertise**, i.e., not having the necessary knowledge or skills for the work required, seems to be the most commonly noted. Most effective plans, therefore, should include requirements for the teacher to acquire and consistently apply new knowledge and skills.
2. **Lack of conviction**, manifested by *debilitating beliefs* regarding student's ability to learn, often interacts with lack of expertise, and the two may be hard to separate. Teachers who lack conviction may commonly be labeled "burned out" (if they have ever been on fire) or "retired on the job." They have ceased learning and readily blame others for their failure to make an impact.
3. **External influences** including marital problems, financial challenges, health problems, or substance abuse may undermine performance.

Though it is appropriate to give teachers time to work through personal issues, months can turn into years of ineffective teaching that significantly impedes student learning. The team cannot address external influences, so it should choose goals that address the symptoms resulting from the teacher's preoccupation with external issues: lack of feedback to students, low-level tasks, or poor planning.

In order to verify causes effectively, teams need to examine current operating assumptions about why the problem exists, brainstorm additional possible explanations, and ask for additional data as needed. The process must include listening to the teacher's explanations. Expect that the well-practiced explanations the teacher provides will include many external factors. It is important not to shut teachers down or accuse them of dodging and excuse mongering even if you, the evaluator, have heard the litany a hundred times. Some of the familiar explanations may be wholly or partially correct and will help you select appropriate strategies. Figure 8B.5 offers some criteria for high-quality cause analysis.

Figure 8B.5 Criteria for High-Quality Cause Analysis

High-quality analysis of root causes
- Strives for honest, open exchanges of information and avoids accusation
- Tries to get beyond symptoms to what underlies or explains the problem
- Surfaces perceptions that are unsupported by data but persist in influencing the teacher's actions
- Reveals evaluator's faulty assumptions—those not supported by data—about what may be causing the problem
- Takes place in the teacher's presence whether or not the teacher agrees to contribute

---

To develop a successful plan, the team needs to learn how the teacher perceives the situation and the narrative s/he has told herself about why the problem is happening. Often the root cause of the problem is hidden under a sea of excuses because the teacher feels s/he lacks the competence required to teach at a high-impact level. The team will likely need to contribute explanations that focus on internal factors within the control of the teacher that can be addressed during the action planning.

Analysis and focusing work takes one or two short, well-organized meetings. Once a focus for the teacher's efforts has been selected, you design a series of interconnected tasks that help the teacher learn new skills and content, apply her learning, and sustain improvement.

REPEATING TASKS TO CARRY OUT PHASES 2, 3, AND 4

Identify Strategies and Actions

Strategies are general, comprehensive statements that tell the teacher what to do in what order. Taken alone, they often do not provide enough scaffolding and guidance for a low-performing teacher. Actions, fleshed out after the strategies have been chosen, tell the teacher how to go about the implementation. They are the "To Do" list of techniques and practices to be carried out by the teacher in order to attain the learning goal(s). In this step, you also identify the resources needed to support plan implementation. These might include any of the following: models, criteria, reference material, assistance from an identified team member, released time for visiting, or money for professional learning.

Strategies and actions should be grounded in solid research and practice. For possible strategies and actions, you can turn to a number of different sources including:

- The expertise of team members
- Support material for implementing new standards and programs provided by the state or the program publishers
- Techniques presented in well-respected training programs the district has provided in the past or available online
- Observations of—or consultations with—highly effective teachers in the building.

- The goals and commitments adopted by a school or professional communities that have been successful in getting the kind of student learning you seek.

As a starting point for identifying instructional resources, please refer to *The Skillful Teacher: Building Your Teaching Skills* (2008).

As you and the team specify strategies and actions, make distinctions between technical and adaptive approaches to tackling performance problems. *Technical approaches* require minimal change in behavior and can be met through implementing routines and procedures such "posting objectives" or "submitting lesson plans every Friday." The advantage of asking for technical adjustments is that they can be easily measured and checked off for compliance. However, do not stop there. Neither posting objectives nor submitting lesson plans by itself improves planning. Design some steps that will require new learning and result in change in behavior and mindsets: *adaptive changes*. Adaptive changes force people out of their comfort zones; they require more resources of time, coaching, and monitoring but are likely to produce longer term, sustained improvement (Heifetz and Linsky 2002). Figure 8B.6 suggests criteria for high-quality strategies and actions in improvement planning.

Figure 8B.6 Criteria for High-Quality Strategies and Actions

High-quality strategies and actions listed in a plan should:
- Be based on research or evidence that they produce good results
- Be organized from simpler to more complex
- Focus on what the teacher will do, not on what helpers or students will do
- Be consistent with practices used by proficient and highly effective teachers within the district
- Cite supporting material and personnel resources when they are necessary for successful implementation
- Be at a reasonable level of task difficulty for the time allocated
- Show what the team thinks are the likely root causes of the teacher's difficulty

Select Data Sources

To avoid confusion later, the team should agree on what sources of data will be used to monitor progress for each strategy and who will collect the data. They also collaborate with the teacher to establish criteria for success. Chapter 4 provides teams with a menu for selection, together with examining questions. Even in the more directive improvement plan level, you will continue to involve the teacher in data collection. However, evaluators assume greater responsibility for gathering information about performance in relation to criteria. Done properly, the data sources listed and their accompanying criteria for success clearly reveal how progress will be monitored and what the team will consider to be evidence of a good performance. In other words, they make transparent what it takes to be rated as proficient. Figure 8B.7 lists criteria for determining good sources of data to monitor each strategy and action area.

Figure 8B.7 Criteria for Sources of Data to Monitor Strategies

Data should
- Come from multiple sources to be collected by both the teacher and the evaluator(s)
- Be carefully aligned with and support the strategies and actions
- Provide evidence about the quality of implementation
- Provide evidence about the impact on student learning
- Be readily available and reasonable to collect as part of implementation

Establish Evidence of Learning

This task requires analyzing the data collected and determining the impact of the teacher's actions both on her own performance and that of her students, i.e., the results of the plan. Criteria for success are frequently listed in this step so that the team members can be clear and consistent about what they will use to assess the teacher's progress and determine whether the plan is working. Figure 8B.8 lists attributes of good evidence to assess a teacher's progress on meeting the goals of the improvement plan.

Figure 8B.8 Criteria for Evidence of a Teacher's Progress

Effective evidence of a teacher's progress:
- Links logically to the teacher and student learning goals.
- Is derived from the analysis of several data sources
- Assesses the extent of progress against clearly identified criteria by answering questions of number, degree, ratio and proportion, duration, or quality
- Highlights what an activity accomplished and what skills the teacher was able to demonstrate rather than the fact that an activity was completed.

POST-PLAN STRATEGIES

The backslider is the bane of an evaluator with conviction. You have undoubtedly encountered individuals who can follow a detailed recommendation or even meet the goals of an improvement plan with extensive support. However, the following year they default to old bad habits when the support and oversight structures have been removed. While you cannot always prevent backsliding, you can reduce it by being strategic about
- Conducting routine supervision and evaluation during the post-plan year
- Influencing and monitoring any required individual or professional growth plans
- Establishing expectations for collaboration and participation in professional learning communities and monitoring the results

Supervision and Evaluation during the Post-Plan Year

During the post-plan year, be vigilant in monitoring teachers' practice to ensure that they can sustain the improvement in performance produced by the improvement plan. District requirements for follow-up or strictures about continued scrutiny of teachers who have been on a plan differ. You may have to conduct your monitoring activities informally as part of your day-to-day leadership activities. Look for opportunities to sustain the work from the plan. Select from the following repertoire:

- **Conduct required formal observations early in the year** and target lessons that teach and assess skills identified as deficits the previous year.
- **Conduct results conferences** where the teacher brings multiple sources of data from a completed unit, e.g.; unit goals, assessments (formative and summative), and work samples from targeted students.
- **Establish checkpoints** during which you have the teacher provide updates on students' progress with supporting data.
- **Use short visits to interview students.** Ask about the skills targeted in the improvement plan and examine work samples. Use questions such as "What skill are you practicing or applying during this task? When or how did you learn to do this work?" (see Chapter 4 C).
- **Compare and contrast grade-level benchmark assessment results** and request that the teacher design appropriate instructional modifications if there are continued discrepancies.
- **Complete a thorough summative evaluation.** Guard against let down or cockeyed optimism. If necessary, document backsliding and prepare for teacher dismissal (see Chapter 10).

Influencing Professional Growth Plans

Almost all districts have professional growth plans based on goal setting. These processes frequently result in a list of low-level activities and deadline-driven compliance. Encourage teachers who are transitioning off a plan to continue their focus on the skills they were learning as part of the plan—or to build student competencies that were identified as lacking during their original goal setting. Specify "next step" goals for professional learning based on Phase 4 results. When possible, align goals with collaborative goals identified by the teachers' team or department.

Collaboration in Professional Learning Communities or Teams

In the post-plan year, expect that the teacher will be a full participant and contributor to his or her team or professional learning community (PLC). Clearly some matching and adjustments may be needed. If you have flexibility, changing the composition of the team, especially the team leader, might be helpful. (For more information on building strong learning teams, see *The Skillful Leader II: Confronting Conditions That Undermine Learning.*) You can also do the following:

- **Adopt a protocol that helps teams to structure collaborative solving of student learning problems.** Several protocols would meet this purpose, including the "short cycle" protocol cited in Phase 4 in the sample improvement plan in Example 8C.9 (Love 2008). Whatever protocol you select should require teachers to examine their own data and those of their colleagues and set collective goals for instruction. Consider using protocols that include analysis of student errors.
- **Observe teams and collect data on the target teacher's participation.** Of spe-

cial interest would be meetings where teachers, based on previously made agreements, individually report on what they did and what they learned.

- **Gather evidence of collaboration in regular pre-post observation conferences** with prompts such as "What will I/(did I) see in the lesson that was influenced by your collaboration with your colleagues? "Talk to me specifically about how your collaboration is impacting your instruction."

In the next section, we will look at how this process is applied to a case. There you will also find a completed model plan (Example 8C.9).

8C

LOOKING AT A SAMPLE IMPROVEMENT PLAN

You have a team. You've reviewed the process we introduced in Section B (repeated here as Figure 8C.1 for your convenience). You're ready to go. So how does this work for a typical case, and what does a sample plan look like?

Figure 8C.1 Overview of Improvement Planning and Monitoring

	Tasks	Estimate of Time Commitment for Team
PHASE 1 **Analysis and focus**	• Identify the target problems. • Develop teacher and student learning goals. • Verify causes for problem(s).	1 to 2 meetings Maximum of 2 hours total meeting time
PHASE 2 **Teacher self-assessment and new learning**	• Identify broad **strategies** and appropriate **actions** to implement them. • Select **data sources**. • Determine **evidence** for teacher and student learning.	2-3 meetings Maximum of 3 hours total meeting time
Analyze data and decide whether to continue.		
PHASE 3 **Application and feedback**	• Design, refine, or review next set of **strategies** and **actions** to implement. • Select **data sources.** • Determine **evidence** for teacher and student learning.	1-2 meetings Maximum of 2.5 hours of meeting time
Analyze data and decide whether to continue.		
PHASE 4 **Independent application and monitoring**	• Design, refine, or review next set of **strategies** and **actions** to implement. • Select **data sources.** • Determine **evidence** for teacher and student learning.	1-2 meetings, including a review of Phase 3 evidence Maximum of 2 hours

In the following pages, we'll apply the four phases to produce a plan for Sally Friendly. Each phase of the plan will be illustrated by an example drawn directly from Sally's plan. At the end of this section, you'll find the complete model, Example 8C.9, with all the pieces put together as they would look in a real plan. So that you can use the plan as a model, we tried to make it sufficiently comprehensive and detailed. It will not, however, suit all situations. For your case, some part of the model may give too much detail and another part too little. As you develop a plan with a team or perhaps simply with a teacher, stop and ask yourself "What does it really mean to do X or to assess Y?" If you and your colleagues answer that question with widely varying interpretations for how to proceed, stop and add as much detail as necessary so that all parties are clear about the expectations.

The Case of Sally Friendly

Mrs. Friendly is the prototypical ineffective teacher whose case was introduced in *The Skillful Leader: Confronting Mediocre Teaching* (2000). She is the classic mediocre performer who needs to be on your radar screen. If you can help Sally and others like her improve their methods, a large number of your students will benefit. Several years ago her evaluator documented and communicated several problems, including Sally's ineffective questioning strategies. He reasoned that improving questioning and discussion techniques would be a high-leverage focus affecting planning, expectations, and the rigor of instruction. Sally responded cheerfully and with minimal compliance. However, there were no real changes to her teaching. Results on three years of standardized tests confirmed parents' concerns about both reading and math instruction with the latter being particularly worrisome. Student performance on 8 of 10 subtests either showed little or no growth or fell below grade-level expectations. Internally adopted benchmark assessments on Common Core math practices such as "making sense of problems" and "persevering in solving them" also showed that Sally Friendly's students were at a distinct disadvantage in relation to students in other sections of fifth grade (CCSS.Math.Practice.MP1).

ANALYSIS AND FOCUS PHASE ILLUSTRATED

Sally's assistance team had three basic tasks to accomplish in this phase: (1) identify the target problem, (2) work with Sally to develop goals for her own improvement on the problem and for her students' growth in the target areas, and (3) explore or verify causes for the problem. They accomplished these tasks by using one, 90-minute meeting. At the end of that first meeting, they assigned a subcommittee to finish drafting the goals with Sally. At the start of their next session, they reviewed and refined the goals for 15 minutes.

Identify the Target Problem

On her final performance evaluation, Sally Friendly's evaluator rated her as unsatisfactory in several areas. The team recognized they could not tackle all of the areas in one plan. Because of the repeated pattern of difference in math scores between Mrs. Friendly's students and those of her colleagues, they decided to focus specifically on addressing the inequities resulting from her weak implementation of the math program. They noted the evaluator's evidence that students routinely encountered low-challenge tasks requiring formulaic computation rather than the rigorous lessons and challenging problems outlined in the curriculum. They also noted that that issue occurred only in Mrs. Friendly's class. It was not pervasive across the grade level or school, which would have indicated more of an institutional problem.

The need to make Sally Friendly's teaching more challenging and more aligned with the curriculum led the team to focus the improvement plan on two high-leverage standards from the district evaluation (Danielson 2013):

Domain 1 Planning and Preparation, Criterion 1a: Demonstrating knowledge
   of content and pedagogy
Domain 3 Instruction, Criterion 3c: Engaging students in learning

Example 8C.1 contains the problem statement that was extracted from the Final Evaluation Summary for Mrs. Friendly.

Example 8C.1 Description of the Problem (s) to be Addressed

Standards Rated as Unsatisfactory:

Domain 1 Planning and Preparation, Criterion 1a: Demonstrating knowledge of content and pedagogy

Domain 3 Instruction, Criterion 3c: Engaging students in learning

Mrs. Friendly does not use content-related pedagogy and skillful instruction to engage her students in rigorous work. She fails to provide opportunities for students to develop deep conceptual understanding and to practice real-world problem solving called for in the district curriculum. The bulk of her questions ask students to recall, identify, and define. Her tasks focus on single-step computational procedures. As a result her students underperform their peers on math items that call for making sense of and solving nonroutine problems (see 2013-2014 Grade 5 _____ Results).

Develop Teacher and Student Learning Goals

Sally Friendly's team prepared to set teacher and student learning goals (see Example 8C.2) by gathering relevant resources, including:

- The past year's performance evaluations
- Student results for the previous three years showing Friendly's trend data compared to that of her colleagues
- Any incident memos drafted by evaluators re Sally Friendly's performance and progress
- Other data: parent letters, disciplinary memos, and conference summaries
- *Webb's Depth of Knowledge* (2005) adopted by school as a source for planning higher level instruction
- The fifth-grade math curriculum
- Common Core math standards for grade 5

To make the plan manageable and give Sally a good chance at success, the team selected three worthwhile "target skills" or competencies that her students would need to master:

1. Identifying and explaining patterns and relationships
2. Explaining math calculations based on models and properties of operations
3. Presenting logical arguments using appropriate mathematical vocabulary

Sally would have to learn what was involved in each of these skills and how to teach them in order to improve students' performance on problem-solving measures. All of the strategies and activities laid out in the various phases of the plan could then be geared to building student capability on these skills.

> ### *Example 8C.2 Learning Goals for Sally Friendly*
>
> **Teacher Learning Goals**
> Mrs. Friendly will demonstrate that she has learned how to
>
> 1. Assess her own tasks, questions, and responses to students for the depth of knowledge they require from students and make changes as necessary to modify the level of challenge when it is not appropriate
> 2. Explicitly teach students three targeted mathematical skills from the grade 5 curriculum that will strengthen their ability to solve problems: (1) identifying and explaining patterns and relationships, (2) explaining math calculations based on models and properties of operations, and (3) presenting logical arguments using appropriate mathematical vocabulary
> 3. Design or faithfully implement math lessons that enable students to make sense of problems and persevere in solving them
>
> **Student Learning Goal(s)**
> As result of improved teacher instruction sustained over the 2nd and 3rd quarter, at least 85 percent of students who have been identified as less than proficient on solving nonroutine problems and explaining their calculations will
>
> 1. Demonstrate significant growth toward proficiency on at least two of the target skills when they are asked to respond orally or in writing during post-assessments
> 2. Demonstrate proficiency in identification of patterns and relationships and application of models and properties of operations on appropriate third-quarter benchmark assessments of nonroutine problem solving

Verify Causes for Problems

Before moving to Phase 2, the assistance team paused to consider the causes for Sally Friendly's poor performance. In earlier encounters with her evaluator or some of the team members, Sally Friendly had offered various reasons for her struggles. They ranged from "kids' poor attention spans as a result of too much screen time" and "no one wants to have fun with math anymore" to "my previous evaluator never gave me any feedback." Her explanations were laced with excuses that placed responsibility on others and revealed her underlying belief that her students would not be able to handle the more challenging math. Mrs. Friendly's team listened to her explanations but also theorized that Sally

- Was afraid she might lose control of class or that students would not like her if she changed her practice
- Lacked the background knowledge and skills needed to effectively teach thinking and improve her questioning. In spite of the professional development, she never learned how to carry out the kind of instruction demanded by the new program
- Had not been provided with sufficient exemplars and experiences to give her models for what she was being asked to do
- Assumed her colleagues' instruction was the same as hers when in fact it was very different

Ultimately, the team decided they had sufficient evidence to suggest that a large portion of Mrs. Friendly's poor performance could be attributed to lack of skill or knowledge. Despite participating in a variety of professional development experiences, she never learned how to apply the training and provide the kind of instruction required. Furthermore, she did not have an image of what rigorous instruction would look like or how differently her colleagues taught. Although it was evident that some of Sally's present beliefs about students' capacities were also interfering with her learning, the team decided to tackle those indirectly. If Sally's students could demonstrate higher levels of performance as a result of better quality instruction, Sally would have evidence to challenge her beliefs. They agreed to keep those underlying causes in mind as they selected strategies and activities for the next phases of the plan.

SELF-ASSESSMENT AND LEARNING PHASE ILLUSTRATED

Phase 2 emphasizes teacher learning. In their second meeting, the assistance team spent 15 minutes reviewing and accepting Sally's goals. Then they moved on to identifying the strategies and actions Sally should undertake, determining the data to be collected, and defining what would constitute evidence for the learning they hoped would occur. Their objective was to help Sally identify and take responsibility for specific discrepancies between her math instruction and its poor outcomes and other methods shown to produce consistently better results. At the end of 75 minutes, they had a good working draft and assigned Sally's coach and evaluator to flesh out the details, clean up the language, and email the plan for comments and approval within three days. Sally's coach then had a brief meeting with her to make sure she understood what she would be doing and to build a schedule.

Identify Strategies and Actions

To help her focus, Mrs. Friendly's team selected three strategies listed in boldface in Example 8C.3. These strategies were matched to the likely causes for her struggles that they had identified in their first meeting. Sally, like many underperforming teachers, could not visualize what a high-level performance looked like. She needed skill building in collecting and analyzing data, and she had to face the reality that her students were underperforming their peers in other classes. Under each strategy, the group discussed and listed action steps to guide Sally's implementation.

Example 8C.3 Strategies and Actions: Self-assessment phase for Sally Friendly

1. **Observe for specific examples of expected performance.**
   - With your designated coach, observe at least two math lessons that demonstrate how to get students actively engaged in abstract reasoning and challenging problem-solving. Target your data collection on the depth of knowledge required by the tasks students are doing, the questions teachers ask, and the kinds of responses students are required to produce. Record the exact questions teachers ask and their responses to student answers.

- Use Webb's DOK chart (2005) dese.mo.gov to independently categorize tasks, questions, and responses to student answers. Compare your analysis with your coach.

2. **Collect and analyze data on your own performance.**
   - Arrange to have a math lesson videotaped or observed by someone who will take literal notes. Analyze and categorize the level of the tasks and demands for abstract reasoning, including:
     — Having students identify and explain patterns and relationships
     — Asking students to explain calculations based on models and properties of operations
     — Requiring students to present a logical argument for strategies selected
   - Review the notes or video. Identify opportunities seized or missed to have students display or practice the skills and reflect on why that happened.
   - Name the teaching skill gaps evident from your analysis.

3. **Identify and pursue further training.**
   - Work with your coach to find and begin participation in appropriately matched coursework, workshops, online resources, and the like.
   - Seek and study print and video resources that illustrate how targeted skills can be taught and assessed.

As you look at the strategies and actions for Phase 2 in Example 8C.3, note the following features of Sally Friendly's plan:

- The team does not just tell Mrs. Friendly to observe someone. They make sure she is accompanied by and has the support of a coach or peer who is skilled at taking literal notes and analyzing the findings so that Sally Friendly will actually be able to see and name the critical elements that are present in the classrooms she visits.

- A common framework adopted by the district—in this case Webb's Depth of Knowledge—anchors the analysis of and reflection on the data.

- To demonstrate ownership of the process, Mrs. Friendly must complete an independent analysis that provides data about her level of understanding. However, a coach will immediately verify that the findings and labels are accurate and give her feedback to correct misconceptions.

- The team makes the teacher jointly responsible for naming the teaching gaps and gives her a say in selecting the methods she uses to learn new skills.

Select Data Sources and Determine Evidence of Learning

The assistance team must align the data collection to the problem and the student skill deficits that Mrs. Friendly will be trying to overcome. As Example 8C.4 demonstrates, the plan calls for her to collect data on the specific aspects of practice that she has not yet mastered. She must also provide artifacts to show her level of understanding of the difference between her own and others' practice. Note that the artifacts also include guidelines for how data should be represented and analyzed so that Sally can gain experience in using data effectively. Ultimately, these artifacts document the quality of effort invested by the teacher. They also identify where new learning or remediation may be needed.

Example 8C.4 Data Sources and Evidence of Learning: Self-assessment phase for Sally Friendly

	Data Source(s) (T)= Teacher prepares and provides (E) = Evaluator or designee provides	Evidence of Learning
Strategy 1 Observe	**Artifact** (T) Chart or other appropriate display that represents the distribution of questions and responses across DOK levels in each classroom observed.	Mrs. Friendly accurately categorizes the tasks students are doing, the levels of questions teachers ask, and teacher responses using Webb's Depth of Knowledge; accuracy to be determined by the designated coach.
Strategy 2 Analyze	**Artifact** (T) Written reflection using the following stems: 1. *Comparing the data from my own performance to data from observations, I can identify the following differences in how the teacher provides opportunities for students to develop the target skills:* 2. *Findings suggest I need support and resources to improve my teaching of the following*	Mrs. Friendly's analysis and reflection . Identifies critical differences supported by data . Accurately notes skills to be strengthened
Strategy 3 Identify training	**Artifact** (T) Learning Activity Log showing . Meetings, course work, and other study undertaken to acquire better knowledge of instruction that builds target skills . Resources used . Implications for instruction	The Learning Activity Log documents . Significant and appropriate effort to learn how targeted skills should be taught . Growth in understanding about how to apply learning and improve instruction going forward

---

As you look at the evidence for learning in Phase 2, keep in mind that this evidence determines whether the teacher can move into Phase 3, Application of New Learning. The team should see clear signs that the teacher

- Has gained new insights about what she needs to do and how she might proceed from the activities and reflections in Phase 2
- Is able to learn new skills and willing to put in the time and effort to do so
- Will admit that the problem exists and take responsibility for actions to fix it

If the evidence of learning is insufficient, the team has two choices: repeat Phase 2 or declare the plan finished and begin the move to dismissal.

In Example 8C.4 note that

- The teacher provides all the evidence
- Evidence in this phase is collected on teacher learning goals on the assumption that teacher learning precedes student learning
- Criteria for success that define a quality performance are clearly designated to move evidence beyond task completion

GUIDED APPLICATION AND FEEDBACK PHASE ILLUSTRATED

The third and fourth assistance team meetings were held within a week of one another. In their third 90-minute meeting, the group reviewed the evidence of Sally Friendly's learning in Phase 2. They agreed that her insights were modest, but she clearly exhibited ownership and a willingness to work at making changes. The evidence showed she could accurately identify the planning and new behaviors that she needed to practice until she could make them automatic. Thus she was ready to move to Phase 3 to determine whether she could translate her learning into making a difference in the classroom. After that review, the team and Sally discussed what strategies and actions she would use to apply her learning and help students acquire one of the target skills identified in her goal and what data she should begin to collect. At the end of the 90 minutes, they had roughed out the strategies, actions, and most of the data to be collected. The team agreed to meet briefly the following week to finish the evidence for learning and make sure this phase of the plan was clear and manageable. To speed up the process, Sally's evaluator and the math curriculum specialist agreed to return with a reaction draft of evidence for learning. Once the plan was adopted, the team set the date, roughly a month away, on which they would review Sally's progress on Phase 3.

Identify Strategies and Actions

Example 8C.5 shows the broad strategies the team identified (in boldface) and the specific actions they outlined in order to help Sally implement those strategies. Requiring three to five successful lessons during which the teacher demonstrates increasing independence and effectiveness sets a realistic target for application. Note the level of detail in the action steps. Teachers whom you refer to improvement planning will need a similar degree of specificity.

Example 8C. 5 Strategies and Actions: Guided application and feedback for Sally Friendly

1. **Plan a series of 3-5 lessons and develop support materials to explicitly teach one of the targeted abstract reasoning skills to mastery and to help students use that skill to improve their performance in solving nonroutine math problems.**
   - With coach or colleague, complete one model lesson focused on direct instruction of thinking skills using the agreed-upon lesson plan framework attached. Use the exemplar to support subsequent independent planning.
   - Develop and routinely use visual supports (e.g., posters or charts) with guidelines and criteria for success for solving nonroutine problems.
   - Submit lesson plans and materials for feedback from math curriculum specialist or designated expert coach; use feedback to make adjustments to the plans prior to implementation and keep a record of those adjustments.

2. **Implement the planned series of lessons and collect formative assessment data on student performance.**
   - Administer, score, and record a pre-test. Use results to fine-tune the first of several lesson plans as needed. Make notes of modifications.
   - Arrange to be taped or observed implementing at least one of the first set of lesson plans and to get feedback on consistency of implementation, particularly of questioning requiring students to use abstract reasoning and mathematical vocabulary. Use feedback to modify subsequent lessons as necessary.
   - Collect samples of student work on tasks designed to provide them with practice on the targeted skills.

The choice of strategies and actions for Sally Friendly follow certain general principles that you can use no matter what content or set of skills you are helping the teacher tackle:

1. Require the teacher to replicate the cycle of thinking, planning, implementation, and analysis expected by whatever performance standard she is trying to meet for multiple iterations.
2. Focus on teaching students something worthwhile or challenging so that the teacher learns how to dig into the content or analyze prerequisites and does not assume you want a "dog and pony show."
3. Provide templates, guidelines, or criteria for what a high-quality artifact such as a lesson plan or homework project would contain.
4. Specifically identify elements of implementation that are essential for student success such as the visual supports (posters or charts) for problem solving in the plan.

As you look at the strategies and actions for Phase 3 in Example 8C.5, notice that Sally Friendly's work was heavily structured to help her practice and internalize the new ways of interacting with and collecting data from her students. The actions required by the plan make her apply formative assessment and use findings to shape subsequent lessons and identify opportunities for re-teaching. Thus both the teacher and team have information about how well the practices are working for students. The team can determine whether the teacher recognizes ongoing student needs and takes responsibility for the next steps.

Select Data Sources and Determine Evidence of Learning

Once the strategies and actions have been determined, the team must decide what data should be collected to reveal how the application of the actions is working and what they should see in the data to tell them the teacher has been successful. Entries in Sally's plan for this phase (Example 8C.6) show that:

- The amount of data the supervisor must collect increases from Phase 2.
- The data sources shift from self-reports and reflections to teacher-developed work products such as annotated lesson plans, lists of criteria, and pre- and post-tests.
- The teacher and supervisor begin collecting student impact data such as students practicing the target skills, interviews with students, and samples of student work.

	Data Source(s) (T)= Teacher prepares and provides (E) = Evaluator or designee provides	Evidence of Learning
Strategy 1 Plan	**Artifact(s)** (T) Annotated lesson plans (T) Samples of guidelines and criteria posters	Lesson plans contain • Clear student learning outcomes that identify the target skills • A short pre-post assessment • Identification of techniques (e.g., graphic organizers, modeling thinking aloud) for direct instruction on skills • Carefully designed prompts and questions to provide students with opportunities to use the targeted skills • Practice tasks to provide students with opportunities to use the targeted skills • Appropriate means of checking for understanding • Annotations indicating changes made after feedback
Strategy 2 Implement	**Artifacts** (T) Pre- and post-tests: samples, results, and teacher analysis and reflections (T) Annotated lesson plans (T) Samples of student work from lessons **Observation and Interview Notes and Feedback** Some combination of (E) Unannounced brief visits with feedback (E) Full lesson observation (E) Students' behaviors and their: 　　1. Understanding of skills to be mastered 　　2. Application of the skills 　　3. Persistence in problem-solving	Lesson plans and discussions with the team show appropriate modifications based on data from pre-tests and observations. Observation notes and conference summary show that Mrs. Friendly provided multiple, well-aligned opportunities for students to learn about and appropriately practice the skill(s) identified in the learning goal. At least 75% of students' work, interview comments, and observed behavior show that they are successfully meeting or making appropriate progress toward meeting the student learning goal.

Example 8C.6 Data Sources and Evidence for Learning:
Guided application phase for Sally Friendly

As you look at the evidence of learning identified for Phase 3, notice that the team is trying to assess whether Mrs. Friendly can transfer some of her coaching and training, first with some support and then independently, at a proficient level. To make sure all members agree on key indicators of proficiency and to make sure that Sally Friendly knows how her progress will be assessed, the team will also do the following:

· Establish explicit criteria to be used to assess the quality of the lesson plan.
· Specify what should be evident in the observation notes, work products, and conference summary.
· Focus attention on student needs such as the need to start to fix skill deficiencies. The team specifies that part of the discussion about success in this phase will be student growth toward meeting the learning goal set by the teacher.

Leader Alert
Make Sure the Team Agrees on and Communicates Criteria
for Success

Especially when it comes to establishing evidence for learning, examine the clarity of the criteria that define successful performance. In Example 8C.5 you might feel a need to specify more clearly what criteria would help the team determine successful learning beyond "Lesson plans and discussion show appropriate responses to data from pre-tests" by defining "appropriate" so that all members assess it in the same way. This might require building a small rubric of indicators to help substantiate "appropriate." ◆

INDEPENDENT APPLICATION AND MONITORING
PHASE ILLUSTRATED

Because they had not met during Sally's guided application phase, the assistance team set aside a 2-hour slot to analyze progress and plan. In the first hour, they listened to reports and reviewed the results of Phase 3. All parties agreed that Mrs. Friendly had needed significant coaching and help for her first two lessons. However by the end of the fifth try, she had demonstrated she was *capable* of designing and delivering more coherent, rigorous instruction. Sally observed that teaching to the standard the team set forth had been difficult and "a lot of work," but she felt she had learned a great deal. Acknowledging her sense of growth and their own assessment that the new way of teaching was not yet automatic or ingrained, the team chair explained the purpose of the final phase. To complete the improvement process, Mrs. Friendly must be able to show (1) that she could continue the more proficient instruction and (2) that she would not revert to old behaviors and undermine the training as she had once before. Sally would therefore use what she had learned in teaching the first of the three target skills to mastery to teach the remaining two skills named in her learning goal. In the second hour of the meeting, the group completed the details of actions and evidence for Phase 4.

Identify Strategies and Actions

As Example 8C.7 illustrates, strategies and actions in the final phase contain fewer detailed guidelines and are less structured. That decision signals the team's assumption that Sally should now know what must be done and be able to function independently or seek appropriate assistance if necessary.

Example 8C.7 Strategies and Actions:
Independent application phase for Sally Friendly

1. Apply the short cycle of improvement process (plan, teach, assess, reflect, plan) independently or in collaboration with your grade-level colleagues to reach the identified student learning goal.
   - Use the cycle for introducing, teaching, and assessing the remaining target skills and for any re-teaching needs that are identified in your analysis of results.

- Keep records of assessments designed/used, new materials created or used, lesson plans, and how you have used data to adjust lessons.

2. Monitor the specific behaviors identified in Phase 1, Problem to be Addressed, to make certain they do not recur.

3. Prepare a final reflection(s) on attainment of student and teacher learning goals.

As you look at the strategies and actions for Phase 4, notice the ways in which the team and evaluator are handing responsibility back to the teacher after the period of intense guidance and support:

- Responsibility for monitoring progress toward meeting the improvement plan goals is shared between the teacher and the evaluator.
- The teacher must assess and report on whether students attained the learning goal that was part of the improvement plan.
- The teacher produces a summary reflection on her own learning and student progress that becomes part of the documentation for her final evaluation.

Select Data Sources and Determine Evidence of Learning

Although it is designed for Sally Friendly's plan, Example 8C.8 also illustrates the general principles that govern putting together a case for successful independent application. Most of the teacher-produced data for the Independent Application and Monitoring Phase come from the normal activities of proficient teaching: lesson plans, assessments, and materials created for students. Because the teacher knows these sources will form part of the record of how the plan has worked, there should be no sense of surprise and some incentive for keeping herself attentive and on course.

This is the point of the plan where the evaluator assumes the most significant responsibility for gathering data. Notes from short visits, longer observations, and conferences with the teacher are key to corroborating or challenging Sally's summary assessment and reflection. The latter should include —without prompting— data about how well she has met the original goals.

Finally, the plan includes a variety of assessments of student learning ranging from district benchmark tests and common grade-level assessments to student work and observer notes about students' performance and perceptions. These assessments serve as the sources of data to help Sally and the team determine whether the student learning goal has been attained or how much progress toward meeting that goal has occurred.

Example 8C.8 Data Sources and Evidence for Learning:
Independent application phase for Sally Friendly

	Data Source(s) (T)= Teacher prepares and provides (E) = Evaluator or designee provides	**Evidence of Learning**
Strategy 1 **Apply** **Strategy 2** **Monitor**	**Artifact(s)** (T) Samples of assessments, materials, annotated plans, and student work **Observations and post-observation conferences** (E) Minimum of 1 short visit and 1 unannounced, 30-minute observation **Impact on Students** (T) (E) Impact data on students' behaviors and understanding of skills to be mastered, application of the skills, and persistence in problem solving	Annotations, teacher presentation to team, and sample artifacts include thoughtful analysis of level of challenge in the instruction, adjustments necessary to help students reach the learning goal, and effects of the re-teaching. The majority of tasks, questions to students, and responses to student answers fall into levels 2, 3, or 4 of Webb's Depth of Knowledge. The teacher capitalizes on (i.e., does not miss) the majority of opportunities to have students practice and demonstrate the targeted math skills in their oral and written responses. The range between high and low student performance on using the targeted skills is narrow. When asked, almost all students can explain the skills and when they should be using them.
Strategy 3 **Reflect**	**Artifacts** (T) Final Reflection (T) Annotated lesson plans **Impact on Students** (E) Common and benchmark assessments of non-routine problem-solving (2nd, 3rd, and 4th quarters)	Final reflection highlights and summarizes • Goal attainment supported by relevant data • Next steps for student and teacher learning At least 85% of students previously identified as less than proficient on problem solving score at proficient or above.

As you look at the evidence of learning required for Phase 4, note that

- The supervisor and perhaps some team members expect to analyze both the assessments and the results to determine whether they have measured the skills identified as needing development in the teacher and student goals.
- Evaluating the level of questioning Sally Friendly used routinely and the tasks that she assigned will allow the team to assess whether her understanding of what rigorous instruction should be like has been maintained, evolved, or regressed.
- The team required a significant number of artifacts and observation notes to allow them to look for patterns over time. They did not want to make a decision based on one single example of when Mrs. Friendly carried out the new practices the plan was designed to help her learn.
- The team expects that the teacher will provide data about her own changes and her students' performance as part of her final summary. If she does not do so, then she has not internalized the thinking required by the plan-teach-assess-reflect cycle of improvement.

At the end of Phase 4, the team must decide if the teacher has made sufficient progress, defined in part by the gains for students, to allow her to return to the regular supervision and evaluation track or whether she will be referred for dismissal. In our sample case, Sally's performance has improved significantly. She will be returned to the regular supervision and evaluation track with some provisions for monitoring, such as those outlined in "Post-Plan Strategies" in Section 8B.

Example 8C.9 shows the complete plan for Sally Friendly.

Example 8C.9 Sample Improvement Plan for Sally Friendly

FOCUS FOR IMPROVEMENT

Standards Rated as Unsatisfactory
Domain 1 Planning and Preparation, Criterion 1a: Demonstrating knowledge of content and pedagogy
Domain 3 Instruction, Criterion 3c: Engaging students in learning

Description of the Problem(s) to be Addressed
Mrs. Friendly does not use content-related pedagogy and skillful instruction to engage her students in rigorous work. She fails to provide deep conceptual understanding and opportunities for students to practice the real-world problem solving called for in district curriculum and in the Common Core mathematical practices. The bulk of her questions ask students to recall, identify, and define. Her tasks focus on single-step computational procedures. As a result her students underperform their peers on math items that call for making sense of and solving nonroutine problems (see 2013-2014 Grade 5 _____ Results).

LEARNING GOALS

Teacher Learning Goals
Mrs. Friendly will demonstrate that she has learned how to
1. Assess her own tasks, questions, and responses to students for the depth of knowledge they require from students and make changes as necessary to modify the level of challenge when it is not appropriate
2. Explicitly teach students three targeted mathematical skills from the grade 5 curriculum that will strengthen their ability to solve problems: identifying and explaining patterns and relationships, explaining math calculations based on models and properties of operations, presenting logical arguments using appropriate mathematical vocabulary
3. Design or faithfully implement math lessons that enable students to make sense of problems and persevere in solving them (CCSS MP 1)

Student Learning Goal(s)
As result of improved teacher instruction sustained over the 2nd and 3rd quarters, at least 85% of students who have been identified as less than proficient on solving non-routine problems and explaining their calculations will
1. Demonstrate significant growth toward proficiency on at least two of the target skills when they are asked to respond orally or in writing during post-assessments
2. Demonstrate proficiency in identification of patterns and relationships and application of models and properties of operations on appropriate third-quarter benchmark assessments of nonroutine problem solving

SELF-ASSESSMENT AND LEARNING PHASE		September 24 to October 30
STRATEGY/ACTION	DATA SOURCE(S) (T) = Teacher prepares and provides (E) = Evaluator or designee provides	EVIDENCE OF LEARNING
1. Observe for specific examples of expected performance. • With your designated coach, observe at least two math lessons that demonstrate how to get students actively engaged in abstract reasoning and challenging problem solving. Target your data collection on the tasks students are doing, the questions teachers ask, and the kinds of responses students are required to produce. Record the exact questions teachers ask and their responses to student answers. • Independently categorize tasks, questions, and responses to student answers using Webb's Depth of Knowledge (DOK) as a framework. Compare your analysis with your coach.	**Artifact(s)** (T) Chart or other appropriate display that represents the distribution of questions and responses across DOK levels in each classroom observed.	Mrs. Friendly accurately categorizes the tasks students are doing, the levels of questions teachers ask, and teacher responses using the DOK framework; accuracy to be determined by the designated coach.
2. Collect and analyze data on your own performance. • Arrange to have a math lesson videotaped or observed by someone who will take literal notes. Analyze and categorize the level of the tasks and demands for reasoning abstractly including —Having students identify and explain patterns and relationships —Asking students to explain calculations based on models and properties of operations —Requiring students to present a logical argument for strategies selected • Review the notes or video. Identify opportunities seized or missed to have students display or practice the skills and reflect on why that happened. • Name the teaching skill gaps evident from your analysis.	**Artifact** (T) Written reflection using the following stems: 1. *Comparing the data from my own performance to data from observations, I can identify the following differences in how the teacher provides opportunities for students to develop the target skills:* 2. *Findings suggest I need support and resources to improve my teaching of the following:*	Mrs. Friendly's analysis and reflection • Identifies critical differences supported by data • Accurately notes skills to be strengthened
3. Identify and pursue further training. • Work with your coach to find and begin participation in appropriately matched coursework, workshops, online resources, and the like. • Seek and study print and video resources that illustrate how targeted skills can be taught and assessed.	**Artifact** (T) Learning Activity Log showing • Meetings, coursework, and study to acquire better knowledge of instruction that builds target skills • Resources used • Implications for instruction	The Learning Activity Log documents: • Significant and appropriate effort to learn how targeted skills should be taught • Growth in understanding about how to apply learning and improve instruction going forward

November 1 to January 15

GUIDED APPLICATION AND FEEDBACK PHASE

STRATEGY/ACTION	DATA SOURCE(S)	EVIDENCE OF LEARNING
1. Plan a series of 3-5 lessons and develop support materials to explicitly teach one of the targeted skills to mastery and help students use that skill to improve their performance in solving nonroutine math problems. • With coach or colleague, complete one model lesson focused on direct instruction of thinking skills using the agreed-upon lesson plan framework attached. Use the exemplar to support subsequent independent planning. • Develop and routinely use visual reminders with guidelines and criteria for success for solving nonroutine problems. • Submit lesson plans and materials for feedback from math curriculum specialist or designated expert coach; use feedback to make adjustments to the plans prior to implementation and keep a record of those adjustments.	**Artifacts** (T) • Annotated lesson plans (T) • Samples of guidelines and criteria posters	Lesson plans contain • Clear student learning outcomes that identify the target skills • A short pre-post assessment • Identification of techniques (e.g., graphic organizers, modeling thinking aloud) for direct instruction on skills • Carefully designed prompts and questions to provide students with opportunities to use the targeted skills • Practice tasks to provide students with opportunities to use the targeted skills • Appropriate means of checking for understanding • Annotations indicating changes made after feedback

2. Implement the planned series of lessons and collect formative assessment data on student performance.
• Administer, score, and record pre-test. Use results to fine-tune first several lesson plans as needed. Make notes of modifications.
• Arrange to be taped or observed implementing at least one of the first set of lesson plans and get feedback on consistency of implementation, particularly of question-ing requiring students to use abstract reasoning and mathematical vocabulary. Use feedback to modify subsequent lessons as necessary.
• Collect samples of student work on tasks designed to provide them with practice on the targeted skills.
	Artifacts
	(T) • Pre- and post-tests: samples, results, and teacher reflections
	(T) • Annotated lesson plans
	(T) • Samples of student work from Lesson 5
	
	Observation Notes and Feedback
	Some combination of
	(E) • Unannounced brief visits with feedback
	(E) • Full lesson observation
	(E) • Students' behaviors and their
	  1. Understanding of skills to be mastered
	  2. Application of the skills
	  3. Persistence in problem solving
		Lesson plans and discussions with the team show appropriate modifications based on the data from the pre-tests and observations.
		
		Observation notes and conference summaries show that Mrs. Friendly provided multiple, well-aligned opportunities for students to learn about and appropriately practice the skill(s) identified in the learning goal.
		
		At least 75% of students' work, interview comments, and observed behavior show that they are successfully meeting or making appropriate progress toward meeting the student learning goal.

INDEPENDENT APPLICATION AND MONITORING PHASE		January 15 to March 15
STRATEGY/ACTION	DATA SOURCE(S)	EVIDENCE OF LEARNING
1. **Apply the short cycle of improvement process** (plan, teach, assess, reflect, plan) independently or in collaboration with your grade-level colleagues to reach the identified student learning goal. • Use the cycle for introducing, teaching, and assessing the remaining target skills and for re-teaching needs that are identified in your analysis of results. • Keep records of assessments designed/used, new materials created or used, lesson plans, and adjustments.	**Artifact(s)** (T) Samples of assessments, materials, annotated plans, and student work **Observation and post-observation conference(s)** (E) Minimum of 1 short visit and 1 unannounced, 30-minute observation **Impact on Students** (T) (E) Impact data on students' behaviors and understanding of skills to be mastered, application of the skills, and persistence in problem solving	Annotations, teacher presentation to team, and sample artifacts include thoughtful analysis of level of challenge in the instruction, adjustments necessary to help students reach the learning goal, and effects of re-teaching. The majority of tasks, questions to students, and responses to student answers fall into levels 2, 3, or 4 of Webb's Depth of Knowledge. The teacher capitalizes on (i.e., does not miss) the majority of opportunities to have students display the targeted math skills in their oral and written responses. The range between high and low student performance on using the targeted skills is narrow. When asked, almost all students can explain the skills and when they should be using them.
2. **Monitor the specific behaviors identified in Section 1, Problem to be Addressed** to make certain that they do not recur.		

CHAPTER 9

USING PROGRESSIVE DISCIPLINE

THIS BOOK focuses primarily on taking action against ineffective instruction, an effort best accomplished by using a continuum of interventions. Formal improvement plans anchor one end of that continuum. Sometimes, however, you face a different problem: teachers who fail to meet their contractual obligations or to comply with official policies, practices, and procedures. Such cases call for a different track of escalated interventions called *progressive discipline*. Like a formal improvement plan, progressive discipline is a red-level intervention that can ultimately lead to charges of insubordination and, in a worst case, to dismissal.

Progressive discipline most often addresses noninstructional areas of performance (see Section 4D). These include the following behaviors:

- Missing paperwork
- Tardiness and poor attendance
- Failure to carry out assigned duties
- Minor examples of conduct unbecoming a teacher
- Unprofessional behavior at staff meetings or during team meetings
- Unprofessional communications to parents or to students
- Failure to implement school policies and team agreements
- Failure to carry out a supervisor's directive such as attending a released-time professional learning event

Progressive discipline can also be used in response to safety issues as well as to address problems affecting the classroom and students' opportunities to learn. Such issues include, but are not limited to:

- Ignoring or failing to carry out safety and security protocols and drills
- Violating grading policies
- Ignoring deadlines or requests for information that affect students or school functioning
- Violating disciplinary procedures or agreements
- Failing to adhere to required formats for lesson or unit plans or to follow specified instructional protocols
- Ignoring the specified curriculum
- Failing to return student work in a timely manner
- Misuse or inappropriate use of materials such as unsuitable text selections or incessant use of videos

Choose progressive discipline when any combination of the problems or needs listed in Figure 9.1 exists.

Figure 9.1 When to Use Progressive Discipline

- The problems identified involve following clearly defined policies and agreements, obeying contract provisions, or carrying out assignments and duties.

- The problems identified involve performance standards that define the teachers' professional interactions outside of the classroom, e.g., communication with parents or community, exchanges with colleagues, or lack of attention to professional responsibilities.

- You want to send a clear message that you have high standards for professionalism and will not tolerate behavior that violates those standards.

- You want to test the individual's willingness to comply with relatively simple requirements before embarking on the more comprehensive improvement plan.

- You suspect that this case may lead in the future to dismissal and you realize that arbitrators are more likely to uphold cases involving insubordination versus cases that attempt to establish incompetence (see Chapter 10).

Documenting problems with policy compliance often involves checking off the presence or absence of identified behavior: the teacher is on time or late, the individual gets paperwork in by the deadline and with the required degree of accuracy or does not. Because it is efficient and not as time-consuming as an improvement plan, it is tempting to try a compliance and checklist-based approach for instructional issues. However, remember that progressive discipline alone does not improve teaching or bring about gains in student performance. An ineffective performer can comply with all policies and still be unable to provide high-quality instruction.

Leader Alert
Integrating Progressive Discipline into an Improvement Plan

Some teacher performance standards contain functions such as adhering to curricular guidelines or carrying out routine duties that could be handled using progressive discipline. If poor performance on those functions is part of a teacher's defined problem, you can include required actions that could be monitored using this approach in the improvement plan. For example, suppose you have a case like that of chemistry teacher Lila Belated in Example 6D.3. Lila needs to (1) increase the range and usefulness of formative assessments and (2) provide students with timely feedback. Therefore, you can include a provision in her improvement plan that requires she comply with all department policies governing timelines and procedures for grading and returning student papers. The hybrid improvement plan integrates the simplicity of progressive discipline with actions that seek more substantive change. ◆

USING A THREE-STEP PROCESS TO IMPLEMENT PROGRESSIVE DISCIPLINE

Ken Chapman, an experienced principal and longtime consultant for Research for Better Teaching, recommends a three-step strategy to deal with compliance problems. His approach, which we have modified slightly, allows you to address substandard professional behavior at a relatively nonthreatening level and then escalate the response if an initial interaction does not result in the necessary change. In the following pages, we describe the escalated steps and illustrate each with examples. This approach will not be appropriate for all problems; you will need to match the number of steps you take to the severity of the problem and to the individual's response. Nothing precludes you from skipping directly to Step 3 if the problem at hand merits that approach.

Before you begin to confront an unmet expectation, decide whether you may eventually need to use the evidence of interactions as part of a formal documentation. If you have any indications that the problem may not be resolved immediately or that the individual may backslide into old, unproductive habits, exercise the option to make a written record of your interactions at every stage. Written records of interactions can be placed in two different kinds of files: an unofficial memory aid file you keep in your office to help you recall what has happened and what informal agreements have been made, or the official personnel file. Be cautious about your file notes (see Legal Notes 9.1 and 9.2).

Procedural requirements govern how and when items may be placed in an official personnel file. Most contracts, for example, require that teachers and administrators sign and date any material that is included in a personnel file to indicate they have seen it. Do not assume that you can convert "unofficial" files later if you have not carefully followed district policies. Do not assume your files are "private." In most cases they are discoverable in a dismissal proceeding. (See Legal Note 10.7 for more information about what constitutes public records.)

Legal Note 9.1 Unofficial File Notes

A first meeting could include hearsay evidence for which you lack solid data although you believe the problem indicated might have a basis in fact. You want to make the staff member aware of potential problems and possible responses "should the information prove to be true." Do not get into a battle as to whether something is in fact true or not. Your conversation can focus on perception—thus the meeting can be seen as an attempt to help the teacher change this "perception." Hearsay evidence is not useful as you progress in your discipline. In legal circles, *hearsay* means A says something to B, B makes a statement to C, and C testifies or reports information. Should you decide to move forward with more formal documentation of the problematic behavior, make sure that anyone who provides you with data knows those data will most likely be shared with the individual being disciplined.

Legal Note 9.2 Hearsay Evidence

Step 1: Communicate a Concern and Collect Data

This first step is designed not to discipline the teacher but to make the school or school district's policies and expectations absolutely clear and thus elicit a change in behavior as early as possible. Disciplinary action may not be needed if you are successful with the following strategy:

- Have a face-to-face meeting with the teacher.
- Be specific about your concern(s).
- Give the supporting data that illustrate those concerns and try to find out what is causing the problem.

At this first meeting, you want to uncover and unscramble any misconceptions the staff member may have regarding your expectations and the actions necessary to fix the problem. If your expectations are widely known and met by all other faculty members, your communication can be straightforward. However, you have a greater responsibility to explain your rationale and the necessary outcomes when you seek to set unique expectations. If, for example, you expect a group of fifth-grade teachers—and no one else—to complete and submit lesson plans two days before the lesson, be prepared to spend time clarifying this expectation. Figure 9.2 lists suggestions on how to conduct a first meeting to communicate your specific concern.

Figure 9.2 How to Conduct a First Meeting to Communicate a Concern

- Assume a positive presupposition that the staff member is a person of good will and good intent who, once informed of a problem, will fix it.

- Minimize power struggles by focusing on the relevant policy or performance standard. At this step the problem can be stated as facts or as a perception that may or may not be accurate but has arisen from certain actions the individual has taken.

- Avoid beginning the conversation with idle chat or a series of social niceties that will later make the staff member feel that he or she was manipulated.

- Establish a clear goal. Say, for example, "The purpose of this meeting is to make sure you are aware of (a concern that I have), (a potential problem), (a perception), to get some additional data from you about what is happening and why. This meeting will also give us a chance to clarify the school (or district's) expectations."

- Write dated meeting notes that summarize what you discussed and what you and the staff member agreed to do as next steps. Typically this would be just a memory aid for the supervisor; the intent of this first meeting is awareness.

- Place your summary in your personal files, those that you use to support your own memory.

Do not feel obligated to create a formal document for a personnel file at this stage of the process. The power of Step 1 is the implied message: "Let's correct this now before getting into formal documentation." Example 9.1 illustrates a statement of concern about a breach of policy.

Example 9.1 First Meeting: Concern re Administrative Policy

"It has come to my attention that you may have been leaving school earlier than the contract permits on grade-level curriculum workshop days. If this is true, I am certainly willing to listen to any explanations but also want to clarify the school committee policy and contract provisions that govern end times on those days."

The teacher may respond to this statement of concern by denying the policy breech. Remember, at this early stage you are not always in a position to claim firsthand knowledge that the breech has occurred. Thus your main goal is to ensure that expectations are clear. Remind the individual that this communication is not presently part of any record or part of his or her evaluation. The conversation is about "If ... then."

The first meeting ends with an understanding that you will look for evidence that the problem (if it exists) is solved satisfactorily and will not happen again. You behave as if you assume there will be no further issue. Often that assumption is justified. The communication is clear; the matter is resolved; and no further action is necessary. Some matters are either concrete enough (punctuality) or easy enough to fix quickly (no use of videos on Friday afternoon) that change should be immediate. If a teacher is learning to master a new technique or internalize a new routine, the administrator may allow four to six weeks for compliance to be complete. If infractions continue and become a pattern, conduct a second meeting.

Step 2: Escalate the Severity of Concern, Check for Understanding, and Establish Guidelines for Improvement and Monitoring

Accidental or deliberate "slippage," for example a teacher who starts arriving at meetings 5, then 10, then 15 minutes late, may be resolved after a first meeting. However, it is also possible that you have inherited a pattern of behavior that has gone on unquestioned during a predecessor's administration and will not be fixed after a first encounter. Perhaps you'll find yourself dealing with a staff member new to the building or district who is testing policies or someone whose personal life is falling apart and affecting his or her ability to meet contract provisions. If the problem is not resolved after a reasonable period of time, shift from an invitational tone to a more directive one. Inform the individual that data indicate a problem still exists, the issue is serious, and change is necessary. In this second meeting, your primary purpose remains fixing the problem. You want to restate your expectation unequivocally and, at the same time, find out why the individual is having difficulty complying. This conference is the second warning shot fired across the ship's bow in an attempt to get it to change direction before real conflict ensues. Figure 9.3 gives suggestions on how to conduct this second meeting.

Figure 9.3 How to Conduct a Second Meeting

- Orally restate the standard and your concern. Don't add extraneous details.
- Cite examples that describe the performance disparity.
- Focus on the impact of the behavior on students and/or colleagues. Highlight how the teacher's behavior is affecting opportunities to learn, the work of a team, or equitable opportunities for students.
- Check whether the teacher understands the severity of the concern and determine what is impeding implementing the policy. Ask the staff member what s/he thinks is interfering with his or her ability to comply with the policy. Checking allows you to diagnose causes and perhaps provide a set of suggestions for action.
- Tell the teacher what kind of data you will be collecting and what data you would like him or her to provide as evidence for improvement.
- Write a summary of your conversation and your agreements for next steps—if possible, with the teacher—at the end of the meeting or immediately after the meeting. Give the teacher a copy and place a copy in your personal desk file. Keep in mind that these notes could be made public during a possible future discovery phase. (See Legal Notes 9.3 and 10.7.)

Example 9.2 shows how a statement of escalated concern could be stated.

Legal Note 9.3 Placing Documents into the Personnel File

Deciding when to place documents in the personnel file is critical. Most supervisors stay with oral communication too long in order to avoid "putting it in writing." If there are not clear signs of willingness to rectify the situation, begin the process of documentation after a maximum of two oral communications.

Example 9.2 Second Meeting: Concern re administrative policy

"I met with you three weeks ago and reminded you of our school expectation regarding full attendance at team meetings, workshop sessions, and curriculum days. Last week when I asked why your name was not on the sign-in sheet, I learned that you were 15 minutes late for the sixth period team meeting on 11/20. I also have a note from Mrs. D. (the school secretary) that you asked her to let me know you had to leave the curriculum session a half hour early yesterday. In both cases you were present for only two-thirds of the time. What's going on? What's causing this pattern?

[Teacher responds.]

My concern is that your absences undermine the team's ability to plan regrouping for acceleration and re-teaching strategies for our students who did not meet benchmarks last quarter. Absences also have a negative effect on the opportunities for your advanced students. For example, you told me you were "not aware" of the two challenge assessments the team reviewed and adopted yesterday. How will you make certain that you meet the full attendance requirement for all team meetings, workshop sessions, and curriculum days?

[Teacher responds.]

Gary, regardless of your personal beliefs, these are school policies followed by all other faculty members. Please make certain that you are present and initial the sign-in sheet at the beginning of every meeting and the follow-up agreements sheet at the end. Put any request to deviate from contract hours in writing to me and make certain you obtain a written okay from me before you modify your arrival or departure time in any way."

If the problem has not been satisfactorily resolved by a substantial change to the requested behavior, conduct a third meeting and write it up for the personnel file.

Step 3: Conference and Document Failure to Respond to Feedback

The third conference is directive with no remaining element of invitation or inquiry. Over time, you have collected data about problematic patterns of behavior that have not been changed despite the clear feedback the individual has received. *Failure to respond to feedback becomes the grounds for establishing insubordination.* You will escalate the communication in order to eliminate all competing interpretations about compliance. Figure 9.4 lists suggestions on how to conduct this third meeting.

Figure 9.4 How to Conduct a Third or "Failure to Respond" Meeting

- Reframe the concern more emphatically as a serious problem—a lapse in performance over time. If possible connect the identified problem to the relevant teacher evaluation standard.
- Elaborate on the negative impact on students or colleagues.
- Emphasize the teacher's failure to alter behavior in spite of feedback and after two distinct requests to do so.
- Keep the focus on the external reference such as the state standard(s), local contractual provisions, school-identified curriculum priorities, or team agreements. Do not use language such as "It's important to me that you…" that suggests the request for compliance is personal: something that you, the supervisor, want.
- Emphasize that the concern is about patterns of behavior, not single events except for serious cases of "conduct unbecoming."
- Obtain the teacher's signature on the memo. In absence of other specifications, use the exact language of your contract, usually located on the final page of evaluation document. "I have read…" language does not signify agreement.

At this third step, it is important to document the previous warnings and failure to comply in a meeting summary. Use the three-part memo format described in Figure 9.5. Inform the individual that the document will be placed in the personnel file and get the individual's signature on the summary. In the unlikely event that the recipient refuses to sign, present the document to him or her in the presence of a witness and ask the witness to sign.

Figure 9.5 How to Document Using the Three-Part Memo

Write a short, three-part follow-up memo that should include the following elements:

1. **What you communicated in the conference.** Summarize information that you presented and, if necessary, identify and cite the direct evidence that supports the communication.

2. **The individual's response.** Quote when appropriate. Summarize the information provided by the teacher and include any written responses by the teacher.

3. **A restatement of the standard and the required expectations for future behavior.** If the information is factual and easily documented, then you can identify what might happen as a result of this incident or what the staff member can expect should it happen again.

If the information is not easily documented or the staff member has denied the situation as an incorrect representation of what happened, then you state the standards and expectations around this behavior and identify what would happen should this behavior ever occur (being careful to use words that maintain the behavior is only an allegation). Example 9.3 cites a standard and states the consequences of repeating the problematic behavior.

> ### *Example 9.3 Third Meeting and Written Documentation: Not complying with an administrative policy*
>
> "On January 30, we had a third meeting to discuss your repeated failure to adhere to the attendance criteria under Standard 6 Professional Responsibilities. When we met on this issue on November 29th, you stated that you understood and would adhere to the attendance policy and standard although you did not agree that they were necessary. Sign-in sheets for December and the first three weeks of January show that you were more than 10 minutes late to three team meetings. You also asked to leave 30 minutes early on January 12 and did not initial follow-up sheets that you were present at the end of the January 19 curriculum development workshop. Your pattern of not being on time and available for a full work session adversely impacts the efficiency of the team as it tries to solve student learning problems. At the January 30 meeting, you told me, "You are nitpicking and out to get me, and we need to cut down on the number of meetings." I responded by restating the attendance policy and your obligation to adhere to that policy and that if you had a competing obligation that might interfere with your attendance, you must check with me first. If you continue the pattern of lateness and early leaving, your evaluation will indicate that your performance is unsatisfactory for Standard 6 Professional Responsibilities."

The key to supervisory responses designed to produce compliance is clear communication about what to stop doing and what to start doing. If an individual cannot or does not comply with repeatedly communicated instructions, this behavior signals a failure to respond to written feedback as well as a failure to meet the standards that describe professional responsibilities and professional interactions. Records of the escalated communication can then also be used to support either a "below standard" rating in a summative evaluation or further escalated progressive discipline.

This chapter can help you structure communication about performance issues that are best handled through progressive discipline, such as breeches of policy or failure to follow accepted practices. Keep the following in mind:

- First decide whether the problem falls into the category of noncompliance and is therefore better addressed through progressive discipline than through teacher evaluation procedures.

- Review your contract carefully and consult with your personnel administrator regarding regulations governing progressive discipline and collective bargaining procedures. Consult with a local school attorney to make sure you are on the right track.

- Begin the process with an approach similar to communicating an "early worry" in Section 6B. Assume a quick solution may be possible, but always verify that assumption by monitoring implementation of the solution.

- Remember that the documentation to support insubordination begins when the notice of a problem is put in writing. Notification that is not in writing does not count!

- Match your response to the gravity of the circumstances. The concept of progressive discipline assumes that most people feel an incentive to avoid being "written up" and would prefer to fix a problem before that happens. Jump to written documentation, however, should the situation require it, e.g., issues of student safety, bullying or harassment, or negligence.

Before embarking on progressive discipline, read carefully Section 4D.

CHAPTER 10

PREPARING FOR
TEACHER DISMISSAL

W E BELIEVE the majority of teachers can and will improve with feedback, direction, and support and that improvements in instruction will lead to better student outcomes. That belief makes the work recommended in previous chapters worthwhile for skillful leaders. We also believe that every child deserves an expert teacher. Thus, if your improvement interventions have failed and students are being adversely affected, you must be ready *and* willing to initiate dismissal proceedings.

In this chapter we focus on establishing grounds for dismissal and anticipating the myriad legal considerations involved. We also consider ways to remove the underperforming teacher from the classroom without resorting to dismissal. As you read, keep the disclaimer and caution in Legal Note 10.1 firmly in mind.

> Laws, regulations, contracts, and local policies differ from state to state and from district to district, therefore legal requirements are not consistent. *This chapter is not intended to replace legal advice that is based on consideration of the facts of your situation and specific provisions of your contract.* Seek guidance from your local school attorney for specific applications to your context.

Legal Note 10.1
Always Consult
Your Local Attorney

Although some contracts may specify the length of improvement plans, there is no prescribed time to wait before commencing dismissal proceedings. Be guided by the concept of a "reasonable period of time," which is determined by the following:

- Opportunity to remediate the deficiency (except for egregious cases of conduct unbecoming)
- The extent of change expected (quick compliance requires less time than substantial changes in formative assessment (see Section 8B)
- A history of high ratings (accurate or not) that may lengthen the time given to a teacher to improve
- The length of service to the district (see Legal Note 10.2)

> "The teacher, by statute, must be given a reasonable period of time in which to correct the deficiencies outlined. Considering this teacher's 17 years of service in the district, in addition to 8 years of teaching elsewhere, it seems harsh and unreasonable to accord her only 5 weeks after the notice of deficiency before the first observation and 8 weeks before the notice of termination to remedy 25 years of teaching practice which was now labeled deficient for the first time." *Joy Ganyo v. Independent School District, No. 832*, 311 N.W. 2d 497 (1981).

Legal Note 10.2
"Reasonable
Period of Time"

Before we examine the specific challenges associated with preparing for dismissal, we need to identify common missteps that can destroy your dismissal case before you begin presenting to *your* attorney.

AVOIDING FIVE UNDERMINING PRACTICES

Know and avoid the five most common traps: (1) not adhering to established procedures, (2) using disparate practices within a district, (3) not understanding the role politics plays in dismissals, (4) mixing formative and summative data collection in improvement plans, and (5) failing to develop a calibrated understanding for unsatisfactory ratings.

1. Not Following Procedures

Cases are usually lost because of procedural failures rather than substance. Procedures governing dismissal are almost always a mandatory source of bargaining. The burden is on you to carry out these procedures: meeting requirements for the minimum number of evaluations, adhering to pre- and post-conference requirements, giving the teacher the opportunity to provide a written rebuttal, and faithfully using the adopted instruments and protocols. Failure to provide timely notice of concerns is one of the most common procedural slip-ups (see Legal Note 10.3). If the evaluator misses deadlines or violates a contractual agreement, arbitrators frequently dismiss cases that have been otherwise well documented and supported.

**Legal Note 10.3
Informing the
Employee**

> Many contracts contain strict timelines for notifying personnel of concerns and complaints. The failure to follow them can compromise the ability to use the information for any personnel action. The timing for informing an employee of a complaint should depend on the nature of the complaint. Timing also depends on whether the evaluator needs to carry out some preliminary investigation or needs to refer the investigation to other administrative or supervisory personnel, as in the case of harassment complaints.

2. Using Disparate District Practices

Conscientious principals might unwittingly employ practices that are inconsistent with collective bargaining contracts. If school sites use different practices, the concept of *disparate practice* could undermine your case. Take, for example, the principal of High Standard High School who has rated a teacher unsatisfactory using several sources of data as evidence. If other principals have not routinely collected these same sources of evidence, the union may claim and arbitrators may later rule that this treatment is inequitable and overturn the dismissal. District leaders must supervise their sites for consistency of practice especially when it comes to data collection.

3. Not Understanding the Politics of Dismissal

The politics of dismissal are as important as the policies of dismissal. As a matter of law, principals can recommend an individual be dismissed. But the economic cost, staff time, and school board politics suggest that the skillful site leader proceed cautiously. For this reason, site-based administrators should not go forward without the full and unqualified support of the superintendent and personnel officer. Many principals have been sacrificed on the altar of accommodation because of a politically connected incompetent teacher who is the son-in-law of the sister of the school board chairman's second wife! In addition, evaluators need to be especially careful when dealing with the politics of dismissing a union activist.

Leader Alert
Dismissing a Union Activist

Principals get exasperated when teachers who have been given poor performance ratings assume active union roles. Suspecting a connection between the teacher's low level of performance and the high number of grievances filed, you may allow personal distaste to cloud your judgment because you so want to get rid of your main pain. If *suddenly* you start giving unsatisfactory evaluations after years of positive evaluations, unions will likely claim unfair treatment. Remember that grievance processes are controlled by collective bargaining agreements and are a protected activity. Focus on the performance in the classroom. Communicate escalated concerns and problems about performance with appropriate evidence the way you would for anybody else. Follow procedures with vigilance. Unless you already have a documentation trail, don't expect that you can dismiss this individual in less than three years, which is approximately the same amount of time as that required for any teacher having a "clean" previous record. ◆

4. Mixing Formative and Summative Data Collection in Improvement Plans

An improvement plan should be structured so that the collection of formative data for purposes of feedback and improvement is kept separate from the collection of data that will be used to make a summative judgment about progress. Cases have been lost by basing a dismissal decision solely on formative data intended to be nonjudgmental assistance (see Legal Note 10.4).

> "Observations during the remediation period could be properly used to evaluate improvement but the absence of any evaluation at the conclusion of the period made it impossible for the Board to make a reasoned decision." [Case overturned] Board of Education of School District No. 131 v. Illinois State Board of Education, 403 N.E. 2d 277 (1980).

Legal Note 10.4 ◈
Mixing Formative and Summative Data

5. Failing to Develop Calibrated Understanding for Unsatisfactory Ratings

States and districts are busy adopting rubrics and their accompanying ratings. A recommendation for dismissal needs to be based on clearly delineated district criteria of what constitutes unsatisfactory performance. Rubrics rarely offer this level of detail and teacher unions skillfully exploit the variations to defend a client. Districts spend considerable time on instrument adoption but little time on establishing evaluator validity and reliability. District-wide calibration training is imperative to reduce invalid or inconsistent ratings between evaluators. Training also helps districts to reduce *rating inflation*, the phenomenon where everyone is found to be excellent and no one is unsatisfactory. Example 10.1 illustrates one way to help all evaluators in a district develop consistent ways of understanding and rating performance.

> ### *Example 10.1 A Process for District Calibration Training*
>
> District teams of three to six evaluators collect data from videos or live classroom visits. Using their performance instrument, they analyze their data to agree on what standards the evidence illustrates and what indicators are important in reaching a rating. Participants then defend and discuss their ratings, offer supporting evidence, and reach consensus about what evidence justifies a particular rating. For example, if they have a four-point rating scale, teams should focus specifically on clarifying the middle ratings such as Basic versus Proficient. These middle categories share a border on a rubric but are miles apart in the teachers' minds; they would most likely prefer to be labeled proficient rather than basic. Most important, teams need to calibrate what they rate as an unsatisfactory performance. Without training, evaluators will almost always inflate ratings and few teachers' performances will ever be judged unsatisfactory.

If your case survives these underminers, you are ready to consider the legal foundations for dismissal.

SATISFYING DUE PROCESS AND JUST CAUSE

All dismissal recommendations should be screened through two legal concepts: due process and just cause. *Due process* refers to requirements that you provide notice and an opportunity for the teacher to respond before you can change an individual's current employee status. All levels of government—federal, state, and local—have added layers and local variations of what due process can mean in your district. You can meet the requirement of due process if you adhere faithfully to your local procedures and deadlines.

Just cause means that you have not acted arbitrarily, capriciously, and discriminatorily or made a decision not based on fact. Just cause is the legal test to determine whether the punishment, in this case dismissal, fits the crime.

Archibald Cox was a well-known Harvard labor and constitutional law expert known for his role in the Watergate crisis. He was chosen as the arbitrator for a Needham Public School (MA) dismissal case. In his decision (see Legal Note 10.5), he modified the Daugherty Test (Koven et al. 1992) that was originally developed in an industrial context and distilled that test into three "just cause" criteria matched to an educational setting. Since it was an arbitration decision, rather than a judicial proceeding, it does not constitute a binding precedent. However, nationally, arbitrators have used the Cox decision as a *persuasive authority* in applying the just cause standard. The misconduct and disciplinary language of Cox's decision on just cause seems at first glance to be a better match to dismissal associated with progressive discipline. However, the "just cause" concept also applies when an unsatisfactory rating in the evaluation process defines shortcomings that become the building block for dismissal based on incompetence.

In order to satisfy "just cause" requirements, you need to be able to answer yes to each of these three criteria:

Legal Note 10.5
Just Cause

1. The employee committed the offense or was guilty of the shortcoming attributable to him or her (the burden of proof).
2. The misconduct or shortcoming justified the disciplinary measure (an equitable standard was applied).
3. The procedure was consistent with fundamental fairness.

Needham Educational Association and Needham School Committee, AAA Case No 1139-2013-83 (Cox 1984).

Figure 10.1 Two Tracks to Dismissal

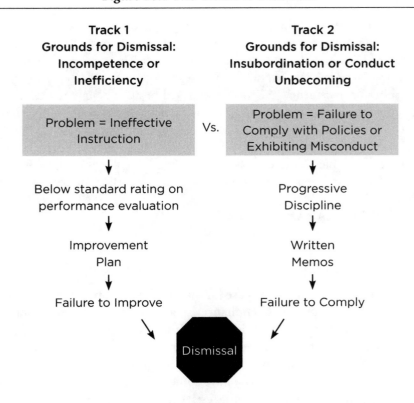

Choosing Tracks for Dismissal

As Figure 10.1 indicates, you typically follow one of two different tracks for dismissal, depending on the grounds cited. Choose Track 1 when a teacher fails to meet standards on an improvement plan. Grounds for dismissal become *incompetence* (lack of requisite skill or knowledge) or its less commonly used cousin, *inefficiency* (failure to achieve intended results in a reasonable period of time).

Choose Track 2 when the teacher fails to comply with policies or behavioral expectations, following a period of *progressive discipline*. Grounds for dismissal under Track 2 are *insubordination* or *conduct unbecoming*. Serious single transgressions are the exception to the principle of providing progressive disciplinary action. Pending dismissal, suspension is immediate, with no opportunity for remediation. Although these two tracks cover the major grounds for dismissal, states use a variety of terms to justify dismissal such as: neglect of duty, moral turpitude, or physical or mental disability.

Consider the following options when you choose the track you will follow in proceeding with dismissal.

Option 1: Throw the Book

Include everything possible in the case for dismissal hoping that a large number of charges will strengthen your case. Know that the more charges you present, the larger the burden of proof becomes. *Burden of proof* means that the onus falls on you, the employer, to provide sufficient evidence in support of the charges. Warranted but weakly supported charges add escape routes to the defense. Since you need only one sustained ground for dismissal, you increase the likelihood of success if you limit the number of charges to one or two that you can clearly support (see Legal Note 10.6).

Legal Note 10.6
Avoid Serial
Grounds for
Dismissal

In a Massachusetts case, a teacher was brought up for dismissal on the oddly worded grounds of "inefficiency, incompetence and conduct unbecoming, failing to discipline students, review IEPs, teach P.E. for the allotted time, and using inappropriate language." These grounds may have been valid, but the arbitrator overturned the dismissal based on insufficient evidence, e.g., the claim of incompetence was based on two brief observations. The arbitrator also found that while the teacher was given an improvement plan, the plan was "barren of advice that failure to improve his performance could result in any penalty—much less his dismissal." Finally, the supervisor acknowledged improvement in some charge areas, further undermining his own case.
(Lynn &PH 1995 AAA# 00573 94).

Option 2: Choose Progressive Discipline

If you have a clear and convincing case for dismissal based on insubordination, this track may be the best choice. Compliance is easier to measure, and insubordination is easier for arbitrators to understand. However, keep in mind that progressive discipline does not correct most of the problems associated with ineffective instruction. If your dismissal process based on progressive discipline fails, you will still own an ineffective teacher. If you have some data from classroom performance but stronger documentation using progressive discipline, go with your strong suit. Your goal is the removal of the teacher from the classroom.

Option 3: Choose Performance Evaluation

Choose this track when you have clearly documented that students are not making expected progress and teaching is below standards despite interventions that include a formal improvement plan. Ineffective performers frequently manage to comply with dictates and demands, thus avoiding progressive discipline. However, if you have faithfully followed and documented the sequence of intervention, and students with the bad luck to draw this teacher are still losing out, you must take action. With conviction and skill, it is time to move to dismissal based on performance.

SELECTING AND CREATING DOCUMENTATION

Documentation will differ, depending on whether you are recommending dismissal on the basis of performance evaluation or progressive discipline. But, in either case, there will be a teacher's personnel file that could include any written record of important information in a person's employment history. Examples of documents include: personnel status changes, incidents that reflect on a teacher's job performance, evaluation documents, memoranda prepared after conferences, and disciplinary actions. These documents are treated as public records (see Legal Note 10.7).

Documents that are created or received by you in the course of your work are presumed to be public records. This also applies to documents that are electronically transmitted and/or received. In addition, all documents created and received by you are potentially subject to "discovery" in litigation, including arbitrations and formal administrative hearings.

Legal Note 10.7
Public Records

If you have been following the policies in your district and the advice in these pages, you will have gathered significant documentation. However, the prospect of dismissal raises the bar for the quality of that documentation. To be prepared for dismissal, your district must establish clear document-retention practices. Policies on document retention are as important as what you say in your documents because you need to be able to locate your records when the need arises. In the age of electronic discovery (the exchange of information before trial), the inability to locate documents like emails and other computer-based information can be extremely harmful to your case. Therefore, it's critical to have a well-organized and well-publicized *document-retention policy*.

Create a document or other record only if you can answer yes to the first two questions and no to the third:

1. Does the school district need this record to serve as a source of evidence for an unsatisfactory evaluation report or disciplinary action? Do I need it?
2. Would I want this document to be seen by a judge, a hearing officer, or an arbitrator?
3. Would I cringe if I saw this document appear on the front page of my local newspaper?

Never guarantee confidentiality to an informant unless you are certain that you can provide other direct supporting evidence. You may be able to withhold the identity of the informant who provided you with the information initially, but if the case proceeds to the discovery phase of litigation, you will not be able to prove your claims without persuasive testimonial and/or physical evidence. In the context of evaluating employee performance, most contracts and evaluation procedures require that all personnel action must be based on documented information that has been communicated with the employee involved.

Legal Note 10.8
Confidentiality

Figure 10.2 provides some tips to help you ensure that you are documenting the various performance issues in your case effectively.

Figure 10.2 Tips for Effective Documentation

- **Write it down.** If it isn't written down it didn't happen. Focus on "just the facts." Be concise. Use simple language free of personal opinion. Avoid inexplicit language such as "seemed" or "appeared." Eliminate "edubabble" jargon such as "assessment for learning," "differentiated learning," or "process-oriented programs."

- **Be careful about confidentiality.** Because of privacy rights, be careful about identifying names of students or other employees at the early stages of the process (see Legal Note 10.8).

- **Avoid inflammatory language.** Judgments like "outrageous," "stupid," and "unbelievable" may be therapeutic for you but will undermine the objectivity of your communication.

- **Avoid cc syndrome.** Circulate information only to people who need to know. Anger may lead you to do a quick email blast that can cause serious "sender's regret." To avoid potential claims of defamation, if copies are sent to parties other than those to whom the document is addressed, that should be so noted.

- **Document the event close to the occurrence, but pause before pressing send.** Early documentation is very important. Nothing undermines your credibility more than a document that was created long after the event occurred. Even though there may be no ill intent behind your delay, the implication is that you may be covering up a mistake. Early documentation is also key because it may signal the need for additional data gathering. Take the time to collect and organize your thoughts. Sleep on your communication for a night to make sure the tone is appropriate, but don't take a month of nights!

- **Cite policies and procedures.** If the document is supported by or created under a certain district policy or procedure, refer to that policy in your writing. Citing the policy or procedure depersonalizes the communication and establishes your credibility as a knowledgeable and objective reporter.

- **Put the document in a context.** For example, if the document relates to a particular meeting, state the date and reason for the meeting, the names of those who attended, the issues discussed, and any type of follow-up required.

- **Sign and date the document.** A document is most useful when you know when it was written and by whom. Therefore always make sure the author can be identified. Make it a practice to date every official document created in your school. This information may be critical in circumstances in which legal or contractual timelines apply.

PREPARING FOR HEARING

If you have followed the guidelines in this book and chapter, you should be well prepared for a hearing; however, in matters of dismissal you should always consult with your personnel officer or attorney. Remember dismissal cases are lost more frequently on procedural grounds than errors of substance. Most dismissals will be upheld if you observe the following guidelines:

1. Adhere faithfully to the deadlines and procedures.
2. Have multiple sources of data to support claims of the teacher deficiency.
3. Provide a notice of deficiency to the teacher.
4. Provide a reasonable opportunity to correct the deficiencies (see Legal Note 10.2).
5. Establish a clear alignment between the ratings given to the teacher and the specific examples provided by the evaluator in describing the teacher's performance.
6. Create consistency in the various reports of the evaluators and observers (see Legal Note 10.9).
7. Produce unbiased, honest documentation.

"In this case, the arbitrator was struck by the commonalities between the observation reports. All of them noted deficiencies in: applying his knowledge of the subject matter to the curriculum; classroom management, including discipline, enforcing basic rules regarding tardiness, attendance, preparedness, and hall passes; and communicating with students. 'When four different evaluators make note of the same areas of concern, over the span of four or five school years, their observations must be deemed as credible.' The arbitrator also noted that the teacher was provided ample feedback, suggestions, support and that despite the support, he continued to exhibit many of the same weaknesses over his two-year period at the school. Therefore, the conclusions of the administration regarding teacher's poor performance were reasonable and warranted his dismissal." *Gerardo and Worcester School Committee*, Dismissal Upheld AAA Case No. 11 390 01520 03, July 21, 2004.

**Legal Note 10.9
Multiple
Evaluators**

Legal Note 10.9 should not imply that you need to have four different evaluators, but it does suggest that in claims of incompetence or inefficiency, multiple evaluators who concur help to build a powerful case. If you have moved into documentation for dismissal mode, consider whether you need to enlist a colleague to conduct independent observations and to act as a critical friend regarding the quality of your documentation.

REMOVING A TEACHER WITHOUT DISMISSAL

Dismissal proceedings are a major commitment of time and resources and should be the last resort. In fact most dismissals processes end up not going to final arbitration. The parties find a way to settle and achieve the central goal of removing the teacher from the classroom so that students can have improved instruction. Several legitimate alternatives may achieve the same end … eventually.

Counsel Out

Confront or have your district level administrator confront the teacher with the data and indicate that you are preparing to initiate dismissal proceedings. (You must be willing to do so.) Ask him or her if s/he would consider resigning. Have a witness with you. It is our experience that skillful leaders have a high success rate using this method if they assume a counseling role and do not browbeat the teacher. Let the facts speak louder than you.

Enlist Outside Help

Sometimes called the "last chance option," this strategy involves hiring an instructional expert to provide the "get better or get out" coaching and counseling. Interactions are confidential, and data are not shared with the district or used as part of an evaluation. The consultant assumes a directive coaching role, collects data, and gives the teacher private feedback, including an honest assessment of his or her skill level. Unless there is sudden improvement, the consultant counsels the teacher to resign to avoid dismissal. If you try this strategy, follow all contract procedures.

Legal Note 10.10
Counseling out
Substance Abusers

> Leaders often seek to counsel out individuals whose performance is adversely affected by substance abuse, frequently alcoholism. Know the ADA (American with Disabilities Act) provisions and be aware that alcoholism is considered a disease and does not justify discipline or dismissal by itself. However, alcoholics or other substance abusers can be held to the same expectations as any other employee, so focus on job performance and lack of capacity rather than the disability.

Buy Out

Although resources are always tight, it is possible that a deal could be achieved by providing a reasonable monetary settlement in exchange for an agreement to resign. This option recognizes the fact that dismissal will have significant costs both in time and money. Taking a paid leave or using sick leave for the rest of the year could be part of a buyout agreement. Depending on the case, putting together a resignation-incentive package may be the right course of action. You pay upfront money but avoid paying more money in legal fees as well as the possibility of losing the case later.

Get a Written Agreement to Resign in the Future

Retirement must happen no later than the end of the following year. Taking this route does lead to another lost year for students, but after years of leaders tolerating poor performance, it might be a cost-effective option. Do not accept oral promises as they inevitably get delayed. In one case we know, a teacher had orally agreed to resign but changed his mind when the principal failed to complete a final performance evaluation. The arbitrator reinstated the teacher who taught five more years before finally retiring. One procedural mistake and the false reliance on oral resignation adversely impacted almost 900 students!

Transfer the Teacher to a Lower Impact Position

Although we rarely recommend this option and it is difficult to accomplish in smaller school districts, assigning a teacher to a nonclassroom setting for a specified number of years without loss of pay is a choice some districts make. It ties up resources that could be used elsewhere to students' benefit and should be implemented only in cases of significant 20+ years of seniority and less than three years before retirement (see Legal Note 10.11).

> You need to be sure that the transfer sought is allowed by the agreements with your local bargaining unit. Even if the teacher agrees to a transfer, unions can block it. Ensure that there is no reduction in compensation or demotion of position, either of which could trigger a successful grievance.

**Legal Note 10.11
Transferring the Teacher**

DEALING WITH BACKSLIDING

Backsliding occurs after a period of genuine improvement and after the teacher has been removed from formal assistance by a principal or a PAR team. In subsequent visits the evaluator notices slippage to previous poor performance. You do not need to restart the clock and begin the improvement process again since a second unsatisfactory rating does not usually entitle a teacher to another remediation period. Although there may be pressure from the union, the district is under no obligation to provide support in the face of backsliding. Arbitrators tend to support the concept that there is a point where the district can release responsibility back to the teacher and that the district can expect the individuals to maintain their own improvement (see Legal Notes 10.12 and 10.13).

> "We have read in detail the evidence in this case.... The record here demonstrates that this teacher during the period would appear to improve and then back-slide into his previous habits.... We fully recognize that the Teacher Tenure Law has as its benign purpose job security for worthy teachers and serves as a protective shield against dismissal for trivial, political, capricious or arbitrary causes. It was not intended to lock a teacher into a school system where efforts over a period of years by the administration to help the teacher in remedial causes fails.... There is substantial evidence in the record to support the conclusion that his period of usefulness in this particular district had waned or perhaps completely evaporated." *Theodore Kallas v. Board of Education of Marshall Community Unit School District No. C-2, Clark County*, 304 N.E. 2d 527 (1973).

**Legal Note 10.12
No Further Remediation Required**

**Legal Note 10.13
No Further
Remediation
Required**

"Given D.'s long history of occasionally remediating but then falling back to her unacceptable teaching performance over a period of three years, and given the inordinate time extended by the system in an effort to assist her in remediation but to no avail, I find the District did not act unfairly in not extending the Tier 2 status for another year.... The evidence shows that her deficiencies are too pervasive and without lasting remediation. It would be patently unfair to the students of Lexington, who have a right to expect the best possible teaching, to subject them to an "experiment" with (D.), with every expectation that it would fail." *Lexington Public Schools*, AAA Case # 11-390-00571-94 (Arbitrator Bruce Fraser, July 14, 1995).

Dismissal is the last-choice intervention and the ultimate action against ineffective instruction or misconduct. The territory comes with a complex set of legal constraints and demand for time. However, leaders set high standards with their responses to the lowest performing teachers. When students continue to lose out after a year or two of lesser interventions, you need to have the conviction to initiate dismissal proceedings. Doing so sends an important message to the entire school and district that students come first and that poor performance will not be tolerated.

Preparation really begins when you commit your first concern to writing. Check yourself if you are tempted to prolong the oral worry period. Do not wait for official formal write-ups. Create your initial documents to provide a timely diagnosis and recommended focus for improvement before you have to make summative judgments. If there is insufficient improvement, you then have the documentation.

The good news is that most teachers will improve with relatively low-intensity intervention. Few cases should or will get to dismissal. If you implement the procedures faithfully and create a good paper trail, you have the best chance of getting improvement, convincing the teacher to retire, or winning the case should you need to move to dismissal.

BIBLIOGRAPHY

Conzemius, Anne E., and Terry Morganti-Fischer. *More than a Smart Goal: Staying Focused on Student Learning.* Bloomington, IN: Solution Tree Press, 2012.

Danielson, Charlotte. *Enhancing Professional Practice: A Framework for Teaching.* Alexandria, VA: Association for Supervision and Curriculum Development (ASCD), 2007.

Danielson, Charlotte. *The Framework for Teaching Evaluation Instrument.* 2013 ed. NYSED.gov. Web. Retrieved 1 June 2013.

Dweck, Carol. *Mindset: The New Psychology of Success.* New York: Ballantine Books, 2006.

Fullan, Michael. *Change Forces.* Bristol, PA: Falmer Press, 1993.

Hattie, John. *Visible Learning.* London: Routlege, 2009.

Heifetz, Ronald A., and Martin Linsky. *Staying Alive Through the Dangers of Leading.* Cambridge, MA: Harvard Business School Press, 2002.

Kennedy, Mary. *Teacher Assessment and the Quest for Teacher Quality.* San Francisco, CA: Jossey Bass, 2010.

Love, Nancy, Katherine E. Stiles, Susan Mundry, and Kathryn DiRanna. *The Data Coach's Guide to Improving Learning for All Students.* Thousand Oaks, CA: Corwin Press, 2008.

Marshall, Kim. *Rethinking Teacher Supervision and Evaluation: How to Work Smart, Build Collaboration and Close the Achievement Gap.* San Francisco, CA: Jossey Bass, 2009.

Marshall, Kim. *Teacher Evaluation Rubrics.* Rev. Nov 2013. NYSED.gov. Web. Retrieved 1 June 2013.

Marzano, Robert, Debra J. Pickering, and Jane E. Pollock. *Classroom Instruction That Works: Research Based Strategies for Increasing Student Achievement.* Alexandria, VA: ASCD, 2001.

Marzano, Robert. *Causal Teacher Evaluation Model.* NYSED.gov. Web. Retrieved 1 June 2013.

Platt, Alexander D., Caroline E. Tripp, Wayne R. Ogden, and Robert G. Fraser. *The Skillful Leader: Confronting Mediocre Teaching.* Acton, MA: Ready About Press, 2000.

Platt, Alexander D., et al. *The Skillful Leader: Confronting Conditions That Undermine Learning.* Acton, MA: Ready About Press, 2008.

Saphier, Jon, Mary Ann Haley-Speca, and Robert Gower. *The Skillful Teacher: Building Your Teaching Skills.* 6th ed. Acton, MA: Research for Better Teaching, 2005.

INDEX

RBT PUBLICATIONS AND PRODUCTS

SKILLFUL TEACHING

 The Skillful Teacher: Building Your Teaching Skills (6th ed. 2008)
Designed for both the novice and the experienced educator, *The Skillful Teacher* is a unique synthesis of the Knowledge Base on Teaching, with powerful repertoires for matching teaching strategies to student needs. Designed as a practical guide for practitioners working to broaden their teaching skills, the book combines theory with practice and focuses on 18 critical areas of classroom performance. A must for instructional coaches and mentors.
by Jon Saphier, Mary Ann Haley-Speca, & Robert Gower

 ***The Skillful Teacher* Interactive Kindle eBook** (2008, Kindle 2012)
Available as complete *The Skillful Teacher* book or in 4 separately-orderable parts. Detailed search options or links to different chapters for instant answers to teaching dilemmas. Go to Amazon.com to purchase.
by Jon Saphier, Mary Ann Haley-Speca, & Robert Gower

 Activators: Activity Structures to Engage Students' Thinking Before Instruction (1993)
This book is a collection of classroom-tested, practical activity structures for getting students' minds active and engaged prior to introducing new content or skills.
by Jon Saphier & Mary Ann Haley

 Summarizers: Activity Structures to Support Integration and Retention of New Learning (1993)
This book is a collection of classroom-tested, practical activity structures for getting students cognitively active during and after periods of instruction.
by Jon Saphier & Mary Ann Haley

 DVDs: *The Skillful Teacher Series* (2012)
Collections of videos that bring to life practical strategies for improving teaching, highlighting high leverage, 21st century skills from our "gold-standard" textbook, *The Skillful Teacher*. Volume 1A & 1B – Motivation skills from the Classroom Climate and Expectations chapters. Volume 2A & 2B – Planning and Error Analysis/ Reteaching skills from the Planning and Assessment chapters. Volume 3 – Instructional Strategies from the Clarity chapter. Included are introductory videos to the Map of Pedagogical Knowledge.
by Jon Saphier et al.

 Poster: *Map of Pedagogical Knowledge Pyramid* (2009)
Full-color, 24" x 36" laminated poster. Support the professional development of your staff with this great visual of the foundation of good teaching. Display in teachers' room and training areas.

 Mini-Posters: *Map of Pedagogical Knowledge Pyramid (pkg. of 25)* (2009)
Full-color, 8.5" x 11" laminated mini-posters, an instructional resource for every teacher.

SKILLFUL LEADERSHIP

 The Skillful Leader: Confronting Mediocre Teaching (2000)
Based on *The Skillful Teacher* framework, this book is targeted to evaluators and supervisors who want a field-tested toolkit of strategies to improve, rather than remove, underperforming teachers. The text includes valuable legal notes and a model contract, case studies, assessment tools, and personal accounts of leaders in action.
by Alexander D. Platt, Caroline E. Tripp, Wayne R. Ogden, & Robert G. Fraser

 The Skillful Leader II: Confronting Conditions That Undermine Learning (2008)
This important "Skillful Leader" book arms administrators and teacher leaders with step-by-step strategies to confront and raise the performance of teams and individuals who undermine student learning. The text includes methods of collecting data, strategies for intervention, and tips for hiring and training. Individual and community profiles, together with legal notes, provide practical tools for busy leaders.
by Alexander D. Platt, Caroline E. Tripp, Robert G. Fraser, James R. Warnock, & Rachel E. Curtis

 Strengthening Teacher Evaluation: Taking Action to Improve Ineffective Teaching (The Skillful Leader III) (2014)
This work serves as a how-to handbook to accompany the best selling *The Skillful Leader: Confronting Mediocre Teaching*. Like its predecessor, the book offers dozens of illustrations, new cases, and sample documents plus legal advice to help evaluators confront ineffective instruction. It is a cover-to-cover guide for solving thorny teacher performance problems.
by Alexander D. Platt & Caroline E. Tripp

Research for Better Teaching, Inc. • One Acton Place, Acton, MA 01720 • Phone 978-263-9449
Web: www.RBTeach.com • Email: pubs@RBTeach.com

RBT PUBLICATIONS AND PRODUCTS

▲ ***Beyond Mentoring: Putting Instructional Focus on Comprehensive Induction Programs*** (2011)
This book emphasizes the critical role of instructional practice in the induction support that is given to new and beginning teachers. Using RBT's model for the comprehensive induction of new teachers, educators are guided through the steps of developing an induction plan for new teachers and integrating the induction program with the district's professional learning community.
by Jon Saphier, Susan Freedman, & Barbara Aschheim

▲ ***Talk Sense: Communicating to Lead and Learn*** (2007)
Barry Jentz shows how leaders can build the requisite trust and credibility for improving organizational performance. Typically, leaders "talk tough" to improve performance. When that doesn't work, they "talk nice" (or vice-versa). By learning to "talk sense", leaders can succeed in their efforts to improve performance.
by Barry Jentz

SKILLFUL DATA USE

▲ ***The Data Coach's Guide to Improving Learning for All Students: Unleashing the Power of Collaborative Inquiry***
(2008)
This resource helps Data-Team facilitators move schools away from unproductive data practices and toward examining data for systematic and continuous improvement in instruction and learning. The book includes a CD-ROM with slides and reproducibles.
by Nancy Love, Katherine E. Stiles, Susan Mundry, & Kathryn DiRanna

▲ ***Using Data to Improve Learning for All: A Collaborative Inquiry Approach*** (2009)
This valuable handbook arms leaders with the tools for using data to improve student learning, with an emphasis on promoting equity within a culturally proficient school environment. The book contains detailed examples of schools that have demonstrated dramatic gains by building collaborative cultures, nurturing ongoing inquiry, and using data systematically.
by Nancy Love, Editor

▲ **Laminated Guide: *Data Literacy for Teachers*** (2011)
For every teacher, Data Coach, and inquiry team. In a fold-out 8.5" x 11" laminated form, ready to be inserted in a notebook, the guide provides a simple framework to help teachers feel comfortable, knowledgeable, and skilled in effectively using a variety of data, including formative assessments.
by Nancy Love

▲ **Laminated Guide: *The Skillful Inquiry/Data Team*** (2012)
For every grade level (elementary) or subject-area (middle and high school) team of teachers, plus school and district administrators. In a fold-out 8.5" x 11" laminated form, ready to be inserted in a notebook, this guide provides a proven-effective inquiry process and practical tools to maximize their impact on student achievement.
by Nancy Love

▲ **DVD: *The Skillful Data Use Series*** (2012) Volume 1 Collaborative Inquiry: Connecting Data to Results. DVD collection of introductory instructional videos based on *The Data Coach's Guide* and *Using Data to Improve Learning for All* provides expert commentary, insights from successful implementations, and views of Data Teams in action.

▲ **Posters: *Unleashing the Power of Collaborative Inquiry*** (2009)
Eight full-color, 24" x 36" laminated posters: (1) Using Data 19 Tasks, (2) Building the Bridge, (3) Using Data Diagram, (4) Data Driven Dialogue, (5) Data Triangle, (6) Logic Model, (7) Verify Causes Tree, (8) Drill Down Deep. Data is power!

OTHER RBT RESOURCES

▲ ***John Adams' Promise: How to Have Good Schools for All Our Children, Not Just for Some*** (2005)
Curriculum reform, structural reform, funding reform, organizational reform—all these 20th-century efforts have failed to make a significant dent in the achievement gap and the performance of disadvantaged students, especially in cities and poor rural areas.
by Jon Saphier

▲ ***How to Bring Vision to School Improvement Through Core Outcomes, Commitments and Beliefs*** (1993)
This practical guide provides a proven step-by-step sequence for generating consensus among parents and staff about a few valued core outcomes they want for all children. Then it shows how to achieve the concrete outcomes in the areas of school and family life.
by Jon Saphier & John D'Auria

Research for Better Teaching, Inc. • One Acton Place, Acton, MA 01720 • Phone 978-263-9449
Web: www.RBTeach.com • Email: pubs@RBTeach.com